ON HUMAN MEMORY:
EVOLUTION, PROGRESS, AND REFLECTIONS ON THE 30TH ANNIVERSARY OF THE ATKINSON-SHIFFRIN MODEL

ON HUMAN MEMORY:
EVOLUTION, PROGRESS, AND REFLECTIONS
ON THE 30TH ANNIVERSARY OF
THE ATKINSON-SHIFFRIN MODEL

Edited by
CHIZUKO IZAWA
Tulane University

 LAWRENCE ERLBAUM ASSOCIATES, PUBLISHERS
1999   Mahwah, New Jersey   London

Lawrence Erlbaum Associates, Inc., Publishers
10 Industrial Avenue
Mahwah, New Jersey 07430

ISBN 0-8058-2952-0

Books published by Lawrence Erlbaum Associates are printed
on acid-free paper, and their bindings are chosen
for strength and durability.

Printed in the United States of America

10 9 8 7 6 5 4 3 2 1

Contents

Indices:

Foreword

Richard C. Atkinson
University of California, U. S. A.

An anniversary like this provides an occasion to reflect on science and on our lives. My own career has had three major phases: about two decades as a professor, mostly at Stanford University; 5 years at the National Science Foundation, having been appointed deputy director by President Ford and then director by President Carter; and the last two decades at the University of California, first as chancellor at UC San Diego, and now as president of the UC System. Each of these phases had its own challenges and rewards, but I recall with special fondness the exhilarating time I spent exploring the complexities of human memory and cognition in the company of some of the brightest young minds in the field.

The Atkinson and Shiffrin model discussed in this book achieved significance and fame far beyond anything we could have imagined at the time it was developed. In hindsight, I am sure that serendipity and timing played major roles. Even my collaboration with Rich Shiffrin arose somewhat by accident. Much of my career at Stanford was spent at the Institute for Mathematical Studies in the Social Sciences, housed in Ventura Hall. The institute was directed by Pat Suppes, a distinguished logician and philosopher, and served as the home for economists, psychologists, statisticians, computer scientists, and political scientists interested in mathematical models in the social sciences. Bill Estes and I, along with Pat Suppes, represented psychology in the institute's array of activities. The institute was a hotbed for the then-evolving field of mathematical psychology, and was populated by postdoctoral visitors and graduate students, too many to name in this foreword, a remarkable number of whom are leaders in the field today. In the early 1960s I began working on mathematical models of memory and used a computer-controlled system to conduct experiments that involved the continuous presentation and testing of items over extended periods of time. This experimental procedure proved to be very adaptable and generated large amounts of data on individual subjects; it was ideal for testing various assumptions embedded in the models. In the fall of 1964 a new graduate student, Richard Shiffrin, arrived at Stanford, having completed a double major at Yale University in psychology and mathematics. He came to work with Gordon Bower, who was housed in the psychology building elsewhere on campus. Shiffrin began developing models of memory applied to list paradigms, particularly free recall experiments. After Shiffrin's first year, Gordon Bower left for a sabbatical year in the United Kingdom, and asked if I would take over as Shiffrin's research advisor, since our more or less independently developed models seemed quite compatible. Thus began an intense and productive collaboration.

Within a few months Shiffrin and I became the hub of a group of students, postdoctoral visitors, and research associates carrying out a wide variety of memory studies suggested by an evolving theory of memory; many of these studies achieved independent publication. Then an invitation to contribute a chapter to *Psychology of Learning and Motivation* provided an opportunity to pull the various empirical and theoretical strands together into a larger framework. In the process, Shiffrin and I realized that the short-term buffer process that we were using in our various models was merely a stand-in for a more complicated set of processes representing short-term memory, leading us to broaden the conception of short-term memory to "control processes," a term standing in for "active memory" or "working memory." This conception in turn allowed us to put together a theoretical framework with relatively autonomous sensory processing, controlled processing in short-term memory, and a permanent long-term memory upon which control processes could operate to produce retrieval. The field was obviously ready to embrace this approach, and the publication of the chapter seemed to act like the nucleus that causes a solution in delicate equilibrium to precipitate.

That this model remains today a widely accepted description of human memory (and a subject for critical attack by continuing generations of theorists) is, I believe, more than a matter of a publication arriving on the scene at a propitious moment. The longevity of the model is most likely due to the parts of the chapter that are unknown to casual readers who learn of the model through secondary sources: namely, the quantitative fit of the model to a wide array of experimental paradigms and conditions. It was this rooting of the model in reality that forced it into a form that remains largely valid today. I believe this is the case for most of the lasting contributions to science, and provides perhaps the best argument for the collection of extensive parametric data and the testing of quantitative models.

It is indeed gratifying to witness this volume celebrating the 30th anniversary of the publication of our chapter. It is satisfying to see the many scientific outgrowths of that model and its use in one form or another in so many diverse fields. It is doubly satisfying to see the way in which Rich Shiffrin's own research has continued the evolution of those concepts, as in the SAM model (Raaijmakers & Shiffrin, 1980) and the REM model (Shiffrin & Steyvers, 1997). It is triply satisfying to see these theoretical efforts continuing into a third generation and beyond of PhDs. Chapters 5, 7, and 10 of the present volume, by Jeroen Raaijmakers, Scott Gronlund, Steve Clark, and their students and associates, provide excellent examples, as does an outstanding contribution by my student, Tom Wickens (Chapter 11). Another member of the circle of PhDs at Stanford in the 1960s, Mike Humphreys, also provides a valuable contribution to this volume (Chapter 7). A theoretical contribution of lasting value requires testing in the fire of intense critical evaluation, as noted by Chizuko Izawa in Chapter 1; over the years such testing has been provided by my friend and colleague, Ben Murdock (Chapter 3). Alice Healy and Tom Cunningham contribute Chapter 8, building upon the ideas of Estes' perturbation model (1972).

I cannot fail to acknowledge my close friend and colleague, Bill Estes, one of the great figures in our field and a recent recipient of the National Medal of Science. He is better placed than anyone to evaluate the last 30 years of progress in memory, and provides an incisive, critical, and telling retrospective in Chapter 4.

It is appropriate to end this foreword with special thanks to Chizuko Izawa, an outstanding scientist, whose idea led to this volume, and whose editing saw it to completion. I recall her as a shy graduate student who arrived at Stanford fresh from the University of Tokyo. She proceeded to surmount the obstacles of culture and language that faced her, and produced a wonderful PhD dissertation in 1965. She has utilized her own experiences involving language learning in her research on memory processes, and has produced significant advances in our understanding of the "efficiency of acquisition," as witnessed by her test trial potentiating model (1971), her retention interval model (1981), her identity model (1985) and her hypothesis concerning the Study-Test-rest (S-T-r) presentation program that is the subject of Chapter 9. Rich Shiffrin and I, as well as all the other contributors to this volume, owe her warm thanks and commendation for her efforts in our behalf.

Preface

The time was 1968, and the place, Ventura Hall, home of the Institute for Mathematical Studies in the Social Sciences at Stanford University. One of our fellow graduate students, Richard M. Shiffrin and his mentor, Richard C. Atkinson jointly devised a new memory model! On the face of it, this was nothing unusual; each graduate student, myself included, participated in creating a model as part of doctoral training.

What was unique about the Atkinson-Shiffrin model, which had been discussed earlier at the regular Friday afternoon Ventura Hall seminars, was its profound scope, depth, quality, and elegance. I clearly remember Rich Shiffrin proudly giving me the draft of his dissertation during one of the seminars I had been regularly attending after my doctorate at Stanford. At that time, I was at Berkeley doing my postdoctoral fellowship at the Institute of Human Learning. Although I did not entirely agree with the rehearsal mechanisms/processes postulated in the model (they did not quite correspond to my personal experiences in the learning of several languages over a number of years), I nonetheless could not help being deeply impressed by the Atkinson-Shiffrin model; an impression that was widely shared by my colleagues everywhere. The model was set forth in a book chapter, and was for decades, one of the most cited contributions to psychology and especially experimental psychology. The model's overall impact has been monumental.

Granted "Nihil est annis velocius [Nothing is swifter than the years] (Ovid, A.D. 7), it is hard to believe that 1998 marks the model's 30th Anniversary! The 1968 Atkinson-Shiffrin model is a resounding victory for the sciences of human learning and memory very close in stature to Ebbinghaus' 1885 *Ueber das Gedaechtnis* which started it all!

That is why Dick Atkinson and Rich Shiffrin's Ventura Hall associates, colleagues, classmates, students, and admirers joined in celebrating the Atkinson and Shiffrin rehearsal buffer model 30 years later. It was my good fortune to have shared the excitement of the model's birth with its creators and now to edit a tribute to this landmark event.

Acknowledgments

Preparation of this volume owes much to the selfless efforts of friends and student volunteers, all with a lively curiosity about research on learning and memory. Special thanks are due to Laura Brown, Emily S. Stitt, Eun-sil Lee, Brian L. Azcona, Jeremy Steckel, Althea Izawa-Hayden, and Lieuko Nguyen who assisted with proofreading and references. The intensive involvement of the latter two are especially appreciated. Both subject and author indexes were greatly benefited from the competent ministrations of Althea Izawa-Hayden, Lieuko Nguyen, and Marc Matrana.

Chizuko Izawa

Chapter 1

On Human Memory: A Brief Introduction

Chizuko Izawa
Tulane University, U. S. A.

In the beginning, there was *Ueber das Gedaechtnis* [On Memory] by Hermann Ebbinghaus (1850-1909). It reflected his decade-long intense personal devotion to create a series of highly original experiments that set enduring precedents for the future scientific study of human learning and memory. It was the first such publication in the history of scientific psychology. The volume was the sweet fruit of highly disciplined hard labor, because after all, Experimenter and Subject were one. This original and masterful oeuvre had a commanding effect on the advancement of psychological science, in part because Wilhem Wundt (1832-1920), the founder of modern experimental psychology (first formal laboratory, Leipzig, 1879), asserted that higher mental processes, such as human memory, were beyond the scope of experimental investigation, and could only be explored through Voelkerpsychologie [folk psychology], which relied primarily on people's casual recollections and traditions, rather than empirical science.

This first definitive stepping stone for theorists and experimentalists of human learning and memory, *Ueber das Gedaechtnis* [On Memory] (1885), set the standard for research on human learning and memory for over three quarters of a century. Henceforth learning/memory was predominantly investigated and measured in reference to the list (the list-design). During the 1985 centennial, Ebbinghaus' unprecedented contributions were celebrated both at home and abroad, at conferences, and via special issues of journals and books (e.g., Gorfein and Hoffman published 1987).

The next decisive advance in human learning and memory was Atkinson and Shiffrin's 1968 rehearsal buffer model. The advent of the cognitive revolution around 1960 promoted human learning and memory workers' investigation of item-design (Brown, 1958; Peterson & Peterson, 1959), opening the path for this second conquest. In 1968, the 107 page chapter, entitled: "Human Memory: A Proposed System and its Control Processes," was the prominent contribution to *The Psychology of Learning and Motivation: Advances in Research and Theory* (Vol. 2 edited by Spence & Spence). It was jointly written by Richard M. Shiffrin, then an outstanding graduate student at Stanford, and his well-known advisor/mentor, Richard C. Atkinson, a professor of psychology at the Institute for Mathematical Studies in the Social Sciences, also at Stanford, a major center for advanced research in psychology.

This seminal masterpiece by Atkinson and Shiffrin (1968), just like Ebbinghaus', is a relatively short thesis packed with innovative ideas and sound methods for testing them. Highly impressive is their synthesis of earlier developments, for example, Estes (1955a, 1955b), Broadbent (1957, 1958), Greeno (1967), and Bower (1967), and the innovative constructions thereon. An effort requiring extensive knowledge of mathematics and statistics, and continuing mastery of the then rapidly developing high speed computer technology utilized as a hypothetical approximation of memory systems.

The Atkinson-Shiffrin model advanced both structural and control processes. First, in terms of memory structures, the model assumes three entities: Sensory register (SR), short-term store (STS, or STM), and long-term store (LTS, or LTM). External input/stimulus may be lost in any of the above three postulated structures which accounts for memory/information losses or forgetting (Fig. 1, Atkinson & Shiffrin, 1968, p. 93; reproduced on p. 18 of this volume as Fig. 2.1). Information in LTS can be transferred to STS, and vice versa.

Second, quite uniquely and importantly, the model emphasizes the role of processes controlled by the participants, for example, rehearsal, coding, and search strategies in human memory as the formal postulates of the theory. Most intriguingly, the model assumes a rehearsal buffer in STS where items may survive by virtue of rehearsals or transfer to LTS (Atkinson & Shiffrin, 1968, Fig. 2, p. 113). This postulate stimulated the imagination of many; because of it the Atkinson-Shiffrin model came to be referred to as "the rehearsal buffer model" or simply "the buffer model."

The buffer model's assumptions regarding coding processes and transfer between STS and LTS, storage in LTS, and long-term search processes are clearly spelled by then extant data. Most impressive of all were the rigorous empirical tests of these theoretical assumptions on 68 of 107 pages. Even today, it is very hard not to be impressed by this monumental early accomplishment. This signal contribution by Atkinson and Shiffrin testifies to the importance of the book chapter format to the advancement of outstanding scientific scholarship. Indeed, Atkinson and Shiffrin (1968) had set the direction for the field of memory during the last 30 years and far beyond.

The influence of the Atkinson-Shiffrin model has been profound; it has become one of the most cited references in experimental psychology. 1998 marks the model's 30th anniversary. Considering its exceptional mastery of the events addressed, a celebration seems eminently proper. According to the 1996 (newest) edition of the unabridged Webster's dictionary, "30" among numerical referents signifies "a mark or sign of completion." And according to the free-association norms I developed for numbers 0 to 100 using well over 400 college students (Izawa, pending), the number 30 immediately elicits associations to youth or youthfulness.

Thus, on this occasion, close associates, mentors, former classmates, colleagues, students, postdoctoral fellows, and all admirers of Dick Atkinson and

Rich Shiffrin are here, assembled to celebrate this 30th anniversary of the buffer model. This anniversary volume's uniqueness is enhanced by the model's architects' contributions to it, through authoring the foreword and the lead chapter (scientific contributions), respectively. The rest of the volume is filled with essays and new experiments of high caliber, including one by the winner of the 1997 National Medal of Science.

The Structure of the Volume

Our 30th anniversary celebration volume commemorates a significant victory for researchers in human memory. The foreword by Richard C. Atkinson was prepared despite his consuming schedule as President of the University of California System. Subsequently, in Chapter 2, Richard M. Shiffrin shares his current psychological and mathematical insights.

In Chapter 3, Bennet B. Murdock presents his 30 years' continued effort to improve on an alternative model, TODAM (theory of distributed associative model). In this editor's eyes, scientific debate is a must for the advancement of knowledge. Such scientific controversy facilitates the healthy growth of a discipline. For instance, the Hullian (response learning) vs. Tolmanian (cognitive map development) debates (Yale vs. Berkeley) in the 1930s-1950s, and the all-or-none (Estes/Bower) vs. gradual learning (Bush-Mosteller/Underwood-Postman) controversy (Stanford vs. Penn/Nortwestern-Berkeley) in 1960s-1970s added not only rigor to our research, they also led to new knowledge. Fortunately for readers, the rehearsal buffer model vs. TODAM (Indiana vs. Toronto) is cast in very much the same mold!

In Chapter 4, the arguably best cognitive psychologist today, William K. Estes, favors our readers with an exceptionally insightful discussion. It allows readers to assess the landscape of human memory models of the past three decades with far greater accuracy than has been possible hitherto.

Starting with Chapter 5, some of Atkinson and Shiffrin's colleagues will delve into current hot issues in their laboratories as part of our 30th Anniversary celebration.

Brief Personal Introduction to Contributors and Chapters

Universal concern with the Atkinson-Shiffrin rehearsal buffer model is well reflected by the diverse origins of contributors to this 30th anniversary volume. They are from Europe, Australia, North America, and Asia. This in itself is no small achievement! The following summarizes both the attributes of contributors to the volume and their chapters. More extensive career histories are, of course, publicly available, inclusive of the Internet. The entries follow the sequence of chapters in this volume, except for Chapter 1; its author and the volume editor is introduced along with Chapter 9, her scientific contribution.

Richard C. Atkinson

The foreword to this volume was written by Richard C. Atkinson, co-author with Richard Shiffrin of the model celebrated here. Since 1995, Dr. Atkinson has served as president of the University of California, one of the largest and most distinguished university systems in the world. Before becoming president of the UC System, he was chancellor of UC San Diego; during his 15-year tenure the campus doubled in size while increasing the distinction of its faculty and breadth of its programs.

From 1975 to 1980, Atkinson served at the National Science Foundation, having been appointed as deputy director by President Ford and then as director by President Carter. He had a wide range of responsibilities for science policy at a national and international level, including negotiating the first memorandum of understanding in history between the People's Republic of China and the United States, an agreement for the exchange of scientists and scholars.

Atkinson began his academic career at Stanford University and was a member of the faculty from 1956 to 1975, except for a 3-year period at UCLA. In addition to serving as professor of psychology at Stanford, he held appointments in the School of Engineering, School of Education, Applied Mathematics and Statistics Laboratories, and Institute for Mathematical Studies in the Social Sciences. Complementing the work discussed in this volume was his more applied work on learning in the classroom. In the early 1960s, he developed one of the first computer-controlled systems for instruction, which served as a prototype for the commercial development of computer-assisted instruction. Reading instruction under computer control for young school children has been an important application of the work.

Atkinson has been elected to the National Academy of Sciences, the Institute of Medicine, the National Academy of Education, and the American Philosophical Society. He is past president of the American Association for the Advancement of Science, former chair of the Association of American Universities, and the recipient of numerous honorary degrees. A mountain in Antarctica has been named in his honor.

Given the remarkable scope of his career, it is fitting to have Dick Atkinson reflect on our field on the 30th anniversary of his and Rich Shiffrin's paper, an exceptional collaboration between mentor and student.

Richard M. Shiffrin

Without him, this volume would never have been possible. In 1968, together with his mentor, Dick Atkinson, Richard M. Shiffrin, a young PhD candidate at Stanford published the Atkinson-Shiffrin buffer model, whose 30th anniversary we celebrate this year (1998). The ideas forged in 1966-1967 were the wellspring for a stream of brilliant contributions to research upon memory. Among others were the Search of Associative Model (SAM, 1980, also published in a volume of *The Psychology of Learning and Motivation*, and co-authored with Jeroen Raaijmakers, now Professor at the University of Amsterdam, who carried out his dissertation research with Shiffrin at Indiana in 1979) and Retrieving Effectively from Memory (REM, 1997).

After his undergraduate education at Yale and doctoral training at Stanford, Shiffrin immediately began his permanent academic career at Indiana University in 1968. Currently, the Luther Dana Waterman Professor of Psychology, Shiffrin is the creator and first director of the Cognitive Science Program there. From 1981 to 1984, he edited the *Journal of Experimental Psychology: Learning, Memory, and Cognition*, and served as Associate Editor for the *Psychological Review* between 1976-1982. He continues to be a major consulting editor for cognitive, experimental, mathematical and theoretical journals, and served as co-editor of several important volumes including the 1992 two-volume Festschrift for William K. Estes. He continues active involvement in numerous scientific bodies for psychology, especially cognitive/mathematical psychology and was called on to chair the Psychonomic Society in 1988. His publications of major importance number about 100 and are growing rapidly.

Rich Shiffrin's work is internationally well known. As a result, he has held Visiting Professorships on three different continents, the University of Queensland in Australia (1988), the University of Amsterdam, the Netherlands (1994-1995) in Europe, and the Rockfeller University (1975-1976) in North America. An Honorary Doctorate from the University of Amsterdam was bestowed on him in 1996 (a Dutch journalist traveled to Bloomington to interview him), and in this country, he was inducted into both the National Academy of Sciences and the American Academy of Arts and Sciences in 1995.

Not surprisingly, Rich Shiffrin had a number of outstanding students. A few of the best known include Bill Geisler (Professor at Texas, a leading theorist in vision), Walter Schneider (Professor at Pittsburgh, and co-author with Shiffrin of the influential articles in *Psychological Review* on automatic and controlled processing), and Sue Dumais (now at Microsoft, and recently co-author with Tom Landauer of a model of the development of word meaning), plus those contributing to this volume, cited later.

Shiffrin presents his own account in Chapter 2, "30 Years of Memory." It commences with the original 1968 Atkinson-Shiffrin buffer model, depicts the evolution of SAM, and the subsequent REM. As is Shiffrin's wont, he continuously refines and advances his models to new levels of sophistication, and with each step, forges the next model. Chapter 2 provides tantalizing hints of forthcoming scientific advancements in human memory research, perhaps the most important ones since *Ueber das Gedaechtnis*.

Bennet B. Murdock

Among the most creative and intensely devoted memory researchers and learning theorists today, Bennet B. Murdock, offers an alternative approach to the Atkinson-Shiffrin buffer model, viz. the theory of distributed associative memory (TODAM). Murdock has also been working on his model and its refinements/improvements for nearly three decades. Among my friends, Ben Murdock is the only one who has had personal contact with Clark L. Hull (1884-1952), a giant who built the most comprehensive hypothetical-deductive theory of learning at Yale. Yale provided Ben Murdock's undergraduate and graduate education, awarding him the doctorate in 1951. After Wesleyan, Vermont, and Missouri, Murdock found a permanent home in 1965 at the University of Toronto. He served on editorial boards of several journals, and many professional organizations, including the presidency of the Mathematical Psychology Society (1993-1994). His volume of publications reached at least 125 as of last count. They include his very successful *Human Memory: Theory and Data* (1974). At his retirement from Toronto in 1991, his students, colleagues, and associates honored him with the *Festschrift, Relating Theory and Data: Essays on Human Memory in Honor of Bennet B. Murdock* (Hockey & Lewandowsky, 1991).

In Chapter 3, "The Buffer 30 Years Later: Working Memory in a Theory of Distributed Associative Memory (TODAM)," Murdock presents an excellent review of the field, and has offered a constructive alternative, TODAM (theory of distributed associative memory) to explain many of the same effects in a different theoretical framework, using a working memory of five storage registers. Here, he discusses both similarities and differences between the Atkinson-Shiffrin's rehearsal buffer and TODAM'S working memory.

William K. Estes

On April 30, 1997, President Clinton announced recipients of the National Medal of Science, the Nation's highest science and technology honor. Among those honored was William K. Estes. He was cited for "fundamental theories of cognition and learning that transformed the field of experimental psychology and led to the development of quantitative cognitive science. His pioneering method of quantitative modeling and insistence on rigor and precision established the standard for modern psychological science." Estes received the medal from President Clinton at the White House on December 15, 1997. (The National Medal of Science was established by the United States Congress in 1959, an American version of the Nobel Prize, publicly recognizing individuals for uniquely eminent contributions to science. Only 11 other psychologists were so honored before Estes.)

We are more than fortunate to have someone of Bill Estes' renown grace our volume. Bill Estes obtained his doctorate at the University of Minnesota in 1943, working with B. F. Skinner (a 1968 recipient of the National Medal of Science). Via Indiana, Stanford, and Rockfeller Universities, Estes came to Harvard in 1979, and retired there 10 years later as the Daniel and Amy Starch Professor Emeritus of Psychology. His nearly 200 publications which include 13 books continue to grow annually.

In the 1950s, Estes pioneered the foundation of the mathematical applications in cognitive psychology and demonstrated its utility for such diverse areas as learning, memory, visual perception, attention, categorization, and conceptualization among many others. In my opinion, his work *Toward a Statistical Theory of Learning* in 1950, and the *Stimulus Fluctuation Model* (1955a, 1955b) were definitive landmarks setting the stage for subsequent developments in cognition and my own research as well.

Estes has a record of notable leadership in all psychological associations and organizations related to his interests as a founder of the Psychonomic Society and the Society for Mathematical Psychology, which he served as Chair and President respectively. His work was recognized not only by the National Medal of Science in 1997 (see above), but also by APA's (American Psychological Association) Award for Distinguished Scientific Contributions (1962), and the Gold Medal for Life-Time Achievement in Psychological Science (1992); he was the first person designated by APS (American Psychological Society) to be a William James Fellow (1990) and numerous other honors.

In Chapter 4, Bill Estes makes a definitive assessment of "Models of Human Memory: A 30-Year Retrospective." Estes incisively summarizes the late 1960s-1970s focus of human memory models on STM processes within the modal model and the 1980s emphasis on LTM processes especially on formats, modes of representation and retrieval processes. Furthermore, he considers that the salient features of diverse current models reflect a composite approach likely to serve the same function as the earlier modal model.

Jeroen G. W. Raaijmakers and R. Hans Phaf

In 1977, an outstanding Dutch graduate student, fresh from his Master's Thesis at the University of Nijmegen came to Indiana University to work with Richard Shiffrin. This was the beginning of Jeroen Raaijmakers' close and productive association with Shiffrin. Together, these two creative minds developed new models, including, for example, SAM (Search of Associative Memory) and, very recently, REM (Retrieving Effectively from Memory). Aspects of SAM appeared in the *Psychology of Learning and Motivation* (1980, edited by Bower) and the *Psychological Review* (1981). An overview of the model was published in Vol. 2 of *From Learning Processes to Cognitive Processes: Essays in Honor of William K. Estes* (1992, edited by Healy, Kosslyn, & Shiffrin) and in the *Annual Review of Psychology* (1992, edited by Rosenzweig & Porter).

Jeroen Raaijimakers, who received his undergraduate and graduate education at the University of Nijmegen, subsequently accepted a faculty position at his alma mater. In 1985, he left the university and moved to the TNO Human Factors Research Institute, setting up a new group in applied cognitive psychology. But in 1992, he was welcomed to the University of Amsterdam, where he currently directs the Graduate Research Institute for Experimental Psychology. Today he is one of the Netherlands' leading psychologists. Raaijmakers' publications, in both English and Dutch, exceed 65 and include a successful graduate text on human memory, as well as some research reports on applied cognitive psychology.

R. Hans Phaf, one of Raaijmakers' best co-workers on memory, was educated at the Leiden University which awarded him a PhD in 1991. Currently an Associate Professor of Psychonomics at the University of Amsterdam, he already has an excellent publication record.

In Chapter 5, "Part-List Cuing Revisited: Testing the Sampling-Bias Hypothesis," Raaijmakers and Phaf report on a series of experiments that directly test SAM's predictions of the counterintuitive part-list cuing phenomenon. They confirm that the effect may be reversed under specific conditions as predicted. These experiments strongly support the SAM explanation for the part-list cuing effect, a gratifying outcome for a task well done.

Scott D. Gronlund and Daryl D. Ohrt

Another of Rich Shiffrin's former graduate students, Scott D. Gronlund, came to Indiana from the University of California at Irvine (B. A. in Psychology, Cum Laude). At Indiana, he pursued cognitive psychology with a minor in mathematics, and 1986 saw the completion of his dissertation. After postdoctoral work at Northwestern with Roger Ratcliff, another eminent cognitive psychologist, he joined the faculty at the University of Oklahoma at Norman. As an Associate Professor of Psychology there, he has been actively pursuing two lines of research: Investigations of the cognitive management of complex systems (especially air traffic control) and the empirical and theoretical evaluation of quantitative models of memory.

Given the importance of the list-length effect (LLE) for SAM, Scott Gronlund and his productive graduate student, Daryl D. Ohrt, who receives his PhD in Fall 1998, titled Chapter 6, "The List-Length Effect and Continuous Memory: Confounds and Solutions." They noted that the simplifying assumptions of Atkinson and Shiffrin (1968) regarding the isolation of the study list were challenged by Murdock and Kahana (1993a, 1993b), who claimed that the null LLE was attributable to confounding variables in prior experiments. The two Ohrt and Grunlund experiments demonstrated an LLE despite the elimination of said confounding factors. A modified version of SAM offered a refined explanation for the LLE and other empirical challenges.

Michael S. Humphreys and Gerald Tehan

After Reed College (B. A., 1964), Michael S. Humphreys received his doctorate in Psychology from Stanford, just at the height of pervasive excitement over the new Institute for Mathematical Studies in the Social Sciences at Ventura Hall where the Atkinson-Shiffrin model first saw the light of day. He became well acquainted with Atkinson then and there as a mentor, and came to know Shiffrin and this editor as classmates. After being on the faculty at British Columbia and Northwestern, he sought new frontiers in Australia. Currently Humphreys is Professor of Psychology at the University of Queensland and a former Head of the Department of Psychology. He is also a Fellow of the Academy of the Social Sciences in Australia. He is one of a few second generation psychologists, a son of famous psychologist, Lloyd G. Humphreys.

A prolific and excellent scientist, Mike Humphreys compiled nearly 80 publications and has served as Consulting Editor for *Journal of Experimental Psychology: Human Learning and Memory* (1976-1980, 1987-1989) and has also served as a referee for other journals in the field of human memory broadly conceived. Mike Humphreys' many research interests include the relationship between recognition and recall, role of context in human memory, memory tests, lexical access and the use of cues in STM, and representation of words. He continues to construct a general theory of human memory (a broad-gauged overview) by utilizing ideas from distributed storage and connectionist models. He is of the view that an understanding of memory tasks starts with an analysis of the bindings that are stored, the cues that are used, and the nature of the decision problem. This sentence describes the latest model, the Bind Cue Decide Model of Episodic Memory (BCDMEM).

Gerald Tehan received his B.A. from the University of Queensland in 1983. He then completed a PhD with Mike Humphreys in 1991. Two years prior to this, Tehan took up a faculty position at the University of Southern Queensland where he is now a senior lecturer. The work in Chapter 7 started with Tehan's PhD thesis and represents their continuing collaboration on the role of cues and codes in short term memory.

In Chapter 7, Mike Humphreys and Gerry Tehan discuss "Cues and Codes in Working Memory." The authors reviewed their recent work on retrieval cues and codes that produce proactive interference (PI) in STM in cued recall tasks. In this chapter, the authors report their findings that PI occurred at very short (2 to 4 sec) retention intervals, that PI depends on the cue, and that short phonological memory codes prevent PI. Their cueing and coding ideas have been extended to understand other working memory tasks.

Alice F. Healy and Thomas Cunningham

We are delighted to welcome one of the most productive cognitive psychologists, Alice F. Healy. A close associate of Shiffrin and the first PhD from William K. Estes at Rockfeller (1973), she did her undergraduate work at Vassar College (B. A., Summa Cum Laude, 1968). Formerly on the faculty of Yale, Professor Healy is currently at the University of Colorado, Boulder. Healy, former Editor of *Memory & Cognition* (1986-1989) and Associate Editor of *Journal of Experimental Psychology, Learning, Memory, and Cognition* (1982-1984), is a prolific author, having output at least 100 publications, including four books. Alice Healy was the senior editor for two volumes, honoring William K. Estes for his retirement from Harvard (in 1989, published in 1992). She served as President of the Rocky Mountain Psychological Association (1994-1995), Chair of the Psychology Section of the American Association for the Advancement of Science (1995-1996) and on the Governing Board of the Psychonomic Society (1987-1992) among many other leadership roles she has played, not to mention being on editorial boards of major cognitive and memory journals.

Truly remarkable is her ability to attract a countless number of students, colleagues, and associates in many areas of memory and cognitive processes, psycholinguistics and reading. A case in point: Thomas F. Cunningham, the co-author of Chapter 8, is a PhD from Oklahoma State University (1966), and post-doctoral at Ohio State (1975-1976), and has been busy at St. Lawrence

University as a faculty member, Associate Academic Dean, and Departmental Chair. Cunningham often publishes with Healy, as is the case here.

"Recall of Order Information: Evidence Requiring a Dual-Storage Memory Model" is the title of Chapter 8. After reviewing relevant literature extensively, Healy and Cunningham addressed the recall of order information and the fundamental distinction between STS and LTS by the Atkinson and Shiffrin buffer model (1968). The authors rightly pointed out that their theoretical base, Estes' perturbation model (1972), requires the second memory store (analogous to LTS) in addition to its original single memory store (comparable to STS). Data supported the authors' position.

Chizuko Izawa

As the editor of and contributor to the present volume, Chizuko Izawa wrote both Chapters 1 and 9; the former as the editor, the latter as a contributor to human learning and memory research. In addition to having the honor of being the first of Bill Estes' PhDs at Stanford (1965), this editor was fortunate to have Richard C. Atkinson as a mentor and a dissertation committee member at Stanford, and is doubly blessed to have Richard M. Shiffrin and Mike Humphreys (Chapter 7) as classmates. We all spent much time at the birthplace of the Atkinson and Shiffrin rehearsal buffer model, Stanford's Institute for Mathematical Studies in the Social Sciences, then housed in Ventura Hall. Izawa came to Stanford with a baccalaureate degree from the University of Tokyo and was subsequently awarded a postdoctoral fellowship at the Institute of Human Learning at the University of California, Berkeley (1967-1968).

Using both her native Japanese and acquired English professionally, she produced nearly 70 publications (including three books) and made about 95 presentations worldwide. Since assuming her Tulane faculty position in 1972, Izawa was elected Chair/President of the Southeastern Workers in Memory (1974-1975), and to the Executive Committees of both the Southwestern Psychological Association (SWPA, 1978-1980) and the Southeastern Psychological Association (SEPA, 1998-2001); and she continues to serve in a variety of ways on many other organizations in psychology.

Aspects of efficiency and optimization of learning and retention, and economy of time utilization have been the backbone of Izawa's work since leaving Stanford. She has extensively utilized her own real-life experiences as a learner of 5 languages (Izawa, 1989), in many of her other research endeavors (e.g., TV viewing effects on children's cognitive development, the psychology of numbers and numerical information processing, cognitive processes of cancer patients, minority and women's issues).

To honor her favorite friends, colleagues, mentor, classmate, Izawa reports on three new concurrent experiments (10 conditions) in Chapter 9 of this Volume. "Efficiency in Acquisition and Short-Term Memory: Study-Test-rest Presentation Program and Learning Difficulty." The total time effects and the total time hypothesis (TTH) were thoroughly examined to evaluate four families of hypotheses (composed of 13 single-factor and 1 multifactor individual hypotheses) by varying S (study), T (test), and r (rest) events under constant (or expanded) total time. Contradicted were all families of Bugelski's total time, presentation duration, and frequency hypotheses and their derivatives. However, Izawa's study-test-rest (S-T-r) presentation program hypothesis was supported. She discovered that efficiency in acquisition was learning-difficult dependent. That is, when learning is difficult, the new item-repetition presentation program is superior to the time honored list-repetition program, whereas the reverse holds when learning is easy. However, when learning is of intermediate difficulty or ease, the two programs differ little from each other.

Steven E. Clark

For decades now, there has been debate concerning the similarities and differences between recall and recognition with many interesting human learning and memory phenomena being pursued in consequence. One of the most recent endeavors was the subject of another young promising PhD (1988) in Richard M. Shiffrin's Indiana laboratory viz., Steven E. Clark, who provided Chapter 10. Clark came to Indiana from Illinois State University (B. S.), and he is now an Associate Professor of Psychology at the University of California, Riverside. His major research activities have been focused on developing and testing comprehensive mathematical models of memory, and he is currently working to develop a mathematical model for eyewitness identification. Supported by NSF, at present he is targeting relationships between recall and recognition, retrieval, search, representation of information, item-specific and associative information, eyewitness testimony, and category representation. He actively publishes and also presents his research at professional conferences, and is a consulting editor for *Memory & Cognition*.

In Chapter 10, Clark discusses an intriguing issue, "Recalling to Recognize and Recognizing Recall." After reviewing theory and data regarding recall processes in recognition memory, he concludes that arguments for recall processes often assume the theoretical alternative to be a very simple local-matching familiarity model. However, he views that recall assumptions for more complex familiarity models may be unnecessary; however, because these models take on many recall-like properties, it is difficult to make the distinction between familiarity and recall.

Thomas D. Wickens

The grand finale of our epochal celebration to honor the Atkinson-Shiffrin rehearsal buffer model is in the competent hands of Thomas D. Wickens who, during the 1970s, had daily contact with Dick Atkinson as a postdoctoral fellow at Ventura Hall at Stanford. For Tom Wickens, psychology is a family enterprise, for his parents were highly regarded psychologists, Delos and Carol Wickens, whose two sons followed their example. The elder of the two, Tom Wickens, was well-educated in both psychology and mathematics. He obtained his A. B. in mathematics at Harvard College in 1964 and his PhD in experimental psychology in 1969 from Brown University. After postdoctoral training with Atkinson at Stanford, he joined the psychology faculty of the University of California at Los Angeles, and is currently Professor and Vice Chair for Graduate Affairs at UCLA. His quality publications include three high-powered books and his research interests are best described as quantitative application in cognitive psychology (particularly perception and memory) and statistics.

In Chapter 11, Tom Wickens presents advanced discussions for those with an appetite for mathematical sophistication entitled: "Measuring the Time Course of Retention." He describes elegant probabilistic arguments to select functional form of time course of retention in human memory. He considers functions with declining hazard function to be more satisfactory than those with the flat or rising hazard functions.

References

Atkinson, R. C., & Shiffrin, R. M. (1968). Human memory: A proposed system and its control processes. In K. W. Spence & J. T. Spence (Eds.), *The psychology of learning and motivation: Advances in research and theory, Vol.2* (pp. 89-195). New York: Academic Press.

Bower, G. B. (1967). A multi-component theory of the memory trace. In K. W.. Spence & J. T. Spence (Eds.), *The psychology of learning and motivation: Advances in research and theory*, Vol. I. (pp. 229-325), New York: Academic Press.

Broadbent, D. A. (1957). A mechanical model for human attention and immediate memory. *Psychological Review, 64*, 205-215.

Broadbent, D. A. (1958). *Perception and Communication.* Oxford: Programming Press.

Brown, J. (1958). Some tests of decay theory of immediate memory. *Quarterly Journal of Experimental Psychology, 10,* 12-21.

Ebbinghaus, H. (1885). *Ueber das Gedaechtnis: Untersuchungen zur experimentellen Psychologie* [On Memory: Investigations in experimental psychology]. Leipzig, Germany: Duncker & Humbolt.

Estes, W. K. (1955a). Statistical theory of distributional phenomena in learning. *Psychological Review, 62,* 369-377.

Estes, W. K. (1955b). Statistical theory of spontaneous recovery and regression. *Psychological Review, 62,* 145-154.

Estes, W. K. (1972). An associative basis for coding and organization in memory in A. W. Melton & E. Martin (Eds.), *Coding processes in human memory* (pp. 161-190). New York: Halsted Press.

Gorfein, D. S., & Hoffman, R. R. (1987). (Eds.), *Memory and learning: the Ebbinghaus centennial conference.* Hillside, NJ: Lawrence Erlbaum Associates.

Greeno, J. D. (1967). Paired-associate learning with short-term retention: Mathematical analysis and data regarding identification of parameters. *Journal of Mathematical Psychology, 4,* 430-472.

Hockey, W. K., & Lewandowsky, S. (Eds.). (1991). *Festschrift: Relating theory and data: Essays on human memory in honor of Bennet B. Murdock.* Hillside, NJ: Lawrence Erlbaum Associates.

Izawa, C. (1989). Introduction. Similarity and differences between anticipation and study-test item information presentation methods. In C. Izawa (Ed.), *Current issues in cognitive processes: The Tulane Flowerree symposium on cognition.* (pp. 201-209). Hillsdale, NJ: Lawrence Erlbaum Associates.

Izawa, C. (pending) The psychology of numbers and numerical information processing: Free association norms of Numbers 0 through 100.

Murdock, B. B., & Kahana, M. J. (1993a). Analysis of the list-strength effect. *Journal of Experimental Psychology: Learning, Memory, and Cognition, 19,* 689-697.

Murdock, B. B., & Kahana, M. J. (1993b). List-strength and list-length effects: Reply to Shiffrin, Ratcliff, Murnane, and Nobel (1993). *Journal of Experimental Psychology: Learning, Memory, and Cognition, 19,* 1450-1453.

Peterson, L. R., & Peterson, M. (1959). Short-term retention of individual verbal items. *Journal of Experimental Psychology, 58,* 193-198.

Raaijmakers, J. G. W., & Shiffrin, R. M. (1980). SAM: A theory of probabilistic search in associative memory. In G. H. Bower (Ed.), *The psychology of learning and motivation: Advances in research and theory. Vol. 14* (pp. 207-262). New York: Academic Press.

Raaijmakers, J. G. W., & Shiffrin, R. M. (1992). Models for recall and recognition. *Annual Review of Psychology, 43,* 205-234.

Shiffrin, R. M., & Raaijmakers, J. G. W. (1992). The SAM retrieval model: A retrospective and prospective. In A. F. Healy, S. M. Kosslyn, & R. M. Shiffrin (Eds.), *From learning processes to cognitive processes: Essays in honor of William K. Estes, Vol. 2.* (pp. 69-86). Hillsdale, NJ: Lawrence Erlbaum Associates.

Chapter 2

30 Years of Memory

Richard M. Shiffrin
Indiana University, U. S. A.

One of the very few benefits of the effects of aging upon memory is the chance to read and comment upon the chapter of Atkinson and Shiffrin (1968) as if it were an unread but important early article, known previously only through secondary sources. That chapter was written while I was a Stanford graduate student with Dick Atkinson as an advisor. This commentary is meant to be a nontechnical look at some of the issues developed in that chapter, and at certain aspects of the present state of the field in relation to that chapter.

The Framework

Our framework organized memory along two dimensions. The first is a distinction between permanent structural features of the memory system and control processes. Structural features include the different memory stores. Control processes refer to the operations that are used to operate and control memory, such as rehearsal, coding, selection of cues for long-term retrieval, retrieval strategies during memory search, and decision rules. These control processes overlap considerably with the concepts of attention and 'working memory', and are a standard component of today's theories.

Memory Structures

The second dimension discussed in the 1968 chapter was a division of the system structure into memory stores: sensory registers, short-term store, and long-term store, as illustrated in Fig. 2.1, taken from the chapter. The nature of retention in long-term store is not made clear by this figure. Although there is a dotted box showing decay or interference as a cause of loss from long-term store, the application of the theory to free recall (later in the chapter) makes it clear that the forgetting seen with longer lists is due not to decay or interference, but instead to the failures of a memory search. Thus this chapter can be seen as making a first step toward an assumption of a permanent store, although this assumption was not stated clearly for a few more years. I will discuss the permanence of long-term store at some length later in this commentary. The other two stores were temporary repositories of information. The sensory registers were posited to be close copies of information arriving at the senses, but copies that decayed rapidly (in under a second, say).

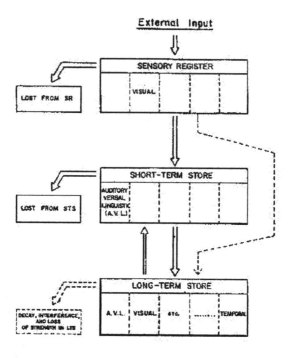

FIG. 2.1. Structure of the Memory System (from Atkinson & Shiffrin, 1968, Fig. 1).

Furthermore, the retention time was not easy or possible to modify with control processes. The short-term store represented "active" memory with longer retention times, and retention in this store could be extended indefinitely by control processes like rehearsal. A typical example would be the rehearsal of a telephone number while looking for a piece of paper to write it down. However, the capacity of short-term store was limited, so only a limited number of items could be maintained. In a typical situation involving verbal materials like words, in which new items continually arrive and demand attention, auditory-verbal-linguistic (or A.V.L.) information would last in the short-term store for about thirty seconds.

The primary division between active and passive memory was an attempt to implement a generally accepted neural metaphor for memory within a cognitive model making specific and testable predications for the then known phenomena of memory. The "metaphor" was the view that neural activity in the form of electrochemical firings represented an active state of memory, but was a poor candidate for long term memory over the course of, say, years; memory for such long periods must be subserved by far longer lasting chemical changes (in the synapses, say), or physical changes (represented by the growth of new neural connections, say). This metaphor has been strengthened considerably over the intervening years and is now a core of the explosively growing field of cognitive neuroscience. Of course there were then (and are now) many ways to represent this general conception within a specific cognitive model, and our chapter probably achieved some of the success it did because it proposed a mapping that seemed plausible to most readers on the one hand, and was capable of predicting and explaining a great deal of behavioral data on the other hand. Within this general conception, it should be noted that the long-term store is an almost unimportant appendage, simply serving as a warehouse for memories—all the important characteristics are part of the active or short-term system. Even when we talk of "long-term retrieval" or "retrieval from long-term store" it is the processes that occur in the active system that play the critical role (in combination with the form in which the memories are "warehoused").

Let me return then to the active memory systems, structurally represented by sensory registers and short-term stores. As illustrated in Fig. 2.1, these structures were populated by few exemplars in 1968—a visual icon in the case of the sensory registers, and A.V.L. information in the case of the short-term store. However, we realized the logical necessity for other types of information in these stores, and reserved slots to be filled in. Indeed, over the intervening years, many types of temporary short-term memories have been identified and studied. In some people's eyes the line between sensory registers and short-term memories have been blurred by this proliferation. However my present opinion is that we may indeed have been correct in drawing this distinction.

Consider for example the visual icon, as studied originally by Sperling (1960): A three by three square of letters is presented very briefly. Subjects can only report about four of these letters. However, in the critical condition the subject is given an auditory signal after a delay ranging up to a second. The signal tells the subject to report just one row. For very brief delays all the letters in that row can be reported, because the icon has not yet decayed. However, the visual icon decays rapidly, so as the delay increases to several hundred ms, performance drops to a low level, representing those letters that had been transferred from the icon to a longer lasting visual short-term memory (the transfer process and/or the longer term visual memory are limited in capacity).

In trying to distinguish between sensory registers and other types of short-term memories, it is important to note that it does not seem to be possible to use internal rehearsal to establish or re-establish an icon; external information arriving at the senses is needed to do so. On the other hand, one of the prime characteristics of what we described as short-term store in the 1968 chapter is the ability to recycle and retain information through control processes like rehearsal. This is true even of visual information, as when we use visual imagery. Thus one can reasonably distinguish sensory short-term stores from more central short-term stores on the basis of the means by which the information is established: Sensory registers are established by external stimulation only, while short-term store is more central, and can be established either by processes initiated by external stimulation, or by internally initiated processes.

This being the case, it is nonetheless true that the primary structural distinction in the memory system is between the active memories (all the short-term and sensory stores) and the passive memory (long-term store). Thus in the following discussion I will generally refer to our system as having two stores.

Although the distinction between an active and temporary short-term memory system, and a passive, and at least relatively permanent long-term store is a critical part of most current memory models, it is not accepted universally. An alternative is a single memory that has a substantial recency component (e.g. Murdock, 1974; 1982). In addition, many modern neural net and connectionist models ignore the possibility of short-term memories (although seldom ruling out their existence explicitly). More recently some researchers have raised objections to our model (which has come to be known as the "modal model of memory"), based on studies showing commonalities between data patterns from studies of short-term retention and long-term retention (e.g. Crowder and Neath, 1991). In my view such results are far from diagnostic (as we discussed in the 1968 chapter), given that performance in a typical short term task is always determined by a mixture of retrieval from short-term store and long-term store.

In looking back at the 1968 chapter, I was struck by the very strong case for the two store approach that was made by the studies of short-term memory studies and the associated quantitative model fits that were summarized in roughly 40 pages of text. The scope of these studies and modeling efforts concerning the interplay of short and short-term systems may not been have been matched since. I believe it is the case that researchers who object to the two-store approach have not provided alternative accounts for this rich set of data. We said then and still believe that any model fit to these data would be hard to distinguish from ours.

Control Processes

Among the control processes emphasized in 1968 were those used to store new information in long-term store. There is probably nothing more important about memory processing in a practical sense. Like most memory researchers, I am often asked what can be done to improve memory. My questioner usually discovers some other pressing appointment when I describe the hard work and long time needed to store information effectively for later retrieval, using various combinations of imagery, mnemonic devices, associative coding and other methods to integrate the new material with what is already known.

Why is integration important? Part of the answer is that essentially all information to be stored consists of a rearrangement and new combination of information already in long-term store. New sensory input plays a relatively small though critical role. For example, if a word like *cat* is presented visually, the external input consists of a pattern of light, and the part of processing not already learned is restricted to simple patterns of contrast and color. The letters, words, meaning, and so forth had all been learned earlier and stored in long-term store. The sensory input serves to prompt the retrieval from long-term store of all this stored information, such as the knowledge of cats. The retrieved information prompted by the sensory input is combined with other information retrieved from long-term store on the basis of internal prompting, such as the stray thought of a Broadway show named *Cats*. It is the combination of all this information that is unique and must be stored during coding. What makes some coding processes effective, and others less so, is still only partly understood; the answer certainly depends on understanding retrieval from long-term store, which I will return to later in this commentary.

Today the Atkinson and Shiffrin article is remembered for only one kind of coding process, a rehearsal buffer, because this was the short term reactivation and coding process that we adopted in all our formal modeling efforts. A rehearsal buffer maintains continuously some fixed number of items (say, four words), and any newly presented input replaces one of the items already in the buffer. Such a model captured two aspects of rehearsal: First it provided a means by which rehearsal maintains items temporarily in short-term store. Second, it provided a means of determining the amount of information transferred to long-term store, since we assumed information stored was related to the amount of time spent in the rehearsal buffer. Thus a rehearsal buffer was a most useful device, but was never intended to exclude a host of more realistic and richer control processes used to facilitate long-term transfer.

Of course, coding processes are only one set among a myriad of others used to carry out the operations of memory. Since the long-term store is simply a passive repository, all the work of memory is in the short-term system, and the processes include decisions, metamemorial decisions, operations used to control the short-term systems, and operations used to retrieve from long- and short-term stores.

The years since the publication of our chapter have seen a great deal of research into the mechanisms of short-term store, although at the same time there has grown a realization that there are numerous short-term stores rather than one (unless one lumps all the active memories together and calls the set short-term store). Thus arguments about which short-term store is the "correct" one are misplaced. Working memory, echoic loops, auditory-verbal-linguistic memory, visual short-term stores, haptic short-term stores (and of course the various sensory registers) are some of the short-term systems that have undergone research over the years. Based on the empirical data, theories have been advanced concerning the mechanisms of each, including time course of retention, causes of forgetting, degree of control, and the ways of coding item, order and position information. Our position in 1968, as depicted for example in Fig. 2.1, was clearly one of positing multiple short-term systems. Certainly a number of details differ from the outline we presented in 1968, and the number of short-term systems is even larger than we guessed at then, but the general characterization we gave in our chapter remains reasonable today.

The Permanence of Long-term Memory

I wish to take up next the control processes used to carry out long-term retrieval, but before doing so it is useful to discuss the question of permanence of long-term storage. Although this was possibility was hinted at in 1968, it was argued directly by Shiffrin and Atkinson (1969). Given that forgetting is the most obvious feature of human memory, it seems strange at first glance to suggest that information is stored permanently in long-term memory. In fact, it might be asked whether anything is stored permanently. Although there are numerous examples of memory for events that occurred many years earlier, it could be argued that what is remembered is not the original event, but subsequent rehearsals of that event. Since the average time interval between the present and the most recent rehearsal of recoverable very old events may be quite small, it could be argued that the existence of old memories has little bearing on the permanence of memory.

This issue has arisen recently in another guise, in which researchers attempt to ascertain whether the recovery of repressed memories is a real phenomenon. For example, someone might claim after treatment that a memory of childhood abuse has been recovered, a memory that had not been available for many intervening years. Is such a thing possible? This has been an emotionally charged issue because it is known that false memories of a variety of sorts are relatively easy to implant in memory (e.g. Loftus & Hoffman, 1989; Roediger & McDermott, 1995; Loftus, 1993). The issue is not whether memory of abuse is possible (of course it is), but rather whether abuse may be forgotten and then remembered or recovered after long periods without access. Unfortunately, we cannot reliably use our own memories to assess whether the so-called repressed memories are memories of the original events or memories of rehearsal at some later point in time; furthermore such rehearsal might or might not reflect the original event (if any) accurately. In an interesting example, Schooler (1994) discussed a case in which a claim was made for recovery of a repressed memory from childhood. It was found that this "repressed" memory had been discussed at length by the person on a number of occasions in the intervening years, but the fact of discussion had itself been forgotten.

Nonetheless, if we move away from repressed memories of traumatic events to normal memories, there is ample evidence that very old memories are sometimes retrievable even after many years of neglect. It is virtually a truism that motor skills are either retained or quickly relearnable after long periods without practice. Some of the evidence in the cognitive domain comes from studies of autobiographical memory (an interesting example comes from Wagenaar, 1986), some from studies of delayed tests of foreign language learned in and not used subsequently school (e.g. Bahrick, 1984), and some from studies of perceptual memory (e.g. Kolers, 1976). Kolers had subjects practice reading text upside down or mirror reversed. They developed considerable skill. More than a year later they retained much of this skill despite little opportunity to practice and little practice in the intervening period. I carried out research (Salasoo, Shiffrin, & Feustel, 1985) in which we gave subjects practice in trying to read briefly presented words and pseudowords. Pseudowords are wordlike but not in the language, like "spet" in English. Fig. 2.2 shows the interesting results.

Both words and pseudowords improved in initial training, until performance came together. We brought the subjects back after a year for a surprise test, and tested them again on the words and pseudowords used in the original training sessions, and words and pseudowords that had not been used in the original training sessions. As can be seen, the trained pseudowords were better than new pseudowords, and as good as words in general. Memory for these had been retained for a year without intervening practice (albeit unconsciously—subjects were not aware that these particular pseudowords had been the ones used in the study a year earlier).

Let us take it as given, then, that at least some memories can be retained over long periods of time without intervening supporting rehearsal. It seems a long step from this position to the position that all memories ever stored in long-term store are retained there indefinitely. Why did we make such an assumption? Part of the answer is based on the fact that retrieval is highly variable and subject to improvements when the period allowed for retrieval is increased. Another part of the answer is the critical role of retrieval cues in accessing long-term memories. We know that some cues are much more effective than others, and numerous game shows are based on the use of "hints" as aids to retrieval. It seems to be a given that good cues are those that were an important part of the initial encoding of an event. Such cues can be specific sights, sounds, or thoughts, or general context, but are critically needed to point retrieval to the right region of memory.

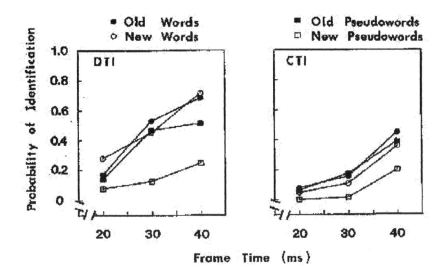

FIG. 2.2. Probability of recall as a function of serial position for Experiment 1, Shiffrin (1970a). Conditions are denoted as follows: the first number is the length of the list *preceding* the recalled list: the second number (underlined) is the length of the recalled list; the third number is the length of the *intervening* list. The means listed are averages of all points in the given serial position curves.

Given that some things in memory can be retrieved at one moment and not another, and given that the use of better cues leads to better retrieval, why not take matters one step further and assume that all forgetting is due to retrieval failure? While this assertion would be almost impossible to prove, it is possible to assemble various sorts of suggestive evidence. For example I published a study (Shiffrin, 1970a) in which subjects were given lists of words and asked not to recall the most recent list, as is typical, but instead the second most recent list. In normal list recall studies, recall drops as the list gets longer. In fact such list-length effects are perhaps the most reliable and universal effects found in the memory literature. Such a list length effect could be due to retrieval failure, or due to some sort of automatic erosion of memory engendered by the competition and interference from the other list words. Fig. 2.3 shows that recall of the words from the penultimate list did not depend on the number of intervening words (that is the number of words in the most recent list), as would be expected on the basis of an erosion account of forgetting. Instead recall depended on the number of words in the list being recalled, as if cues were being used to focus on the relevant list, with the number of words in the region of focus determining the level of retrieval.

Resistance to the permanence hypothesis is due in part to a conceptual argument: Given a finite substrate for memory (the nervous system) there has to be a limit on the amount of information that can be stored, before degradation begins to set in due to overwriting of earlier information. In the limit this must be true, but no one knows whether this is an important limitation during human lifespan. A version of this argument appears in certain attempts to model memory as a highly composite/distributed neural network, in which new memories are laid down in the same neural connections as earlier ones. Although there is merit in such theories, we have learned that degradation produced by superimposition of traces is most unlikely to account for the kinds of forgetting seen in typical laboratory experiments (Ratcliff, Clark, & Shiffrin, 1990; Shiffrin, Ratcliff, & Clark, 1990).

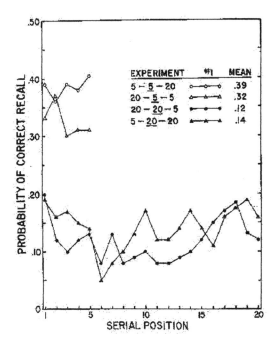

FIG. 2.3. Probability of identification as a function of frame time, for first presentations of items in Experiment 3 from Salasoo et. al., (1985). DTI and CTI refer to two different methods for testing threshold identification.

How Is Information Retrieved from Long-term Store?

My models of long-term retrieval began in the late 1960s and have continued to evolve to the present day. In the 1968 chapter, we introduced the idea of a search model for free recall, a notion that was elaborated in Shiffrin (1970b). The cue-dependent sequential search theory for free and cued recall reached full development in the SAM model of Raaijmakers and Shiffrin (1980, 1981). The basic idea was simple: First we assumed that memories are represented in long-term store as distinct and separate events called images. Retrieval cues are placed in short-term store and serve as the probe of long-term memory. Cues could be words and their associated meanings, category membership, context, internal feelings and moods, sounds and visual patterns, to give a few examples. Each cue is associated with a wide range of images stored in long-term store. The idea behind the SAM model that Raaijmakers and I developed was the notion that retrieval would be focused on the intersection of the memory regions accessed by each cue separately. A multiplication of the separate cue to image strengths produced this focusing, because multiplication meant that the net retrieval strength for an image would be highest for those images that had a high strength of association to all the cues in the probe, not just one.

The final key part of the model was the assumption that recall proceeds as a sequential search. In each cycle of the search, an image is sampled with replacement, in proportion to the retrieval strengths. An attempt is made to recover as much information as possible from the sampled image, and the results are examined. If the correct image is sampled, and if enough information is recovered, then a correct response will occur. A number of other possible outcomes may lead to an incorrect response being made. However, it will often be the case that no response will be made. If so, another sample is made and the process continues. The whole search will continue until a response is made or a decision is made to give up.

Why should the subject ever give up? There are several factors in the model that make such a decision rational. First, sampling with replacement causes decreased retrieval success as time passes: After a while, most images sampled will have been sampled already earlier in the search and have been proven useless. Second, the strongest images tend to be sampled, and hence tend to be resampled, even if useless. Third, there is a tendency to store more information about an image that has just been sampled, so useless samples are strengthened and tend to be sampled again with even higher probability.

In free recall the subject is simply asked to recall all the members of a group in memory, such as the words from a list just seen. This task extends over time, and is inherently sequential. Cued recall need not involve sequential sampling, but was assumed to do so in the SAM model. The key to retrieval in both paradigms is the use of appropriate and specific cues to activate as many as possible of the desired images, and as few as possible of any other images. In both free and cued recall tasks, longer lists produce poorer performance because the proportional sampling rule leads to a lower probability of sampling the desired image(s).

In the SAM model, then, forgetting occurs when retrieval does not succeed. As time passes, several factors tend to harm retrieval: One is that it is harder to find and use appropriate cues. For example, one always has available current context, and it is usually hard to reconstruct past contexts, even if one knows that a memory is old. I may know that something occurred on one of my early birthdays, but the difficulty of reconstructing appropriate temporal context may produce a cue that targets a multiyear window of events (a set of images vastly larger than that accessed by the context cue used for the list just seen).

There may well be a tendency to use present context to probe memory, whether or not it is entirely appropriate, because it is readily available. Combined with the fact that context tends to change over time, these factors make retrieval poorer for older memories. On the one hand the cues used may be less well associated to the memory in question; on the other hand, the cues used may target a much larger region of memory when a memory is old.

Retrieval in Recognition versus Recall

The idea that retrieval during recall operates as a memory search has been accepted for free recall, an inherently sequential process, but has been debated in the case of cued recall, which could in principle occur in one retrieval step. The issue is highlighted by the fact that recognition is almost universally acknowledged to operate as a parallel process of memory activation producing something like a feeling of familiarity. This idea was laid out in greatest detail by Gillund and Shiffrin (1984). Our model was quite simple: we assumed that the decision whether a test item had been, say, on a recent list was determined by summing the activations (that is the retrieval strengths) of all memory images, and responding "old" if the sum was greater than a criterion. Such a model worked quite well (at the time) for recognition data. However, if recognition operates as a global and parallel process, and if free recall as a sequential search process, where does that leave cued recall? One of my students, Peter Nobel, and I have looked into this question recently (Nobel, 1996). We discovered in a series of studies that the response times in cued recall were substantially slowed and spread out in time relative to recognition. Typical results are given in Fig. 2.4. These and related results strongly supported the assumption that cued recall operates as a sequential search.

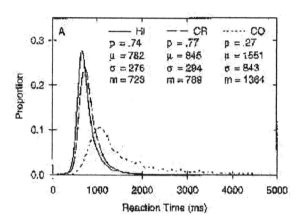

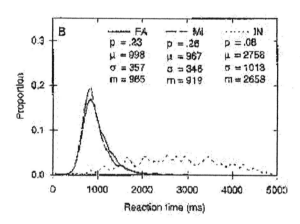

FIG. 2.4. Response time distributions conditionalized for correct (panel A) and incorrect (panel B) responses for recognition [hits (HI), false alarms (FA), correct rejections (CR), and misses (MI)], and cured recall [corrects (CO), and intrusions (IN)]. Data are collapsed over length and strength, and taken from Experiment 1 of Nobel (1996).

Are Memory Traces Separate?

All the models of long-term store with which I have been involved have assumed distinct and separate memory images. There are alternatives to this assumption that deserve discussion. For example, there may be a tendency to merge memory traces together. Consider the following scenario: suppose I hear a story containing a description of a red car; later I hear the same story, but one change is made (of which I am unaware): the car's color is described as yellow. Would the memory of the car then contain a combination so that the car's color is now stored as yellow-red? Note that this idea is quite distinct from alternatives in which memory contains both colors stored either separately in one memory image, or in separate memory images. This idea is carried much further in the case of many (but not all) neural net and connectionist models of memory. These models use composite storage. The idea is that memories are stored in superimposed fashion. Such a model seems a bit bizarre to most observers at first glance, because it seems as if the superimposition of multiple events would soon make any individual memory inaccessible. However, if the length of the vector is very large in comparison with the number of separate events stored, the system can produce reasonable predictions for memory phenomena.

A similar principle underlies the use of holograms to store several different patterns in the same photographic emulsion.

In 1990 I published research (Ratcliff, et al., 1990; Shiffrin, et al., 1990) dealing directly with this issue. We discovered that repeating some items within a list did not harm retrieval of other items in that list (the list-strength effect), even though adding items to a list did produce harm (the list length effect). It was not possible to explain both list-length and list-strength effects by degradation due to composite storage. Indeed all accounts to date of our findings have been forced to assume separate image storage: In frameworks like the SAM model, the images are already separate. In neural net and connectionist accounts, the equivalent of separate storage is assumed: sparse storage. In sparse storage, events may be superimposed, but it is seldom the case that a feature of one event actually lies atop a feature of some other event. Within either approach, repeating or strengthening an item can better differentiate it from alternatives, producing less interference in memory, thereby accounting for the observed data. At least as of this date, therefore, it seems best to assume that event images are stored as separate memory images. There are some potential practical applications of this view. For example, suppose that an eyewitness to a crime reports some memory that is cast into doubt by the testimony of others or by objective evidence. In some of these cases, the "false" memory might be due to sampling an incorrect image, and the "correct" image may also be in memory and potentially retrievable.

Knowledge, Explicit Memory, and Implicit Memory

Some of our memories are identifiable by personal relevance, context, and details concerning the time of storage, such as memory of a word on a recent list, of a visit to the Grand Canyon, or of the place where I parked my car at the airport (if I am lucky). We call such memories episodic or explicit. On the other hand, much of our memory is filled with general knowledge, facts and procedures that we know, but are not identifiable by point of origin. Examples are arithmetic tables, the spelling and meaning of common words, the dates of historic events, the correct method for walking and balancing, and so forth. Over the last 15 years, research into memory for knowledge has grown rapidly. Even more important, research into the interaction between the two forms of memory has evolved as an important subfield. The basic phenomenon is that the occurrence of a recent event, such as presentation of a word in a list to be remembered, affects our retrieval of general knowledge. For example the time to say that a displayed string of letters is a word or a non-word is shortened if the word displayed had been studied in a list twenty minutes earlier. Such demonstrations, and there are many different types, are known as implicit memory phenomena, because they demonstrate the occurrence of a recent event indirectly, through the effect upon access to general knowledge. This phenomenon often occurs without explicit recollection of the recent occurrence, and even occurs in amnesics who can remember little or nothing of recent events when asked explicitly.

All of the models I have discussed thus far, including the 1968 chapter and the SAM models, have been aimed at episodic, explicit memory only. In a recent sabbatical at the University of Amsterdam I worked with Jeroen Raaijmakers to extend our theory to memory for general knowledge and implicit memory. Our first step was to modify the SAM model for recognition to fix some problems that had arisen over the years (see Shiffrin & Steyvers, 1997). There won't be space in this commentary to discuss the modifications. However, in the broadest sense the model remains the same, with activations of memory images, and sampling of these for recall, and summation of these for recognition. What changed was the underlying conception and the mathematical form by which the activations were calculated. The new model correctly predicts those phenomena that were previously fit by SAM, and some new ones that had proved difficult for SAM to handle.

Our second step was to extend this model to memory for knowledge and implicit memory phenomena. We developed the new system in such a way that general knowledge could grow out of the storage of individual events. I only have space to describe it in the broadest possible terms. The idea is that images of individual events are always laid down in long-term store, events marked by contextually specific information. However the storage of such events tends to be incomplete and error prone, depending on the amount and quality of coding given to the event. The memory images stored in this way are the images that have been described, say, in the SAM theory. However, the critical idea is that not only does storage take place in such images, but also in images that had been stored earlier, if the similarity between the two is high enough.

Thus old images tend to accumulate information from subsequent occurrences. For example, storage of a newly encountered word might produce a weak trace. This trace contains contextual information about the conditions of storage. When this word is next encountered a new weak trace is stored again, with new contextual information. In addition, however, some of the new information may be added to the previous trace, both filling it out, and perhaps making it more accurate. In this way, a memory image of a word develops that tends to accumulate information over time, becoming richer and less error prone. In addition, this accumulated trace contains many sorts of context information, from many different occurrences, so that no one context dominates, and the image seems decontextualized—it is not associated with any particular origin. In the case of words, say, we refer to such images as lexical/semantic images. More generally, it is in this way that we assume knowledge develops.

Finally, the same mechanisms can explain implicit memory findings. When an event occurs, such as the presentation of a word, not only is a new image stored for this event, but some of the information about this event is stored in the lexical/semantic image. In particular, what is stored in the lexical/semantic image is some of the current context information, since it is this information that is not already stored in that image. Later, when a general knowledge test is given for that word, some of the probe information will include the current context. Words that have been studied recently will therefore have lexical/semantic traces that better match the current context, and hence will be retrieved more readily.

Final Remark

This brief mention of our new model of memory does no more than hint at its actual implementation, but may give the general idea. Its development is still in early stages, and will be continuing for several years. To me it appears to be a natural successor to the series of models that began with Atkinson and Shiffrin (1968) and have continued to the present day. Thus, in my research the 1968 chapter has not really been supplanted by recent alternatives, but rather amended. Starting with the 1968 framework, the successive models have evolved in a fairly natural way, each model building upon what has gone earlier.

Acknowledgment

The research reported in this chapter was supported by Grant NIMH 12717. Requests for reprints should be sent to Richard M. Shiffrin, Department of Psychology, Indiana University, Bloomington IN 47405, or by email to: shiffrin@indiana.edu.

References

Atkinson, R. C., & Shiffrin, R. M. (1968). Human memory: A proposed system and its control processes. In K. W. Spence & J. T. Spence (Eds.), *The Psychology of Learning and Motivation: Advances in Research and Theory* (Vol. 2, pp. 89-195). New York: Academic Press.

Bahrick, H. P. (1984). Semantic memory content in permastore: 50 years of memory for Spanish learned in school. *Journal of Experimental Psychology: General, 113,* 1-29.

Crowder, R. G., & Neath, I. (1991). The microscope metaphor in human memory. In W. E. Hockley & S. Lewandowsky (Eds.), *Relating Theory and Data: Essays on Human Memory in Honour of Bennet B. Murdock, Jr.* (pp. 111-125). Hillsdale, NJ: Lawrence Erlbaum Associates.

Gillund, G., & Shiffrin, R. M. (1984). A retrieval model for both recognition and recall. Psychological Review, 91, 1-67.

Kolers, P. A. (1976). Reading a year later. *Journal of Experimental Psychology: Human Learning and Memory, 2,* 554-565.

Loftus, E. F. (1993). The reality of repressed memories. *American Psychologist, 48,* 518-537.

Loftus, E. F., & Hoffman, H. (1989). Misinformation and memory: The creation of new memories. *Journal of Experimental Psychology: General, 118,* 100-104.

Murdock, B. B., Jr. (1974). *Human Memory: Theory and Data.* Hillsdale, NJ: Lawrence Erlbaum Associates.

Murdock, B. B., Jr. (1982). A theory for the storage and retrieval of item and associative information. Psychological Review, 89, 609-*626.*

Nobel, P. A. (1996). *Response Times in Recognition and Recall.* Unpublished doctoral dissertation, Indiana University.

Raaijmakers, J. G. W., & Shiffrin, R. M. (1980). SAM: A theory of probabilistic search of associative memory. In G. H. Bower (Ed.), *The Psychology of Learning and Motivation, Vol. 14,* 207-262. New York: Academic Press.

Raaijmakers, J. G. W., & Shiffrin, R. M. (1981). Search of associative memory. *Psychological Review, 88*, 93-134.

Ratcliff, R., Clark, S., & Shiffrin, R. M. (1990). The list-strength effect: I. Data and discussion. *Journal of Experimental Psychology: Learning, Memory, and Cognition, 16*, 163-178.

Roediger, H. L., & McDermott, K. B. (1995). Creating false memories: Remembering words not presented in lists. *Journal of Experimental Psychology: Learning, Memory, and Cognition, 21*, 803-814.

Salasoo, A., Feustel, T. C., & Shiffrin, R. M. (1985). Memory codes and episodes in models of word identification: A reply to Johnston, van Santen, and Hale. *Journal of Experimental Psychology: General, 114*, 509-513.

Schooler, J. W. (1994). Seeking the core: The issues and evidence surrounding recovered accounts of sexual trauma. *Consciousness and Cognition, 3*, 452-469.

Shiffrin, R. M. (1970a). Forgetting, trace erosion or retrieval failure? *Science, 168*, 1601-1603.

Shiffrin, R. M. (1970b). Memory search. In D. A. Norman (Ed.), *Models of Memory* (pp. 375-447). New York: Academic Press.

Shiffrin, R. M., & Atkinson, R. C. (1969). Storage and retrieval processes in long-term memory. *Psychological Review, 79*, 179-193.

Shiffrin, R.M, Ratcliff, R., & Clark, S. (1990). The list-strength effect: II. Theoretical mechanisms. *Journal of Experimental Psychology: Learning, Memory, and Cognition, 16*, 179-195.

Shiffrin, R. M., & Steyvers, M. (1997). A model for recognition memory: REM: Retrieving effectively from memory. *Psychonomic Bulletin and Review, 4*(2), 145-166.

Sperling, G. (1960). The information available in brief visual presentations. *Psychology Monographs, 74*, No. 498.

Wagenaar, W. A. (1986). My memory: A study of autobiographical memory over six years. *Cognitive Psychology, 18*, 225-252.

Chapter 3

The Buffer 30 Years Later: Working Memory in a Theory of Distributed Associative Memory (TODAM)

Bennet B. Murdock
University of Toronto, Canada

The buffer model of Atkinson and Shiffrin (1968) was a milestone in our understanding of human memory. In *Perception and Communication* Broadbent (1958) had laid down a framework for an information-processing view of memory, and the buffer model fleshed this out. Contemporary with the two-store model of Waugh and Norman (1965) and a similar memory model by Bower (1967), it described a possible set of mechanisms for short-term memory and how short-term memory could interface with long-term memory. Further, it had many testable implications, and these were the subject of a very active period of experimentation in the 1970s. This research, dealing with the interactions of short-term and long term-memory and their experimental separation, led to the development of the so-called "modal model" (Murdock, 1967), and this modal model is still presented as the standard view of human memory in many introductory textbooks today.

The theoretical development, however, has certainly not stopped there. The search of associative memory (SAM) model of Raaijmakers and Shiffrin (Raaijmakers, 1979; Raaijmakers & Shiffrin, 1980, 1981) was a detailed extension of the buffer model, and it can account for an impressive array of experimental findings in both recognition and recall (Gillund & Shiffrin, 1984). At more or less the same time distributed memory models such as the linear associator model LAM of Anderson (Anderson, 1970), and the theory of distributed associative memory (TODAM; Murdock, 1979, 1982, 1983) were being developed, and these distributed memory models took a rather different point of view. In contrast to semantic-memory node-and-link models such as the spreading-activation model of Collins and Loftus (1975), distributed-memory models assumed that all items were stored in a common content-addressable memory system and retrieval was achieved by direct access not search. It was a slow-acting parallel system in contrast to a fast-acting serial system and forgetting or memory degradation was gradual not sudden; see Anderson, Silverstein, Ritz, and Jones, (1977) for a more detailed comparison.

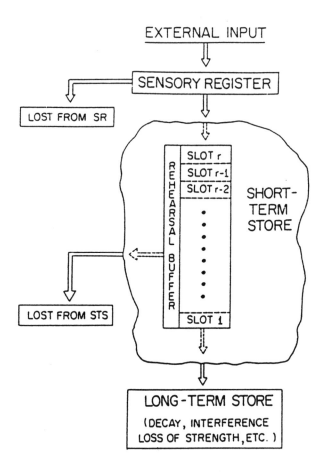

FIG. 3.1. The Atkinson and Shiffrin rehearsal buffer showing the sensory register, the short-term store, and the long-term store. Fig. 2 from Atkinson & Shiffrin (1968).

In addition to LAM, and TODAM, other "global-matching" models include the MINERVA2 model of Hintzman (1988), the matrix model of Humphreys, Bain, and Pike (1989), the composite holographic associative recall model (CHARM) model of Metcalfe-Eich (1982, 1985), and the resonance-retrieval model of Ratcliff (1978). Unlike the buffer model of Atkinson and

Shiffrin, they are global-matching models because all items in memory (or at least all relevant items) enter into the comparison process on recognition tests. However, without going into detail, suffice it to say that some of them (LAM, the matrix model, CHARM, and TODAM) all need a working memory and working memory was an essential feature of the buffer model.

The rehearsal buffer played the role of working memory in the Atkinson and Shiffrin model, and a schematic diagram of the model is shown Fig 3.1. The rehearsal buffer played a maintenance function; it consisted of some r slots which held the few items currently activated. The value of r was typically four for single items and two for paired associates. Items (or associations) were transferred to long-term memory, and that was a second and much more permanent storage system. Items could be recycled if rote repetition was required, but when new information (new items or new pairs) occurred the old items or pairs were displaced from the buffer. If there were four items, and each item occupied one slot in the buffer, when the next item came along one of these four items was displaced. And so it went; once the buffer was full, as each new item came along, one of the old items was displaced.

A probabilistic version of this scheme was reported in Phillips, Shiffrin, and Atkinson (1967), and it had considerable explanatory power. It could explain why there was often a brief (2-3 item) primacy effect in single-trial free recall. List presentation started with an empty buffer, so the first few items had more time for rehearsal; further, this primacy effect should both be graded and hold up in final recall because the greater rehearsal time should lead to more transfer to long-term memory. There should be a more extensive (7-8 item) recency effect which should also be graded but not hold up in final recall, and this prediction was subsequently confirmed by the negative-recency effect reported by Craik (1970). It even explained the asymptotic middle part of the serial-position of free recall; there was equal rehearsal time in the buffer for middle items and, consequently, equal transfer to long-term memory. It is also critical in explaining output-order effects in free recall (Kahana, 1996). In short, primarily because of the assumed operation of the rehearsal buffer, the Atkinson and Shiffrin model predicted all the details of the serial-position effect of free recall and, according to Norman (1970), this was a key test for any model of memory.

This achievement, and the whole utility of this kind of approach, was seriously undercut by the levels approach of Craik and Lockhart (1972) which focused on encoding rather than storage and retrieval. The levels approach turned much memory research into other directions in the late 1970s and early 1980s. However, the notion of a rehearsal buffer and many of its characteristics were incorporated into the SAM model (see Gillund and Shiffrin, 1984), and are still an essential part of the SAM model today (Shiffrin & Raaijmakers, 1992). I think it is fair to say that the current SAM model is basically an extension of the

Atkinson and Shiffrin model; the long-term memory has been spelled out in more detail but the operation of the buffer, while more complex, is still very much in the spirit of the original Atkinson and Shiffrin model.

Distributed-memory models (or at least LAM, the matrix model, CHARM, and TODAM) need a working memory but it is somewhat different from the rehearsal buffer of Atkinson and Shiffrin. According to all these models (and many connectionist models as well) items are represented as random vectors; that is, vectors whose elements are random variables. These elements are abstract characteristics of items like genes at the time of Mendel or elementary particles in high-energy physics today. One can think of them as features or computational units and, as an ensemble, the item vectors are the basic information the memory system must store and retrieve. Exactly how this is done differs according to the model; here we will focus on TODAM and the operations involved in working memory.

TODAM

TODAM, an acronym for Theory of Distributed Associative Memory, is based on the convolution-correlation formalism of Borsellino and Poggio (1973). Items are assumed to be represented as random vectors.They are associated by the operation of convolution and retrieved by the inverse operation of correlation. For the purposes of this chapter it is not necessary to understand exactly what convolution or correlation is; the interested reader could see Metcalfe-Eich (1985) or Murdock (1996). All that is necessary is to understand that convolution is a way of combining two vectors into a third vector which is different from either of its constituents. Correlation is a way of retrieving one of them given the other as the probe. Symbolically, if we represent the item vectors as **f** and **g** then the convolution (denoted by *) is **f*g**. The retrieved item will be an approximation to the target item and we denote an approximation by a prime. Then, if **f** is the probe, the correlation (denoted by #) of **f** with the pair is

$$\mathbf{f} \# (\mathbf{f} * \mathbf{g}) = \mathbf{g}' \ \rightarrow \ \mathbf{g}$$

where the arrow denotes the deblurring or cleanup of the fuzzy **g'** into the target item **g**. (Deblurring in TODAM is like recovery in SAM; it is an additional step required to map the retrieved information into a list item.) Since convolution is commutative (**f*g = g*f**) it is also the case that

$$\mathbf{g} \# (\mathbf{g} * \mathbf{f}) = \mathbf{f}' \ \rightarrow \ \mathbf{f}.$$

Where do these operations take place? They must take place somewhere, and we call this place Working Memory. The system architecture consists of the P-System (P for perceptual), the Q-System (Q for query; this is the long-term memory system), the R-system (R for response), and Working Memory (Fig 3.2). Note that Working Memory interacts with all three systems (P, Q, and R) and the double-headed arrows indicate the bidirectionality.

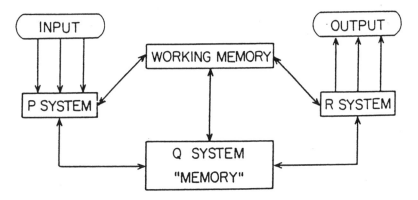

FIG. 3.2. The system architecture in TODAM showing the interaction of Working Memory with the P-system, and Q-system, and the R-system. Fig. 2 from Murdock (1983).

Working Memory

For a complete account, it seems to be necessary to assume that Working Memory consists of five storage registers. These registers are specialized for array processing, and we need five of them if we are to account for the storage and retrieval of item, associative, and serial-order information in simple episodic-memory tasks. Suppose we have to remember an A-B pair. Item A, represented by the random vector **f**, goes in one slot (storage register), Item B, represented by the random vector **g**, goes in another slot, and the association or convolution (**f∗g**) requires a third slot. We cannot use the **f** or **g** slot for the convolution because that would overwrite the **f** or **g** item during the process of the convolution.

Denote the five slots as **v**, **w**, **x**, **y**, and **z**. Then we can schematize this simple process as follows:

$$v \leftarrow f, \quad w \leftarrow g,$$
$$x \leftarrow v * w.$$

The vector f is written to register v, the vector g is written to register w, and the contents of v (i.e., f) and the contents of w (i.e., g) are convolved and the result ($f*g$) is stored in x. We assume that f can be written to v and g to w at the same time (i.e., in parallel) which is why they are written on the same line.

Is there anything special about these registers? That is, do v and w have to store the items and x the association, or could any register play any role? There may be some specialization, but here we will assume complete flexibility; any register can play any role.

Now let us consider a slightly more complex case. Suppose a list of paired-associates is presented, and the subject stores both item information and associative information. (Item information allows us to remember single items or events such as names and faces while associative information allows us to remember their pairing; e.g., which name goes with which face.) If we disregard differential attention to items and pairs and probabilistic encoding (any given feature is only encoded with some probability), then the basic storage equation is:

$$M_j = \alpha M_{j-1} + f_j + g_j + f_j * g_j$$

where M is the memory vector (in this case, Working Memory) and α is the forgetting parameter, $0 \leq \alpha \leq 1$. The contents of Working Memory (i.e., M) after the j_{th} pair in the list has been presented are exactly the same as the contents of Working Memory after the $(j-1)_{th}$ pair except that M has been decremented slightly (α is generally quite close to 1.0) and the new items (f_j and g_j) and their convolution (f_j*g_j) have been added to M. How can this be implemented in Working Memory?

$$v \leftarrow f, \quad w \leftarrow g,$$
$$x \leftarrow v * w,$$
$$y \leftarrow v + w + x.$$

Thus, all it takes is one more register and one more step. We now need a fourth register (y) and assume that the three additions can be done in parallel. The result is that at the end of the list what we called M in our storage equation is really one particular register (in this case, y) in Working Memory and it holds the item and associative information for all the pairs in the list. As a result, we can discriminate between items in the list and items not in the list, discriminate between intact and rearranged pairs, and recall B_j given A_j as the probe or recall A_j given B_j as the probe.

A question that immediate arises is whether the addition (i.e., $\mathbf{v} + \mathbf{w} + \mathbf{x}$) involves displacement (i.e., $\mathbf{f}$, $\mathbf{g}$, and $\mathbf{f*g}$ displace the previous contents of $\mathbf{y}$) or whether it is more like superposition (i.e., a "store $+$" operation where the contents of $\mathbf{v}$, $\mathbf{w}$, and $\mathbf{x}$ are simply added to the previous contents of $\mathbf{y}$). The same question arises in the original assignment of $\mathbf{f}$ to $\mathbf{v}$ and $\mathbf{g}$ to $\mathbf{w}$. My personal opinion is that superposition with attenuation is more likely, but so far I have only investigated the displacement alternative.

Finally, take the chunking model (Murdock, 1992), which is one possible model for serial-order information. We must store the item information because subjects can recognize items that had been presented in the list, but we also need multiple convolutions and n-grams to form chunks. A multiple convolution is an n-way convolution of the form $f_1*f_2*...*f_n$ where n could be 2, 3, 4,... This idea comes from Liepa (1977) in his CADAM model (the forerunner of both TODAM and CHARM) where an (n-1)-way multiple convolution is the retrieval cue for an n-way multiple convolution. Thus,

$$a \# (a*b) = b',$$
$$(a*b) \# (a*b*c) = c',$$
$$(a*b*c) \# (a*b*c*d) = d', \text{ etc.}$$

Where do the multiple convolutions come from? With two items (a pair) you only have to associate A and B but with three items you have to associate A with B with C to form a three-item chunk. With four items you have to associate A with B with C with D to form a four-item chunk, etcetera. These n-item chunks arise from n-grams, the n-way convolution of the sum of n items. If we symbolize n-grams as $G(n)$ then

$$G(2) = (a+b)^{*2} = a*a + b*b + 2(a*b),$$
$$G(3) = (a+b+c)^{*3} = a*a*a + b*b*b + c*c*c + 3(a*a*b + a*a*c + ... + b*c*c) + 6(a*b*c),$$

or, more generally,

$$G(n) = \sum_{i=1}^{n} \left(f_i \right)^{*n}.$$

Since an n-gram will always include an n-way convolution involving each of the n items (and this n-way convolution will always be the strongest component in the chunk), we need to have the n-grams sitting in Working Memory waiting for the next multiple convolution to come along as a retrieval cue. How can Working Memory do all this?

To set up a chunk (the sum of n n-grams) we need five registers: one to hold the sum of the items presented to date, three to do the multiple autoconvolutions required for the n-grams, and one to hold the sum of the n-grams which constitute the chunk. For more details, see Fig. 10.1 in Murdock (1992). We only need four registers to use multiple convolutions as probes in serial recall. Store the chunk in register **w** and store "context" (the probe for the recall of the first item) in register **x** then

$$z \leftarrow x \# w,$$
$$\text{Recall } z,$$
$$y \leftarrow z,$$
$$z \leftarrow x * y,$$
$$x \leftarrow z,$$
$$\text{Repeat.}$$

The fifth register (**v**) could be used to keep track of the items recalled to date.

It is a bit vague to use "context" as the retrieval cue for the first item, and at this point we cannot be too clear about exactly what this means. In the original chunking paper we simply used the delta vector, where the delta vector (δ) is a center-justified vector with 1 in the middle position flanked by zeros on both sides. This does in fact retrieve the first item because **a** in the only single item in the chunk, but then this sidesteps the problem of how you get the right chunk in register **w**. This is not a problem for immediate recall but could be a problem for delayed recall, especially if other chunks were learned or used during the retention interval.

Recall and Recognition

Can the chunking model do recall and recognition? More particularly, does it show primacy for ordered recall and recency for item recognition? These are prominant characteristics of recall and recognition that show up consistently in the experimental literature. An example of the primacy you get in serial recall is shown in Fig. 3.3; note that as the list length increases so do the slopes. At any given serial position, the correct recall level decreases monotonically as list length increases. An example of the recency you get in item recognition is shown in Fig. 3.4, which shows reaction time to a probe test for an immediate and delayed test as a function of backward serial position.

Figure 3.5 shows the results from a simulation of the chunking model in which we varied chunk size (list length) and ran both recall and recognition after each list presentation. (With computer simulations you do not have to worry about contamination from one task to another.) In the simulation we formed chunks of the requisite size (2 to 7) as described above. For recall we followed the described retrieval process, correlating the convolution of the items retrieved to date with the chunk and scoring the retrieved information by a best-match criterion; see Murdock (1995) for details. For item recognition we compared the probe item to register x (this register held the accumulated item information) using the dot product operation, the standard comparison operation in TODAM.

For recognition, we did not compute reaction time because that requires a decision process. Instead, we determined d' for each item in each chunk, and that is what is plotted in Fig. 3.5. The d' values decrease with lag and this corresponds to the increase in reaction time with backward serial position shown in Fig. 3.4. The important point is that the curves in the recognition panel of Fig. 3.5 essentially lie on top of each other, just as they do in Fig. 3.4.

One of the problems of the chaining model noted by Mewhort et al (1994) and Nairne and Neath (1994) is what you use as the cue (probe) for the multiple convolution for the next probe regardless of whether the best match was right or wrong. If the best match had a negative dot product we used whatever

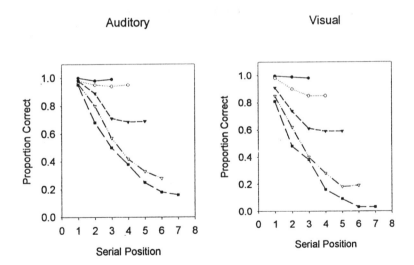

FIG. 3.3. Proportion of correct recalls as a function of serial position for auditory and visual presentation for list lengths 3-7 Data from Drewnowski and Murdock (1980).

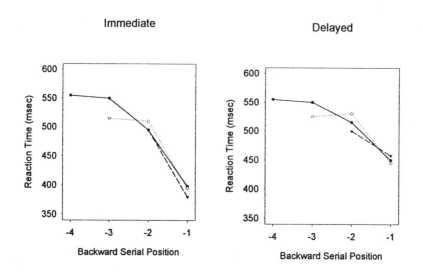

FIG. 3.4. Mean reaction time at a function of backward serial position for a delayed or immediate test for set sizes 2-4. Data from Monsell (1978).

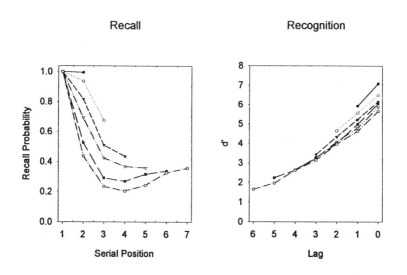

FIG. 3.5. Results from a simulation of the chunking model for recall and recognition for list lengths 2-7. Fig. 4.7 and 4.8 from Murdock (1995).

had been retrieved even though it was not a proper item. While the correspondence between the simulation results and the experimental results for recall is quite good, there is one clear discrepancy. At the later serial positions, the recall simulation curves for the long lists do not fan out the way the experimental data do. A likely reason is that experimental subjects form several chunks but in the simulation we only used a single chunk for all lists.

In the simulation, why is there primacy in recall and recency in recognition? With recall there is output interference. Quite apart from the increase in error probability as recall proceeds (with its attendant deleterious effects on subsequent recall), the variability of the retrieved information increases with each step because the multiple convolution used as the probe gets larger. For the item recognition, we actually used a relatively small value of α (0.8) which guaranteed a marked recency effect. While this might be questionable, our justification was that we wanted to see if the same encoding algorithm and the same set of parameter values could result in primacy for recall and recency for recognition. The answer was clearly affirmative; this small value of α had no noticable effect on recall. Apparently TODAM can produce a clear experimental separation between serial recall and probe recognition.

Before we get too complacent about our good fits, we should acknowledge a possible problem noted by one of our colleagues (thanks to Gus Craik for this point). While the experimental data differentiating recall and recognition are very clear, these studies are almost always either between experiments or, if within experiments, then precued. Consequently, subjects know what kind of test they will get and can prepare (encode) accordingly. Will we get the same results with postcuing?

The answer seems to be no (or at least partly no). In several recent experiments (Duncan & Murdock, under revision) we have found that recall is exactly the same (and follows the pattern shown above) regardless of whether it is precued or postcued. On the other hand, recognition is definitely not the same. With precuing, the typical recency result occurs but with postcuing the recognition serial-position curve is essentially flat (Fig.3.6). Not only that, but it is about level with the slowest performance of the precued group, not the fastest performance.

Why does this happen? Subjects say that, when postcued, they prepare for recall and somehow this is different from when they prepare for recognition. The converse of this is certainly true; a subsequent experiment showed that when subjects expect recognition and are very occassionally given a recall test their recall performance is abysmal. But this does not tell us how their recognition encoding differs in the two cases (precuing and postcuing).

A possible explanation is as follows: when subjects expect recall, or when they are postcued and prepare for recall, they form chunks as described above. As the simulations show, TODAM can generate the right pattern of data with no difficulty. When they are precued on recognition they do not form chunks; there is no need to. They use some other means of encoding, yet to be specified. But the critical question is what explanation can we give for the recognition results when they are postcued (and so presumably form chunks). An

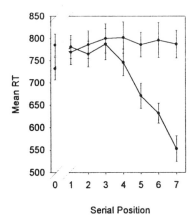

FIG. 3.6. Mean reaction time as a function of serial position for postcued and precued recognition. Experiment 1 from Duncan and Murdock (under revision).

easy answer is that they have to unpack the chunk(s) and this is not only slow (explaining why the latency curve is so high) but also there is only a single comparison process (so the curve is flat). However, there is a problem with this interpretation. The item information is contained in register x so why do they have to unpack the chunk? They can treat register x as a simple matched-filter (Anderson, 1973) and run the comparison process on that.

Now we have less grounds for complacency. Our overall analysis has suggested a particular answer to an interesting question, but when we look at the hypothesized operation of Working Memory we find that our tentative conclusion does not hold up. Either our overall analysis is wrong or our analysis of Working Memory is wrong; this remains to be seen. But the theoretical analysis has led to some interesting experimental results, and the experimental results reflect sharply on the theoretical analysis. In the best tradition of the buffer model, this is what models are supposed to do.

Item and Assocative Information

How can the nature of Working Memory help us to understand better item and associative information? Again, item information refers to the information in memory that enables us to remember single items or events such as names and faces; associative information is the information in memory that enables us to remember how pairs of items go together (e.g., which name goes with which face). Data on short-term memory for single paired associates provide another look at the possible operations of Working Memory.

Paired Associates

Shortly after the breakthrough experiments on the retention of single items by Peterson and Peterson (1959), we embarked on an extensive study of the short-term memory for single pairs. The usual procedure involved the single presentation of a short list of pairs of randomly selected common words followed by a single-item probe for one of the pairs. Thus, we would present A-B, C-D, E-

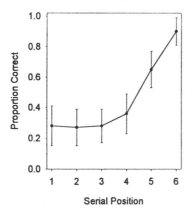

FIG. 3.7. Proportion correct as a function of serial position for a probe paired-associate recall task. Data from Exp. 3 of Murdock (1963a).

F, G-H, I-J, and K-L (list length was typically six) and then immediately probe for the cued recall of one of the pairs (e.g., G- ?). A number of subjects would be tested on several sessions with many lists per session so we could obtain stable data. Study time per pair was relatively short (usually 2 sec/pair) to minimize rehearsal.

Typical results from such a procedure are presented in Fig. 3.7 which shows recall probability as a function of the serial position of the probe. There is a very precipitous recency effect. The last pair is almost always recalled correctly, the next-to-last pair is recalled less frequently, and the first four pairs in the list are recalled with about the same probability which is much lower still. Note that these results occur with practiced subjects. With naive subjects who are only given one trial, there is a one-item primacy and a one-item recency effect but all the other pairs are at asymptote.

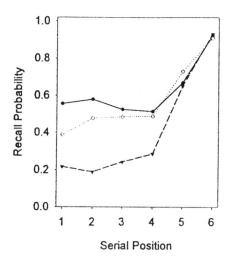

FIG. 3.8. Recall probability as a function of serial position following one (triangles), two (open circles), or three (filled circles) resentations of a list of six paired associates. Data from Experiment 3 of Murdock (1963c).

Output interference is very much like input interference What is critical is the lag between study and test (Murdock, 1963b; Tulving & Arbuckle, 1963). For lag zero (last pair studied, first pair tested) recall probability is very high. For lag one (either the next-to-last pair tested first or the last pair tested second) recall probability is intermediate, and from lag two on recall probability is at asymptote. It does not matter whether an early pair is tested first or the last pair tested later; recall probability is essentially the same.

Repetition boosts the asymptote but does not seem to change the recency effect. At least up to three presentations, the asymptote increases but the recency effect (relative to the asymptote) stays the same (Fig. 3.8). In this study, the list was presented once, twice, or three times (always in the same order) before the probe was presented, and the subjects did not know in advance how

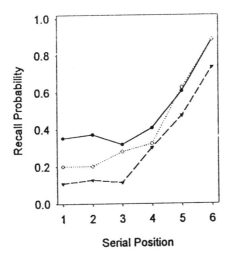

FIG. 3.9. Recall probability as a function of serial position following presentation of a list of six paired associates for 1 (triangles), 2 (open circles) , or 3 (filled circles) sec per pair. Data from Experiment 2 of Murdock (1963c).

many list presentations there would be.

A similar result occurs when you vary presentation rate. When lists are presented at a slow (3 sec/pair), medium (2 sec/pair), or fast (1 sec/pair) rate, the recency effect is much the same, but the asymptote drops down (Fig. 3.9). Thus, repetition and presentation rate seem to affect the asymptote but not the recency effect.

With a single presentation there is a definite modality effect; auditory presentation is much better than visual presentation for the next-to-last pair, but the asymptote is essentially the same (Fig. 3.10). If vocalization is not prevented modality differences are greatly reduced (Murdock, 1966, Fig 1) but this is typical of modality effects in short-term memory (Penney, 1989).

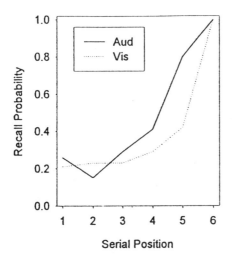

FIG. 3.10. Recall probability as a function of serial position following auditory or visual presentation of a list of six paired associates. Data from Experiment 1 of Murdock (1967).

Our results always supported the principle of associative symmetry proposed by Asch and Ebenholtz (1962). Performance is the same regardless of whether the left-hand item was the cue for recall of the right-hand item or vice versa (Murdock, 1966). There are exceptions to this principle (Kahana, submitted), but with a single presentation where the left- and right-hand items are drawn from a common word pool the symmetry principle seems to apply.

Finally, one can wipe out the recency effect for paired associates without affecting the asymptote, much like free recall (e.g., Glanzer & Cunitz, 1966). Fig. 3.11 shows the results when an unfilled interval of 0, 5, or 10 sec. preceding the probe (left-hand panel) or the retention interval was filled with shadowing (right-hand panel). Overall, the free-recall analogy is quite striking; the recency effect is transitory but the asymptote is sensitive to experimental manipulations such as presentation rate and number of repetitions.

What do these data tell us about the operation of Working Memory? At first glance, the two-item recency effect seems strikingly consistent with the analysis we have presented above. Convolution (for association) takes three

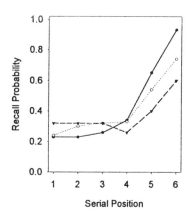 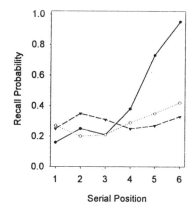

FIG. 3.11. Recall probability as a function of serial position following a 0 (open circles), 5 (closed circles), or 10 (triangles) sec unfilled (left panel) or filled (right panel) delay. The data in the left panel come from an unpublished study while the data in the right panel come from Experiment 2 of Murdock (1967).

registers, and there are a total of five registers available. Like the buffer model of Atkinson and Shiffrin, Working Memory is a push-down stack so, in a sense, the last item is always on top. Consequently, the last pair will always be recalled and that is no surprise. But then why is the penultimate pair at half strength compared to the asymptote?

Suppose the two items always went in the same registers (e.g., v and w) but there was double-buffering of the convolution; that is, the convolution alternated in a regular fashion between two other registers (e.g., x and y). Then the item and associative information would both be stored in the last register (e.g., z). In particular:

$$v \leftarrow f_1 \qquad\qquad v \leftarrow f_2, \qquad\qquad v \leftarrow f_3,$$
$$w \leftarrow g_1, \qquad\qquad w \leftarrow g_2, \qquad\qquad w \leftarrow g_3,$$
$$x \leftarrow v*w, \qquad\qquad y \leftarrow v*w, \qquad\qquad x \leftarrow v*w,$$
$$z \leftarrow v+w+x, \qquad z \leftarrow v+w+y, \qquad z \leftarrow v+w+x, \text{ etc.}$$

This would certainly work for two-pair lists; we could recall either of two pairs with essentially perfect accuracy and the item information could be retrieved relatively accurately from register z. Some relevant data are shown in Table 3.1, which gives the results from three different experiments in which list length varied in an unpredictable fashion. We analysed the data as a function of the number of prior pairs (proactive inhibition, or PI) and the number of subsequent pairs (retroactive inhibition, or RI). For two pairs recall was essentially perfect regardless of which pair was tested. As you go to three pairs the results change, and recall of the first pair (and, to a lesser extent, the second pair) drops markedly. Thereafter the results quickly turn into the typical results shown in Fig. 3.7.

This would explan why recall of two pairs was essentially perfect and why recall of three pairs shows a big recency (RI) effect. However, why is the recall of the next-to-last pair in the longer lists less than perfect? One could argue that, as list presentation starts, the double alternation works perfectly but becomes somewhat erratic as list presentation continues so sometimes (in fact about half the time) pair j overwrites pair j-1. This could be, but it is clearly ad hoc.

Why is recall of the next-to-last pair so poor with visual presentation? Even worse, if Working Memory is the antechamber to long-term memory and the asymptote reflects long-term memory, how can mode of presentation have no effect on the asymptote given this large difference at the next-to-last serial position? It does not help to have separate Working Memories for auditory and visual presentation if they both have the same transfer function.

Table 3.1

Results of Three Different Experiments Investigating the PI x RI Interaction in the Short-Term Retention of Single Paired Associates. The Rows are PI, and the Columns are RI.

			RI		
PI	0	1	2	3	5
0	.96	.81	.36	.46	.28
	.98	.82	.48	.40	.35
	.99	.89	.43	.43	.35
1	.86	.61	.31	.21	.11
	.98	.70	.38	.23	.26
	.97	.78	.35	.30	.26
2	.94	.59	.23	.18	.25
	.96	.65	.32	.22	.21
	.97	.68	.42	.16	.21
3	.94	.43	.21	.23	.20
	.94	.60	.30	.28	.26
	---	---	---	---	---
4	---	---	---	---	---
	---	---	---	---	---
	.88	.69	.31	.27	---
8	---	---	---	---	---
	---	---	---	---	---
	.90	.62	.20	.23	---

Discussion

Clearly our analysis of Working Memory leaves something to be desired. It captures some aspects of the data but there are also some glaring inconsistencies. Our analysis highlights the fact that, if one is going to propose a process model for human memory, it is necessary to specify how these processes are being carried out. In the present case, that means specifying the operations of Working Memory. Just as a computer simulation of a process model requires one to be more specific than a verbal formulation and is useful in highlighting inconsistencies or contradictions, an analysis of Working Memory may raise issues that a simple enumeration of the processes involved might overlook.

Thirty years ago Atkinson and Shiffrin introduced the rehearsal buffer as part of short-term memory. Since then we have learned a lot about it, but we do not have the final answers yet. The rehearsal buffer, now known as Working Memory, is still vital to the understanding of how human episodic memory works.

Acknowledgements

Preparation of this chapter was supported by Research Grant APA 146 from the Natural Science and Engineering Research Council of Canada. I would like to thank Mike Kahana for many helpful comments on the chapter.

References

Anderson, J.A. (1970). Two models for memory organization using interacting traces. *Mathematical Biosciences*, *8*, 137-160.

Anderson, J.A. (1973). A theory for the recognition of items from short memorized lists. *Psychological Review*, *80*, 417-438.

Anderson, J.A., Silverstein, J.W., Ritz, S.A., & Jones, R.S. (1977). Distinctive features, categorical perception, and probability learning: Some applications of a neural model. *Psychological Review*, *84*, 413-451.

Asch, S.E., & Ebenholtz, S.M. (1962). The principle of associative symmetry. *Proceedings of the American Philosophical Society*, *106*, 135-163.

Atkinson, R.C., & Shiffrin, R.M. (1968). Human memory: A proposed system and its control processes. In K.W. Spence & J.T. Spence (Eds.), *The psychology of learning and motivation: Advances in research and theory, Vol. 2* (pp. 89-195). New York: Academic Press.

Borsellino, A., & Poggio, T. (1973). Convolution and correlation algebras. *Kybernetik*, *122*, 113-122.

Bower, G.H. (1967). A descriptive theory of memory. In D. P. Kimble (Ed.), *Learning, Remembering, and Forgetting*, Vol. 2. (pp 112-185). New York: New York Academy of Sciences.

Broadbent, D.E. (1958). *Perception and communication*. New York: Pergamon Press.

Collins, A.M., & Loftus, E.F. (1975). A spreading-activation theory of semantic processing. *Psychological Review, 82*, 407-428.

Craik, F.I.M. (1970). The fate of primary memory items in free recall. *Journal of Verbal Learning and Verbal Behavior, 9*, 143-148.

Craik, F.I.M., & Lockhart, R.S. (1972). Levels of processing: A framework for memory research. *Journal of Verbal Learning and Verbal Behavior, 11*, 671-684.

Drewnowski, A., & Murdock, B.B. (1980). The role of auditory features in memory span for words. *Journal of Experimental Psychology: Human Learning and Memory, 6*, 319-332.

Duncan, M., & Murdock, B.B. (under revision). Recognition and recall with precuing and postcuing.

Gillund, G., & Shiffrin, R.M. (1984). A retrieval model for both recognition and recall. *Psychological Review, 91*, 1-67.

Glanzer, M., & Cunitz, A.R. (1966). Two storage mechanisms in free recall. *Journal of Verbal Learning and Verbal Behavior, 5*, 351-360.

Hintzman, D.L. (1988). Judgments of frequency and recognition memory in a multiple-trace memory model. *Psychological Review, 95*, 528-551.

Humphreys, M.S., Bain, J.D., & Pike, R. (1989). Different ways to cue a coherent memory system: A theory for episodic, semantic, and procedural tasks. *Psychological Review, 96*, 208-233.

Kahana, M. J. (1996). Associative retrieval processes in free recall. *Memory & Cognition, 24*, 103-109.

Kahana, M.J., & Caplan, J. (under revision). *Memory for serial order: Effects of compound cueing, target ambiguity, and recall direction.*

Liepa, P. (1977). *Models of content addressable distributed associative memory (CADAM).* Unpublished manuscript, University of Toronto.

Metcalfe-Eich, J.M. (1982). A composite holographic associative recall model. *Psychological Review, 89*, 627-661.

Metcalfe-Eich, J.M. (1985). Levels of processing, encoding specificity, elaboration, and CHARM. *Psychological Review, 92*, 1-38.

Mewhort, D.J.K., Popham, D., & James, G. (1994). On serial recall: A critique of chaining in TODAM. *Psychological Review, 101*, 534-538.

Monsell, S. (1978). Recency, immediate recognition memory, and reaction time. *Cognitive Psychology, 10*, 465-501.

Murdock, B.B. (1963a) Short-term retention of single paired associates. *Journal of Experimental Psychology, 65*, 433-443.

Murdock, B.B. (1963b). Interpolated recall in short-term memory. *Journal of Experimental Psychology, 66*, 525-532.

Murdock, B. B. (1963c). Short-term memory and paired-associate learning. *Journal of Verbal Learning and Verbal Behjavior, 2*, 320-328.

Murdock, B.B. (1966). Foward and backward associations in paired associates. *Journal of Experimental Psychology, 71*, 732-737.

Murdock, B.B. (1967). Recent developments in short-term memory. *British Journal of Psychology, 58*, 421-433.

Murdock, B.B. (1979). Convolution and correlation in perception and memory. In L.G. Nilsson (Ed.), *Perspectives in memory research: Essays in honor of Uppsala University's 500th Anniversary* (pp. 105-119). Hillsdale, NJ: Lawrence Erlbaum Associates.

Murdock, B.B. (1982). A theory for the storage and retrieval of item and associative information. *Psychological Review, 89*, 609-626.

Murdock, B.B. (1983). A distributed memory model for serial-order information. *Psychological Review, 90*, 316-338.

Murdock, B.B. (1992). Serial organization in a distributed memory model. In A.F. Healy, S.M. Kosslyn, & R.M. Shiffrin (Eds.) *From learning theory to connectionist theory: Essays in honor of William K. Estes, Vol 1* (pp. 201-225). Hillsdale, NJ: Lawrence Erlbaum Associates.

Murdock, B.B. (1995). Primacy and recency in the chunking model. In C. Weaver, S. Mannes & C. Fletcher (Eds.), *Discourse comprehension: Essays in honor of Walter Kintsch* (pp. 49-63). Hillsdale, NJ: Lawrence Erlbaum Associates.

Murdock, B.B. (1996). Item, associative, and serial-order information in TODAM. In S. Gathercole (Ed.), *Models of short-term memory* (pp. 239-266). Hove, Sussex, England: Lawrence Erlbaum Associates.

Nairne, J.S., & Neath, I. (1994). A critique of the retrieval/deblurring assumptions of TODAM. *Psychological Review, 10*, 528-533.

Norman, D.A. (1970). Appendix: Serial position curves. In D.A. Norman (Ed.), *Models of human memory* (pp. 511-518). New York: Academic Press.

Penney, C.G. (1989). Modality effects and the structure of short-term verbal memory. *Memory & Cognition, 17*, 398-422.

Peterson, L.R., & Peterson, M.J. (1959). Short-term retention of individual verbal items. *Journal of Experimental Psychology, 58*, 193-198.

Phillips, J.L., Shiffrin, R.M., & Atkinson, R.C. (1967). The effects of list length on short-term memory. *Journal of Verbal Learning and Verbal Behavior, 6*, 303-311.

Raaijmakers, J.G.W. (1979). *Retrieval from long-term store: A general theory and mathematical models.* Unpublished doctoral dissertation. University of Nijmegan, Nijmegan, The Netherlands.

Raaijmakers, J.G.W., & Shiffrin, R.M. (1980). SAM: A theory of probabilistic search of associative memory. In G.H. Bower (Ed.), *The psychology of learning and motivation: Advances in research and theory, Vol. 14* (pp. 207-262). New York: Academic Press

Raaijmakers, J.G.W., & Shiffrin, R.M. (1981). Search of associative memory. *Psychological Review, 88*, 93-134.

Ratcliff, R. (1978). A theory of memory retrieval. *Psychological Review, 85*, 59-108.

Shiffrin, R.M., & Raaijmakers, J. (1992). The SAM retrieval model: A retrospective and prospective. In A.F. Healy, S.M. Kosslyn, & R.M. Shiffrin (Eds.), *From learning theory to connectionist theory: Essays in honor of William K. Estes, Vol. 2* (pp. 69-86). Hillsdale, NJ: Lawrence Erlbaum Associates.

Tulving, E., & Arbuckle, T.Y. (1963). Sources of intratrial interference in immediate recall of paired associates. *Journal of Verbal Learning and Verbal Behavior, 1*, 321-334.

Waugh, N.C., & Norman, D.A. (1965). Primary memory, *Psychological Review, 72*, 89-104.

Chapter 4

Models of Human Memory:
A 30-Year Retrospective

William K. Estes
Harvard University, U. S. A.

The crest of an unprecedented wave of activity in the formulation of models of memory that had begun in the early 1960s was marked by the appearance of the compilation assembled in Norman (1970). A first scan of that volume yields an appearance of astonishing diversity. A second look reveals some interesting commonalities. Perhaps most conspicuous among these is the pervasive influence of the information-processing movement and the computer metaphor, manifest in the central role of information storage and retrieval processes in the majority of the models. Almost as conspicuous is a distinction between short-term and long-term memory in the basic frameworks of many models. Among the seven previously published and currently influential models reviewed in the volume, four (those of Bernbach, Kintsch, Shiffrin, and Sperling & Speelman) are marked by both of these attributes and only two (those of Morton and Wickelgren) by neither; the remaining entry, Feigenbaum's computer-simulation model implements storage and retrieval processes in a network format but without an explicit short-term, long-term distinction.

For readers of the Norman (1970) volume, myself included, a prime question was which, if any, of the models represented would move into a position of leadership and reduce the clutter of the model landscape by providing a common framework for continuing development. One might have thought that the prime candidate would have been the opening chapter, written especially for the volume, on "A system for perception and memory," (Norman & Rumelhart, 1970). This chapter presented a broad framework for theory ranging from tachistoscopic perception through short- and long-term memory, but it never served its apparently promising integrative function and quickly dropped from view, not even being cited in a 1975 volume in which Norman and Rumelhart, with other collaborators, reported extensive new studies focused on the role of long-term memory in language processing and problem solving (Norman & Rumelhart, 1975).

An Integrative Model of Memory: 1968

For the much needed integrative function, one should have looked instead to the chapter by Shiffrin, which was entitled "Memory Search," but actually reviewed a rapidly developing theoretical framework comparable in breadth to that of Norman and Rumelhart. Along with a number of other investigators from all parts of the world, I had my first introduction to this development in the summer of 1966 when I organized and chaired a symposium on Mathematical Models of Psychological Processes at the XVIII International Congress of Psychology in Moscow, to which Richard C. Atkinson contributed a paper on "Models for short-term memory.[1]" The centerpiece of this presentation was a multistore model with a computer-like architecture, first outlined in a preliminary form by Atkinson and Shiffrin (1965). The general schema of Atkinson and Shiffrin's approach was in the air. Within weeks of Atkinson's Congress paper, Bennet Murdock gave an invited paper to Division 3 of the American Psychological Association[2] in which he outlined a "modal model" that synthesized several currently active approaches. The instantly popular appellation *modal model*, later given wide visibility by Baddeley (1976, 1986), denoted a model incorporating conceptions of processing stages, memory stores and a buffer mechanism similar to those of Atkinson and Shiffrin's approach. However, Murdock "did not particularly favor" the approach (Murdock, 1974, p. 202), whereas in Atkinson and Shiffrin's hands it led directly to their enormously influential 1968 article, which was the principal basis of Shiffrin's chapter in the Norman volume.

The model fully described, with much supporting evidence, in Atkinson and Shiffrin (1968), henceforth denoted A&S, brought together numerous ideas drawn from the just subsiding wave of research on verbal associative learning and memory (Postman, 1961; Underwood, 1957), models of attention and visual persistence (Broadbent, 1958, Sperling,1967), concepts from information-processing theory (Broadbent, 1963), computer models of language processing and thought (Feigenbaum, 1961; Newell, Shaw, & Simon, 1958), and new research paradigms with associated models for short-term memory (Conrad, 1964; Conrad & Hille, 1958; Peterson, 1966; Peterson & Peterson, 1959; Sternberg, 1966). The architecture of the A&S model was based on a conception

---

[1]The paper was a surprise to me although Shiffrin was a graduate student and Atkinson and I were faculty colleagues at Stanford, where all three of us were heavily involved in a mathematical psychology program. In fact, Atkinson and I had neighboring offices in Ventura Hall at Stanford and talked shop almost every morning on topics ranging from students' thesis problems to new developments in cognitive theory. These conversations contained premonitions of the evolving Atkinson and Shiffrin system, but I had no idea how rapidly the evolution was proceeding.

[2]September 5, 1966.

of three principal memory stores -- a set of sensory registers, a short-term buffer of limited capacity, and a long-term store of virtually unlimited capacity. The sensory registers were assumed to receive input directly from sensory channels, the contents of the registers being subject to rapid decay with all information quickly lost unless passed to the short-term buffer. The buffer had the character of a push-down stack in a computer, but with the modification that its contents could be manipulated by control processes such as rehearsal. The contents of each cell in the buffer were encoded representations of information from the sensory registers in the form of unitary items, such as digits, letters, or words. A critical aspect of the system was that items in the buffer could be transferred incrementally to the long-term store as a consequence of rehearsal without disturbing their continued maintenance in the buffer. Thus, for a short time after input of an item to the system, its recall or recognition could be mediated either by its representation in the buffer or by its representation in long-term store.

The properties of the short-term buffer were critical to many novel predictions whose empirical confirmations yielded rapidly mounting support for the model. One of the first major supportive studies was reported by Phillips, Shiffrin, & Atkinson (1967). The task was a modification of the standard paired-associate paradigm. On each trial, the subject viewed a series of cards, varying in number from 3 to 14, marked with color patches, the cards being turned over and placed in a row after viewing, then a test was given on which a randomly selected card was pointed to and the subject attempted recall of its color. Curves depicting proportions of correct responses as a function of serial position, though quite complex in form, with asymmetrical recency and primacy effects, were well predicted by the model. In the A&S monograph itself, several new experiments were designed to bear on particular properties of the buffer; results were largely confirmatory but also led to refinements of the assumptions. A particularly striking tour de force appeared a few years later (Atkinson & Shiffrin, 1971). Like many other investigators, these authors had noted an apparent contradiction between implications of the A&S model, with its assumption of a permanent long-term store, and those of the large body of interference theory (Postman, 1961), which assumed that information was lost from memory following storage over an interval during which new learning occurred. A source of apparent support for interference theory had been the *list-length effect* -- a negative relation between length of a study list of words and accuracy of free recall. This relation would be predicted from interference theory because with increasing list length, the number of item presentations intervening between study and test of any given item must increase on the average, thus increasing the opportunity for interference effects. In the A&S model, however, the key factor is the opportunity for transfer of an item from the short-term buffer to long-term store. As length of a study list increases, constituent items will have increasing probability of being dropped from the buffer before being transferred to long-term store. In a neatly designed experiment, a subject was presented on any trial with two successive study lists, one containing 5 and one 20 words, then attempted recall of the first list. The result was that, as implied by the buffer model, probability of any given word in the first list being recalled was higher for 5 than for 20 word lists, independently of the length of the second list.

On the whole, I think it is fair to say that the many tests of the model, not only those conducted by the A&S group but also those reported by other investigators, were largely confirmatory and very few pointed to the need for more than fine tuning of the model.

An important point missed by many later critics was that Atkinson and Shiffrin did not treat their model as a fixed structure to be either accepted or rejected but rather as an evolving system to be shaped and refined by interactions between theory and experiment. Thus, it did not make sense to continue conducting tests of the model as originally formulated, and over ensuing years the frequency of such studies declined as both of the originators and their associates diverged on new paths. Other investigators with continuing interest in evaluating the A&S system focused mainly on the assumptions concerning encoding of items in the short-term buffer and transfer from the buffer to long-term storage. In the former category was a series of studies initiated by Craik and Lockhart (1972), who proposed that items presented to a subject for study are encoded to different levels, for example that of visual or auditory features, that of semantic features) as a function of task demands, and that the level of encoding determines the resistance of an item representation to forgetting. In the latter category were some highly ingenious experiments indicating that rote rehearsal of items in the short-term buffer does not necessarily enhance transfer to long-term storage (Craik & Watkins, 1973; Woodward, Bjork, & Jongeward, 1973) These studies yielded some striking findings that motivated highly fruitful new lines of research. However, they need not be viewed as undermining the A&S model. As later reviewers (Healy & McNamara, 1996; Raaijmakers, 1993), have pointed out, A&S anticipated the new concepts emanating from the levels-of-processing and rehearsal studies and their theoretical framework requires no basic modification to accommodate them.

Models of Memory: 1998

The diversity of present-day memory models equals or exceeds that of three decades ago but is marked by a somewhat different character. The models represented in Norman (1970) all had a common basic architecture: During learning, items of information are stored in memory; when a task calls for action based on the information, recognition, recall, classification, or whatever, a memory search locates relevant stored items and they enter into a decision process that yields a response. The items may be relatively simple in structure (e. g., digits) or very complex (e.g., propositions), but in either case they serve as the units on which information-processes operate. For brevity, I will refer to models of this type as *item-processing models*. The present scene includes many of these, some holdovers from the 1960s and some new entries, but also a rapidly proliferating class of models with a different architecture, commonly termed *global memory models*. In the following sections, I briefly review some representatives of each class and discuss problems of differential testing and assessment. To be practical, I will need to be quite selective and will limit consideration to models that have been developed with reference to much the same range of phenomena and the same level of definition of informational units as those included in Norman (1970). In particular, I will exclude the class of models in which propositions are the basic units of information storage (e.g., Anderson 1976; Anderson & Bower, 1973; Kintsch, 1974), important in their own right but not feasible to discuss in this article.

The central question that shapes this review is whether the striking diversity of current models reflects increasing fragmentation of memory theory or whether it reflects varied approaches to central issues that may be yielding some convergence on a common body of basic theory. If convergence is the answer, what is being converged on? A new "modal model"? If so, is its form apparent, at least in outline, as of 1998? I will return to this question after reviewing the present scene.

The A & S Tradition

Current Status of A&S. In any compilation of influential models of memory as of the late 1990s, A&S would certainly merit inclusion, but how to fill the bill would be a problem. The 1968 article still has a high citation rate, but the references are mainly to particular concepts (most frequently control processes) rather than to the A&S model per se. Also, though I have done no actual counting, I suspect that the citations are more frequent in textbooks of general and cognitive psychology than in the technical literature (see also Greene, 1986). In fact, the model no longer appears as an entry in the perennially popular activity of conducting differential empirical tests of memory models (Hintzman, 1991; Ratcliff & McKoon, 1991; Shiffrin, Ratcliff, & Clark, 1990). Lacking in the current scene is a thorough revision of the A&S model, preserving the original framework and basic concepts but refining and elaborating particular mechanisms to meet the more cogent criticisms of the original formulation. Unlike many suggestions for alternative systems that have appeared in the literature, a revision would need to account for the data, rich though limited in scope, that supported the original model but also handle such matters as recency effects in long- as well as short-term memory, the absence of forgetting from short-term memory under conditions in which forgetting would be predicted by the buffer model, and phenomena relating to temporal discriminability and item distinctiveness (Crowder & Neath, 1991; Glenberg & Swanson, 1986; Murdock, 1960).

This last group of phenomena, apparently quite well accounted for by concepts that seem incompatible with the buffer mechanism of A&S (Baddeley, 1976, 1986; Baddeley & Hitch, 1993; Crowder, 1993; Glenberg, 1987), may have had a major role in discouraging any comprehensive revision of A&S. More important, I suspect, is a shift in the Zeitgeist from that of the 1960s, when the general approach of memory theorists was based on retrieval of information contained in individually stored item representations, or images, by a search process to one based on retrieval by parallel activation of a composite memory. The former was most strongly influenced by analogies of human cognitive function to that of information-processing by digital computers, the latter by analogies to processing by parallel computers and by conceptions of parallel processing in the brain derived from developments in neural science.

Just as the denotation *item search* captured the spirit of the earlier tradition, the appellation *global memory* characterizes models developed in the newer tradition, including the matched filter model of Anderson (1973); the matrix model of Humphreys, Bain, and Pike, (1989); the TODAM (Theory of Distributed Associative Memory) model of Murdock (1982) and the closely related model of Eich (1982); the resonance model of Ratcliff (1978, 1981); and the array model developed by myself and associates (Estes, 1994; Estes & Maddox, 1995). The SAM (Search of Associative Memory) model of Raaijmakers and Shiffrin (1980, 1981), described in the next section, reflects a mixture of the two traditions.

The reasons for the hegemony of global memory models are mixed. One important factor clearly has been a shift of interest on the part of cognitive psychologists from phenomena of short-term memory that are especially amenable to search models to phenomena of long-term memory that have appeared to be more naturally treated by global models. Also, the idea of simply extending the search models developed in connection with the short-term recognition paradigm of Sternberg (1966) in the 1960s to long-term recognition, always involving much longer study lists, ran into difficulties. One was that consideration of the time scale of cognitive operations (Newell, 1990) indicated that searches requiring comparison of a test item with hundreds, in some cases thousands, of stored item representations could not be accomplished within the duration of the reaction times typical of long-term memory tests. Another was that, whereas it had been possible to specify a mechanism that could actually accomplish search and retrieval for short lists (Newell, 1973), no one has reported progress in doing the same for lists of the length used in many experiments (e.g., Shiffrin, Huber, & Marinelli, 1995; Standing, Conezio, & Haber, 1970).

Direct empirical tests of the class of global memory models versus the class of non-global models would be desirable, but success at accomplishing such a test is not in sight. In the only relevant study I have encountered (Humphreys, Pike, Bain, & Tehan, 1989), it was shown that simplified versions of several global models share a parameter-free quantitative prediction that would apparently differentiate them from nonglobal models. However, problems in constructing a feasible empirical test of the prediction have not yet been solved. For the present, the situation is that search and retrieval continues to be the process of choice for models of short-term memory but activation of global memories has taken over for treatments of long-term memory. The remainder of this section sketches three of the global models now under active development preparatory to some comparisons among them.

SAM. Although the main focus of the SAM model is on the formerly little elaborated conception of long-term store, the route from perception to long-term store still includes the short-term buffer of A&S as a constituent. Assumptions about its character as a push-down stack are relaxed, but the probability that a perceived item passes to long-term store is still assumed to be an increasing function of its time in the buffer. Several new assumptions bear on the processes of long-term memory storage and retrieval.

1. What is stored is not a replica of a perceived item but an *image*, which contains information about the item, the amount of information depending on the duration (and presumably the nature) of rehearsal. This elaboration of A&S allows for a potentially wider range of applications, but in research to which the model has so far been applied, the stimuli have been familiar unitary items like digits, letters, and words, so for the present one may as well continue speaking of the storage and retrieval of items.

2. An important extension of the A&S is the assumption that the unit of storage may be not a single item, but a relation between two items, for example, between two items present simultaneously in the buffer or between an item in the buffer and a component of the background context in which the item was perceived. Thus, although I have not seen a discussion of the point, for logical consistency, it must apparently also be assumed that components of the background context must be encoded in the buffer and rehearsed just as are stimulus items. The stored relation apparently does not take the form of a new image, but rather is represented as a level of strength of association between images.

3. Retrieval from long-term store is achieved by using retrieval cues to sample images. A cue for retrieval of an item I_k may be the image of another item or of a contextual element, and the choice of cues to use in any situation may be determined by a voluntary strategy of the learner. Formally, strength of activation of an image I_k in a memory test is the product of the tendencies of all cues being used to activate I_k individually, and the probability of sampling image I_k is the ratio of the activation strength of I_k to the sum of activation strengths of all images in memory (presumably just all of those formed in a given situation), that is,

$$P(I_k) = A_k/S(A_m), \qquad (4.1)$$

where A_k is the activation strength of the image I_k, and $S(A_m)$ is the total activation of all images in memory by the cues currently being used. A simple transformation of Equation 4.1 yields the expression for predicted probability of recall. The treatment of recognition, requiring an auxiliary process, was spelled out by Gillund and Shiffrin (1984). According to these authors, subjects could voluntarily choose to perform a recognition task by searching memory for the image of a test stimulus and generating an "old" response if recollection (recall of the stimulus) occurs, in accord with Equation 4.1. However, subjects do not ordinarily resort to a search, but rather, respond "old" to a test stimulus if the value of the quantity $S(A_m)$ in Equation 4.1 exceeds a criterion; otherwise they respond "new." When this latter mode is employed, the treatment of recognition in SAM closely parallels the treatment by the global memory models of Hintzman (1988), Murdock (1982), and Estes and Maddox (1995).

The distinctive difference between search and global memory models lies in the basis for responding on memory tests. In search models, perception of a test item initiates a search of the item representations, *or images*, currently stored in memory, which terminates with retrieval of some one image that serves as the basis for a recognition judgment or other response appropriate to the task. In global memory models, perception of a test item leads to activation of all currently stored images in parallel, and response to the test item is some function of the level of activation.

There is some ambiguity as to how the SAM model should be classified. In its first presentation, SAM was introduced as " a theory of retrieval from long-term memory" (Raaijmakers & Shiffrin, 1980, p. 207), and the formalism developed and applied to free recall and paired associate paradigms was that of a global memory model. However, the authors comment that this model may usefully be viewed as an elaboration of the long-term component of the A&S system, the short-term component of that system being retained as a search-and-retrieval submodel that provides an interface with perception. This theme is echoed, without further elaboration, in later presentations (Raaijmakers, 1993; Shiffrin & Raaijmakers, 1992).

Another problem in classification is that the long-term retrieval component of SAM is a hybrid, including aspects of both classical search models and strictly global memory models. In applications to recognition, the currently favored interpretation is essentially that of Gillund and Shiffrin (1984), in which assumptions about memory storage and access are very close to those of the global models, in particular the array model and the MINERVA model of Hintzman (1988). But in applications of SAM to recall, it is assumed that a test stimulus initiates a search of memory that may result in activation of only a subset of the stored images. Nonetheless, for purposes of comparison with other models, I will henceforth classify SAM as a global model except when some finer distinction is specified.

The SAM model, augmented by paradigm-specific assumptions as needed, has been applied to a large array of experiments on recall and recognition, some of them new experiments generated in the course ot testing implications of the model, with an impressive record of successful results ("...there are potentially multiple ways [some of them not intuitively apparent], in which SAM can be falsified by failures of predictions generated from its assumptions. In fact, however, the model has been remarkably successful in its predictions, both qualitatively and quantitatively...," Ratcliff, van Zandt, & McKoon, 1995, p. 371).

A decade and a half earlier, SAM's authors remarked that "...a general and complex model such as SAM cannot be judged a success simply on the basis of predicting the results from one or two studies or paradigms. We have therefore embarked on a program of evaluation in which the model (in essentially unchanged form) is applied to as many paradigms and results as possible. Reports on these applications are forthcoming (Raaijmakers & Shiffrin, 1981, p. 133)." The promise has been kept, and at present SAM is one of the models of memory most fully worked out in quantitative detail and stands alone as the one demonstrated to account for the greatest range of phenomena of recognition, free recall, and cued (paired-associate) recall.

Without in the slightest discounting this record of accomplishment, one looking back over the nearly 30 years of evolution of the model may note that the formulation of SAM's basic assumptions, or axioms, required some strategic decisions that have had little discussion or effort toward explicit evaluation. One of these is the nature of memory activation; others bear on the format of memory storage. In the following sections, I discuss problems of evaluation of these axioms, using as a vehicle comparisons of SAM with models that differ from it with respect to one or more basic axioms. In this task, I rely mainly on comparisons with two models, TODAM and the array model, that have been developed as fully as SAM and applied to much the same range of phenomena.

TODAM: Distributed Memory with Parallel Processing. TODAM differs widely from SAM on several theoretical dimensions, in particular, the mode of memory storage and the mechanisms of retrieval. Whereas SAM includes no assumptions about format of memory images, in TODAM stored representations of items in memory take the form of vectors of features (a vector being essentially a list in a form permitting manipulation by mathematical and logical operations). In many theories, it is assumed that the features entering into item codes are values of the items on attributes (in simple cases, sensory dimensions), but the features assumed in TODAM are purely hypothetical. The vector representating any stimulus item has some number N of these features, sampled randomly from a normal distribution; N and the mean and variance of the normal distribution are free parameters to be estimated for any experiment by fitting the model to the data. The vector for any perceived and remembered item does not appear in memory as a unit, like a memory image in SAM, however; rather, the vector is added into a cumulative composite memory by an operation termed convolution, losing its identity in the process (like a lump of sugar dropped into a glass of water).

A bit more formally, the current state of an individual's composite memory for the events of an experiment, M_t, is transformed on a learning trial for any single item by the function:

$$M_t = aM_{t-1} + pf_t \qquad (4.2)$$

where M_t and M_{t-1} are the memory states on trial t and the previous trial, respectively, f_t is the vector representing the item learned on the trial, and p is the probability that learning (memory storage) occurs. The + sign in Equation 4.2 denotes an operation termed convolution, not the same as arithmetical addition. On a recognition test when some item with vector f_x is presented, the degree of match, s, between f_x and f_t (the basis for a recognition judgment) is computed by

$$s = f * M, \qquad (4.3)$$

where * denotes a mathematical operation termed *correlation* (not the same as correlation in statistics) and M is the state of memory at the time of the test.

If the items studied on a learning trial are stimulus pairs, for example the stimulus and response members of paired-associates, each constituent member of a pair is added into the composite memory, M, and so also is a vector representing the relation between the two constituents (technically, their convolution). Then, if the stimulus member is presented alone on a recall test, its correlation with M yields as output an approximation to the response member, which is the basis for recall.

Array Model: Instance Storage in a Global Memory. Two global memory models currently under active development, the array model and the MINERVA model of Hintzman (1988), differ from both SAM and TODAM in similar ways with respect to format of memory storage and mode of memory access. I use the array model in this discussion because it allows a greater number of contrasts with the other two models.

The array model differs from all of the others mentioned in that its origins were not in memory theory but in classification theory. The model, derives from exemplar models (also termed *context models*) of categorization (Estes, 1986; Medin & Florian, 1992; Medin & Schaffer, 1978; Nosofsky, 1984, 1988). The extension to recognition that we employ in this chapter has been presented, with experimental applications, by Estes (1994) and Estes and Maddox (1995). In a categorization experiment, the subject views a series of stimuli together with their category labels, for example, plants labelled either fruit or vegetable and on test trials tries to assign new instances appropriately to categories. In an exemplar model, it is assumed that whenever the subject perceives a stimulus during a learning series, a featural representation of the stimulus, in its current context, is stored in the appropriate section of a memory array. In the example, each instance of a fruit would be stored in one section and each instance of a vegetable in another section. When presented with a test stimulus, the subject mentally computes its total similarity to all of the stored representations in each section separately and responds on the basis of the relative values of the two total similarities. With the categories denoted by F or V, the probability, $P(F)$, of assigning the test stimulus to category F would be

$$P(F) = Sim(F)/[Sim(F) + Sim(V)], \tag{4.4}$$

where $Sim(F)$ and $Sim(V)$ are the total similarities of the test stimulus to the stored entries in the F and G sections of the memory array, respectively.

Recall in the framework of the array model may be viewed as a special case of categorization. Consider, for example, the learning of associations between names and faces. In what is termed a cued recall experiment, a subject might view a series of photos of people, each labelled with the name of the person depicted, then on a test trial be asked to recall the appropriate name when shown a photo alone. By analogy to categorization, the photos correspond to category exemplars and the names to category labels. The probability of recall of the name appropriate to a test photo is given by a function of the same form as Equation 4.4,

$$Sim(N_i) = Sim(N_i)/S(N_k), \tag{4.5}$$

where $Sim(N_i)$ denotes total similarity of name N_i to the contents of the corresponding section of the memory array and the summation on the right of the equation is over the similar similarities for all other admissible names.

In the array model applied to recognition, (described in essentials by Estes, 1994 and Estes & Maddox, 1995) the processing assumptions regarding stimulus processing, memory storage, and memory access are essentially identical to those for categorization. On each study trial of a typical recognition experiment, a subject views a series of stimuli and stores featurally encoded representations in a memory array, which may be regarded as labelled Old, figuratively speaking. On an old-new test for recognition, the similarity of the test stimulus to the contents of the Old memory array is computed, and the probability, $P(Old)$, of a positive response (judging the stimulus to be Old) is equal to the total similarity divided by that quantity plus a background value,

$$P(Old) = Sim(Old)/[Sim(Old) + B\}, \tag{4.6}$$

where Sim(Old) is the total summed similarity of the test stimulus to the entries in the Old array and B is a background constant whose value reflects any bias the subject may have toward using the response "old" regardless of the familiarity of the stimulus.

It is important to distinguish two versions of the array model that differ only with respect to the mode of similarity computations. In what I will term the *standard* version, it is assumed that perceived items are encoded in memory as vectors of values on empirically specifiable stimulus attributes, or features, (as those having to do with form, color, size, phonetics) and computations of similarity between items are accomplished by feature-by-feature comparisons. Thus, when the standard version is applied to a memory experiment, the memory array generated for a list of items contains representations that differ from each other in varying degrees of similarity. However, for some types of applications, most notably experiments with words as stimuli, there is no known way of specifying an adequate set of features. The procedure used in such cases is to simplify the model by assuming that items are stored in memory as images that lack any specifiable format but that can be characterized by an average level of inter-item similarity (a "similarity parameter," s, that can be estimated from data and used in computing predictions). For present purposes, I will call this simplified form of the model the *image* version. The array memory model has had its most intensive and detailed applications to effects of stimulus properties, stimulus base rates, informative feedback, and stimulus familiarity in recognition (Estes & Maddox, 1995; Maddox & Estes, 1997). A generalized version of the array model also deals with phenomena of retention loss, memory for temporal order, and distortions of recall and reproduction (Estes, 1997).

Models and Issues

Comparisons of the models reviewed above with respect to some issues concerning processes and structures will be useful preparation for consideration of the question of convergence.

Examined at the surface level of verbal characterizations, the basic concepts of SAM, TODAM, and the array model appear so disparate that deciding among them by means of empirical tests might seem to be a routine task. In many instances, however, it proves to be unexpectedly difficult to find testably different implications of apparently quite distinct concepts. In this section, I examine several cases of this kind.

Tripartite Classification of Memory Stores. In broad outline, the contempory models being compared do not exhibit any gross departure from the assumption of three principal memory stores - sensory registers, short-term working memory (successor to the rehearsal buffer of A&S), and long-term store

- that became generally accepted in midcentury. However, the idea, popular for a time owing to analogies with early digital computers, that items of information input move through the three stores in strict succession has been progresssively relaxed. All of the contemporary approaches recognize that patterns registered in sensory systems during perception of any item must be encoded in a form resistant to interference and amenable to rehearsal before they can enter working memory. Similarly, it is generally recognized that for items in working memory to transfer to long-term memory, they must become associated with contextual elements or retrieval cues that may be available in later test situations; however, at present the formal elaboration of this assumption in the current models remains largely programmatic.

Item Encoding in Perception and Memory. Some form of featural representation is the mode in contemporary models. However, assumptions about the nature of features take two distinct forms. In the version employed in several distributed-memory models, features are purely abstract entities with no assumed correspondence to specific stimulus properties. This approach is typified by TODAM, in which a to-be-stored item is represented by a vector of abstract features sampled from a normal distribution. The mean and variance of the distribution are important parameters of the model, basic to such procedures as predicting the variances of signal and noise distributions in recognition experiments; however, the particular sets of features that enter into the memory representations of different items bear no relation to stimulus properties of those items. In the other version of featural representation, employed in the array model and others (including Drewnowski, 1980; Nosofsky, 1988; and Underwood, 1969, 1977), the features, or attribute values, making up a memory representation are assumed to correspond to observable stimulus properties. The former mode is convenient for the kinds of computations associated with distributed models, but leaves the treatment of generalization and transfer to be handled by added "curve-fitting" parameters[3]. A prime advantage of the latter mode is that it provides the basis for computing similarity relationships among items and thereby for deriving predictions about generalization and transfer of training.

It must be recognized that applications of models that assume stimulus-related features are constrained by the current state of knowledge about the feature systems appropriate for different kinds of stimuli. For some situations, it has proved feasible to arrive at a characterization of the features or attributes used by subjects for item encoding by scaling studies applied to similarity-judgment data (Nosofsky, 1984, 1986). For others, it has been necessary to rely on more

---

[3]Possibly the advantages of both versions could be obtained by defining macro- and micro-features, the macrofeatures being those of the array model, but with each macrofeature represented by a vector of abstract features as in TODAM. I have not looked into the feasibility of this approach.

informal heuristic devices. In one recent study, for example, an objective was to apply the array model to data on recognition of three kinds of stimuli -- digit strings, consonant strings, and common English words (Estes & Maddox, 1995). For the first two types, it proved satisfactory to apply the model with an assumption that features of the strings corresponded to the constituent digits or consonants. But for the word stimuli, that assumption was neither sensible nor fruitful, so we had to be content to assume that words were stored in vectors of unknown features and to implement the model by defining an average similarity parameter to be applied when computiong similarity beween perceived words and stored word representations.

In some models, notably SAM, items are assumed to be stored in memory as images that have no specific formal structure and may contain an almost indefinitely large variety and amount of unformatted information. I think a choice between the image representation of SAM and the other types must reflect the conceptual level of model construction and the intended domain of application. Defining the basic unit of information storage as done in SAM may be convenient if the main goal of the theorist is to allow for a wide range of potential applications of a model, most necessarily being qualitative in character. But more specific assumptions about format of memory representations seem essential if one's goal is to use a model as a tool for aiding in the resolution of theoretical issues in the borderland between perception and memory and and may be advantageous when the goal is to mediate interconnections between cognitive concepts and those of neural science. The preference of the developers of SAM is to present rather open definitions of concepts bearing on memory format in their basic model and then spin off more limited submodels with more restrictive assumptions for particular applications. Maintaining testability of the basic model in that approach obviously depends on close attention to formal relationships among the submodels.

Although my preference is for representations in terms of stimulus-related features, in applications of the array model, practicality can demand compromises. In some situations (for example, experiments with words as stimuli), the assumption that words presented to subjects are represented in memory as feature vectors lacks force because at present we lack knowledge about the nature of the features. In such applications, the procedure has been either to define average similarities among the items within experimentally-defined classes and estimate these similarities from the experimental data (Maddox & Estes, 1997) or to estimate the inter-item similarities by means of separate scaling experiments (Nosofsky, 1984).

Mode of Memory Storage. The models being compared fall into two categories with regard to mode of memory storage: distributed or nondistributed. For the latter, I will follow Clark and Gronlund (1996) in using the term *separate-storage.* In TODAM, it is assumed that the representations of items that occur in a learning episode are entered in a distributed, composite memory, losing their separate identities in the process. In the other models, the stored representation of each item is a distinct entity (image in SAM, feature-vector in the array model). Thus, in the latter two models, but not in TODAM, it is appropriate to conceive of cognitive operations such as comparison being applied to individual representations.

Attempts to differentiate distributed and nondistributed storage on the basis of behavioral observations have met with frustration. The effort appeared to be off to a good start when it was observed that both of the currently familiar distributed-memory models (the "matched-filter model" of Anderson, 1973, and TODAM as presented in Murdock, 1982) yielded the surprising prediction that repetition of an item in the study series of a recognition experiment would have no effect on performance (Murdock & Lamon, 1988; Murdock, 1989). This prediction was contrary to the ubiquitous finding that repetition of an item improves accuracy of performance on recognition tests, which is readily accommodated by all or nearly all other extant models (Gillund & Shiffrin, 1984; Murnane & Shiffrin, 1991). However, this apparent refutation of the distributed memory models was not accepted docilely by Murdock and Lamon (1988), who amended the detailed assumptions of the matched-filter model regarding the learning that occurs on a study trial (replacing an assumption of deterministic encoding by one of probabilistic encoding of stimulus features) with the result that the revised model could predict a repetition effect. Shortly Murdock (1989) extended this analysis to his TODAM model, with a similar conclusion.

The hope of securing decisive evidence on modes of storage surfaced again almost immediately in a flurry of studies aimed at distinguishing among global models by comparing their abilities to handle the *list-strength effect* in recognition (Ratcliff, Clark, & Shiffrin, 1990; Shiffrin, Ratcliff, & Clark, 1990; Yonelinas, Hockley, & Murdock, 1992). This effect is defined as a tendency for recognition of an item to be affected by the presence of stronger (better learned) items in the same study list. In the experimental paradigm that yields the data for comparisons, recognition is tested following study on three kinds of lists termed pure weak, pure strong, and mixed. In a typical instance, the lists might all contain 10 items (usually unrelated words); in the pure weak list, each item would occur once during study; in the pure strong list, each would occur twice; and in the mixed list, 5 items would occur once each and 5 items twice. One would speak of a list-strength effect if weak (once-presented) items in the mixed list were significantly more or less well recognized than items in the pure weak list and strong (twice-presented) items in the mixed list were more or less well recognized than items in the pure strong list. Apparently the common intuitive expectation is that recognition of weak items should be impaired if they are included in a mixed list, perhaps because they suffer increased competition for limited-capacity attention or reduced relative contrast with new items included in tests; recognition of strong items would be enhanced by their inclusion in a mixed list because of reduced competition or increased contrast (Murdock & Kahana, 1993a; Ratcliff et al., 1990; Shiffrin et al., 1990). Following Ratcliff et al. (1990), I will refer to this pattern as a *positive* list-strength effect.

Prior to 1990, a positive list-strength effect had been found in free recall (Tulving & Hastie, 1972), but no relevant studies had been reported for cued recall (as paired associates) or recognition (Ratcliff et al., 1990). The study reported by Ratcliff et al. (1990) immediately eliminated that lacuna, however, with a series of seven recognition experiments all focussed on list-strength. and all showing either negligible or negative effects. One of those experiments included a free recall and a cued recall condition; the latter yielded a small but significant positive effect, the former a larger positive effect. The theoretical import of these results was pointed up by Shiffrin et al. (1990), who demonstrated in a searching analysis that extant global memory models, including, in particular, SAM and TODAM, uniformly predicted positive list-strength effects.

Was this demonstration taken to be fatal to the models? It was not so viewed in the case of SAM, at least, for Shiffrin et al. (1990) proceeded immediately to show that the recognition results could be accommodated by a revision of SAM in which psychological similarity between a test stimulus and a stored image of a different stimulus was assumed to be diminished as the strength of the latter increased (an assumption termed the *differentiation hypothesis*). These investigators reported no success in finding comparable emendations of a number of other models, including TODAM, that yielded satisfactory handling of list-strength effects. But SAM 's new status as the only global model that could predict null list-strength effects in recognition (coupled with significant list-length effects) was only temporary. Shortly, Murdock and Kahana (1993a) apparently saved TODAM by showing that it too can yield this prediction if one replaces its assumption that an individual's memory system is reinitialized at the start of each study list by an assumption of continuity over lists, and even over successive experiments. A later interchange of criticisms and responses between adherents of SAM and TODAM (Shiffrin, Ratcliff, Murnane, & Nobel, 1993; Murdock & Kahana, 1993b) makes it clear to an impartial reader only that specific versions of both models can handle the basic list-strength results and that for TODAM, and perhaps also SAM, to be able to handle all of the auxiliary findings of the list-strength studies, further development will be needed.

Whether continued research does or does not yield a generally acceptable decision on the relative merits of the various currently popular models, one who has been following the scenario can foresee that the outcome may yield no answer to the question of distributed versus distinct-item storage. One difficulty is that each of these two models is being taken to represent a class and within each class the storage assumption may be implemented in different ways. For example, in both the matched-filter model and in TODAM it is assumed that storage is ditributed,. However, in TODAM it is assumed that newly learned items are entered into the composite memory by the operation of convolution whereas in the filter model newly learned items are entered in memory by matrix multiplication. Thus, a finding of superiority or inferiority of TODAM to SAM with respect to the list-strength effect, or indeed any other empirical relationship, could not be taken to imply superiority or inferiority of the class of models assuming distinct-item storage to the class assuming distributed storage. A second, and perhaps even more severe difficulty is that the SAM and TODAM models, in any incarnation, differ in more respects than type of storage, and therefore a finding of superiority of one model or the other on an empirical test cannot unequivocably be attributed to any one difference (and the same is true for comparisons on other sets of models). To obtain decisive evidence on the mode of memory storage from behavioral observations, if it can be done, clearly will require more sharply focused comparisons of models, or versions of models, that differ with respect to only a single assumption.

Pending some decisive empirical test of distributed versus nondistributed storage, we must look to other bases for a decision between these conceptions. There are plausible arguments for both, but on balance I think the field will go with local storage in the sense assumed in the SAM, MINERVA, and array models, among others. Distributed storage as implemented in TODAM and CHARM is appealing on grounds of formal elegance and offers at least one heuristic advantage, namely more effective handling of the problem of response generalization. It has been well known since the work of Osgood (1949) that when recall or reproduction of items on memory tests is not veridical, the response characteristically bears some resemblance to the correct item (*response generalization*). This phenomenon is ignored in much current theorizing but is handled naturally in TODAM as an automatic consequence of retrieval from distributed memory by the operation of correlation (Murdock, 1982, 1989). However, it seems unlikely that the mathematics of convolution and correlation are going to become popular, and there are other ways of handling response generalization. In the array model, for example, it arises as a special case of category similarity (Estes, 1994), and it would be possible to augment other models, such as SAM, to allow a treatment of that kind.

Memory Access. It appears that several modes of access to memory are available and will be used under appropriate circumstances.

1. Items in short-term working memory can be accessed by a serial, self-terminating search initiated by presentation of a test item. This assumption is included programmatically in expositions of the SAM (Shiffin & Raaijmakers, 1992) and array (Estes, 1994, 1997) models but has not been formally implemented in published applications of the models.

2. In all of the global models, it is assumed that, beyond the temporal limit of working memory, items of stored information reside in a memory array whose contents are activated in parallel by a test item presented for recognition or cued recall.

3. In these models, probability of recognition is a function of the total

level of activation of the array; probability of cued recall is directly related[4] to the probability that presentation of a test stimulus reactivates a stored vector including representations of the test stimulus and the response it evoked during learning. For free recall, the best-supported conception of memory access is the combination of search and parallel activation of global memory assumed in SAM.

4. The degree of activation of any stored representation by a test item is assumed to be a joint function of strength and similarity. This assumption is embodied in many current models, including the array model, TODAM, CHARM, and MINERVA. Strength is an increasing function of the number of times instances of the test item have been stored in memory and similarity a function of the featural overlap of test and stored items. In SAM, level of activation depends only on strength, which in turn is a function of number of repetitions and study time per occurrence during learning, but activation does not depend on similarity. Quite direct evidence is available on the advantage of including similarity in the activation function (Estes & Maddox, 1995).

Retention Loss. In all of the global memory models I have discussed, SAM, TODAM, and the array model in particular, retention loss following a learning experience depends on a variety of factors. Foremost among these is a property common to all of the models that has to do with memory load and competition of memory traces for output channels: Other factors equal, accuracy of recognition or recall of an item on a memory test is a decreasing function of total memory load (the size of the relevant memory array) at the time of the test (Atkinson & Shiffrin, 1971; Estes, 1994, p. 211). Representations of events occurring during a retention interval are likely to be stored in the same memory array that contains those of items of the study series preceding the interval; and as the number of stored "extraneous" items increases, the memory load at the point of a subsequent test also increases, producing a reduction of the difference between probabilities of positive responses to targets and nontargets. The specific functions relating probability of retrieval of targets to levels of activation of targets and nontargets in the memory array differ among the models being compared, but the common result is that, as duration of a retention interval increases, the accuracy of recognition or recall is predicted to decrease.

This "competitive" property of the models will in itself tend to produce effects that are known in the memory literature as proactive and retroactive interference, but under some conditions, differences in amount of retention loss are observed between tests when memory load is held constant, and then some other property must come into play. For example, it is well known that accuracy on a single test of memory for a target item given at a fixed interval following a study list decreases with increasing distance of the occurrence of the target item

---

[4]This relation is simply equality in the array model, a more complex function in SAM.

from the end of the study series (Murdock, 1974; Murdock & Anderson, 1975). To enable prediction of this and related findings, all three of the models include a "forgetting parameter" that reduces the accessibility of a target representation in memory upon each occurrence of any item between study of the target and the memory test.

The assumption of some kind of autonomous decay of stored representations of items following learning, preventable or even appreciably delayable only by rehearsal, has broad support (Baddeley, 1976, 1986; Cowan, 1993), although the rubric "decay" may include several distinct processes all of which contribute to a decline in item retrievability (Cowan, 1993; Crowder, 1993). One of these processes is a continuous loss of information resulting from random perturbations of the values of item representations on sensory or other dimensions (Estes, 1997; Nairne, 1991, 1992). The rate of perturbation varies with type of dimension (highest for temporal), with stimulus class (relatively high for visual forms and low for verbal items), and with time frame (relatively high within the span of short-term memory and lower thereafter).

It is almost universally assumed in memory theory, including all of the models being compared here, that stored representations of items include elements of the context (temporal, spatial, sensory) in which the items appeared during learning. Partial reinstatment of the learning context on a later test of memory tends to reactivate the full item representation and thus to mediate responses such as recognition and recall; and at least for recall, accuracy of test responses is an increasing function of the degree of reinstatement of the learning context. The detailed nature of contextual elements is largely unknown[5], but it is uniformly assumed that subsets of elements occurring close together in a list or series are more similar than those occurring further apart, and that those occurring near the beginning or end of a list or series or near other boundary markers are especially distinctive and thus are especially important determiners of retrieval (Bower, 1972; Crowder & Neath, 1991; Glenberg, 1987; Lee & Estes, 1981; Murdock, 1960).

The parameter for loss of item retrievability with increasing time after storage that is included in SAM, TODAM, and the array model, among others, can be interpreted as a heuristically convenient substitute for the functions representing effects of contextual drift in the models of Bower (1972), Baddeley and Hitch (1993), and Mensink and Raaijmakers (1988, 1989).

---

[5]Our inability to specify the physical properties of the local contexts in which items occur on learning and test trials has been seen as an all-but-fatal weakness of extant models of memory (Crowder & Greene, 1987; Underwood, 1977). However, in an interesting new development, theoretical mechanisms have been proposed for interpretation of drift and reinstatement of context that embody no assumptions about physical characteristics of elements of context, only assumptions about its dynamic properties (Brown, Vousden, & Hulme, 1996; Burgess & Hitch, 1992).

Outline of a Composite Model for 1998 and Beyond

My examination of a selection of current models in the preceding sections provides grist for a new effort toward organization and integration. The one that follows is offered in much the same spirit as that of the "modal model" proposed some 30 years ago by Murdock (1967). I eschew the term *modal* on this round, however, because the model I sketch in outline represents only my own set of choices on the various debatable theoretical issues, and not a consensus of current opinion. This presentation, replacing the customary "conclusions" section of a chapter, will take the form of an annotated listing of aspects of the proposed composite model. All of the concepts and issues pertaining to this effort have been introduced in the preceding review so in this section I limit discussion of them to amplifications of the earlier treatments where needed. For brevity, I use the term *item* throughout to refer to objects or events of any kind that may be perceived and remembered.

Item encoding. Stimulus items are encoded during perceptual processing in terms of their features, or values on attributes, and their representations in memory take the form of feature vectors whose elements are assumed to correspond to stimulus properties.

Memory stores. In broad outline, the composite model reflects the assumption of three principal memory stores -- sensory registers, short-term memory and long-term store -- that became generally accepted in mid-century. However, it is recognized that individual items do not move through the stores in strict succession; rather, the form of item representations is progressively modified by clusters of distinct processes whose time courses overlap but whose durations correspond to the earlier tripartite conception.

Mode of memory storage. The composite model embodies separate, or local, storage in the sense assumed in the SAM, MINERVA, and array models, among others. That is, stored items preserve their distinct identities and can be compared individually to a test item during a search process. However, evidence from psychological research on memory does not seem in any way contrary to an emendation of this conception suggested by developments in neural science: As information processing proceeds beyond the time frame of the experimental work on which current models are based, there may be a shift from separate to distributed representations (McClelland & Goddard, 1996; McClelland, McNaughton, & O'Reilly, 1995; Squire, 1986; Shadmehr & Holcomb, 1997).

Memory access by search or global activation. Several modes of access to memory are available and are used under appropriate circumstances.

  1. Items in short-term working memory can be accessed by a serial, self-terminating search initiated by presentation of a test item.

  2. Beyond the temporal limit of working memory, items of stored

information reside in a global memory array whose contents are activated in parallel by a test item presented for recognition or cued recall.

3. The degree of activation of any stored item by a test item is assumed to be a joint function of strength and similarity. Strength is an increasing function of the number of times instances of the test item have been stored in memory and the study time per occurrence of the item during learning. Similarity is a function of the featural overlap of test and stored items.

4. Probability of recognition is a function of the total level of activation of the array; probability of cued recall is directly related[6] to the probability that presentation of a test stimulus reactivates a stored vector including representations of the test stimulus and the response it evoked during learning. For free recall, the best-supported conception of memory access appears to be the combination of search and parallel activation of global memory assumed in SAM.

Forgetting. Retention loss following a learning experience is assumed to be the result of a combination of factors: Memory load, memory trace decay, and shifts in context between learning and test.

Summary

In the late 1960s, models of human memory focussed on short-term phenomena and processes within a framework known informally as the *modal model*, which motivated and guided research for another decade. By the early 1980s, the focus had shifted to long-term memory, with major attention to formats and modes of representation and processes of retrieval of information. Although contemporary models are diverse in many respects, it has been possible to abstract from them a set of salient features - a *composite model* - that may serve much the same functions as the modal model of the earlier period.

Acknowledgment

Preparation of this chapter was supported by Grants SBR 93-17256 and SBR 96-10048 from the National Science Foundation.

---

[6]This relation is simply equality in the array model, a more complex function in SAM.

References

Anderson, J. A. (1973). A theory for the recognition of items from short memorized lists. *Psychological Review, 80*, 417-438.

Anderson, J. R. (1976). *Language, Memory, and Thought.* Hillsdale, NJ: Lawrence Erlbaum Associates.

Anderson, J. R., & Bower, G. H. (1973). *Human Associative Memory.* Washington, DC: Winston.

Atkinson, R. C., & Shiffrin, R. M. (1965). *Mathematical models for memory and learning.* Technical Report No. 79, Institute for Mathematical Studies in the Social Sciences, Stanford University.

Atkinson, R. C., & Shiffrin, R. M. (1968). Human memory: A proposed system and its control processes. In K. W. Spence, & J. T. Spence (Ed.), *The Psychology of Learning and Motivation* (pp.89-105). New York: Academic Press.

Atkinson, R. C., & Shiffrin, R. M. (1971). The control of short-term memory. *Scientific American, 224*, 82-90.

Baddeley, A. D. (1976). *The Psychology of Memory.* New York: Basic Books.

Baddeley, A. (1986). *Working Memory.* Oxford: Oxford University Press.

Baddeley, A. D., & Hitch, G. (1993). The recency effect: Implicit learning with explicit retrieval? *Memory & Cognition, 21*, 146-155.

Bower, G. H. (1972). Stimulus-sampling theory of encoding variability. In A. W. Melton, & E. Martin (Eds.), *Coding Processes in Human Memory* (pp. 85-123). Washington, D C: Winston.

Broadbent, D. E. (1958). *Perception and Communication.* New York: Pergamon Press.

Broadbent, D. E. (1963). Flow of information within the organism. *Journal of Verbal Learning and Verbal Behavior, 4*, 34-39.

Brown, G. D. A., Vousden, J., & Hulme, C. (1996). An oscillator-based model for serial order. *Abstracts of the Psychonomic Society, 1*, 45.

Burgess, N., & Hitch, G. J. (1992). Toward a network model of the articulatory loop. *Journal of Memory and Language, 31*, 429-460.

Clark, S. E., & Gronlund, S. D. (1996). Global matching models of recognition memory: How the models match the data. *Psychonomic Bulletin & Review, 3*, 37-60.

Conrad, R. (1964). Acoustic confusions in immediate memory. *British Journal of Psychology, 55,* 75-84.

Conrad, R., & Hille, B. A. (1958). The decay theory of immediate memory and paced recall. *Canadian Journal of Psychology, 12,* 1-6.

Cowan, N. (1993). Activation, attention, and short-term memory. *Memory & Cognition, 21,* 162-167.

Craik, F. I. M., & Lockhart, R. S. (1972). Levels of processing: A framework for memory research. *Journal of Verbal Learning and Verbal Behavior, 11,* 671-684.

Craik, F. I. M., & Watkins, M. J. (1973). The role of rehearsal in short-term memory. *Journal of Verbal Learning and Verbal Behavior, 12,* 599-607.

Crowder, R. G. (1993). Short-term memory: Where do we stand? *Memory & Cognition, 21,* 142-145.

Crowder, R. G., & Greene, R. L. (1987). In D. S. Gorfein, & R. R. Hoffman (Eds.), *Memory and Learning.* (pp. 191-199). Hillsdale, NJ: Lawrence Erlbaum Associates.

Crowder, R. G., & Neath, I. (1991). The microscope metaphor in human memory. In W. E. Hockley, & S. Lewandowsky (Eds.), *Relating theory and data: Essays on Human Memory in Honor of Bennet B. Murdock (*pp. 111-125). Hillsdale, NJ: Lawrence Erlbaum Associates.

Drewnowski, A. (1980). Attributes and priorities in short-term recall: A new model of memory span. *Journal of Experimental Psychology: General, 109,* 208-250.

Eich, J. M. (1982). A composite holographic associative recall model. *Psychological Review, 89,* 1-38.

Estes, W. K. (1986). Array models for category learning. *Cognitive Psychology, 18,* 500-549.

Estes, W. K. (1994). *Classification and Cognition.* Oxford: Oxford University Press.

Estes, W. K. (1997). Processes of memory loss, recovery, and distortion. *Psychological Review, 104,* 148-169.

Estes, W. K., & Maddox, W. T. (1995). Interactions of similarity, base rate, and feedback in recognition. *Journal of Experimental Psychology: Learning, Memory and Cognition, 21,* 1075-1095.

Feigenbaum, E. A. (1961). The simulation of verbal learning behavior. *Proceedings of the Western Joint Computer Conference (WJCC), 19,* 121-132.

Gillund, G., & Shiffrin, R. M. (1984). A Retrieval model for both recognition and recall. *Psychological Review, 91,* 1-67.

Glenberg, A. M. (1987). Temporal context and recency. In D. S. Gorfein, & R. R. Hoffman (Eds.), *Memory and Learning.* (pp.173-190). Hillsdale,NJ: Lawrence Erlbaum Associates.

Glenberg, A. M., & Swanson, N. C. (1986). A temporal distinctiveness theory of recency and modality effects. *Journal of Experimental Psychology: Learning, Memory and Cognition, 12,* 3-15.

Greene, R. L. (1986). Sources of recency effects in free recall. *Psychological Bulletin, 99,* 221-228.

Healy, A. F., & McNamara, D. S. (1996). Verbal learning and memory: Does the modal model still work? *Annual Review of Psychology, 47,* 143-172.

Hintzman, D. L. (1988). Judgments of frequency and recognition memory in a multiple-trace memory. *Psychological Review, 95,* 528-551.

Hintzman, D. L. (1991). Why are formal models useful in Psychology? In W. E. Hockley, & S. Lewandowsky (Eds.), *Relating theory and data: Essays on Human Memory in Honor of Bennet B. Murdock* (pp. 39-56). Hillsdale, NJ: Lawrence Erlbaum Associates.

Humphreys, M. S., Bain, J. D., & Pike, R. (1989). Different ways to cue a coherent memory system: A theory for episodic, semantic, and procedural tasks. *Psychological Review, 96,* 208-233.

Humphreys, M. S., Pike, R., Bain, J. D., & Tehan, G. (1989). Global matching: A comparison of the SAM, MINERVA II, Matrix, and TODAM models. *Journal of Mathematical Psychology, 33,* 36-67.

Kintsch, W. (1974). *The Representation of Meaning in Memory.* Hilldale, NJ: Lawrence Erlbaum Associates.

Lee, C. L., & Estes, W. K. (1981). Item and order information in short-term memory: Evidence for multilevel perturbation processes. *Journal of Experimental Psychology: Learning, Memory, and Cognition, 7,* 149-169.

Maddox, W. T., & Estes, W. K. (1997). Direct and indirect stimulus-frequency effects in recognition. *Journal of Experimental Psychology: Learning, Memory, and Cognition, 23,* 539-559.

McClelland, J. L., & Goddard, N. H. (1996). Considerations arising from a complementary learning systems perspective on hippocampus and neocortex. *Hippocampus, 6,* 654-665.

McClelland, J. L., McNaughton, B. L., & O'Reilly, R. C. (1995). Why there are complementary learning systems in the hippocampus and neocortex: Insights from the successes and failures of connectionist models of learning and memory. *Psychological Review, 102,* 419-457.

Medin, D. L., & Florian, J. E. (1992). Abstraction and selective coding in exemplar-based models of categorization. In A. Healy, S. M. Kosslyn, & R. M. Shiffrin (Ed.), *From Learning Processes to Cognitive Processes: Essays in Honor of William K. Estes* (pp. 207-234). Hillsdale, NJ: Lawrence Erlbaum Associates.

Medin, D. L., & Schaffer, M. M. (1978). Context theory of classification learning. *Psychological Review, 85,* 207-238.

Mensink, G. J. M., & Raaijmakers, J. G. W. (1988). A model for interference and forgetting. *Psychological Review, 95,* 434-455.

Mensink, G. J. M., & Raaijmakers, J. G. W. (1989). A model of contextual fluctuation. *Journal of Mathematical Psychology, 33,* 172-186.

Murdock, B. B., Jr. (1960). The distinctiveness of stimuli. *Psychological Review, 89,* 16-31.

Murdock, B. B., Jr. (1967). Recent developments in short-term memory. *British Journal of Psychology, 58,* 421-433.

Murdock, B. B., Jr. (1974). *Human Memory: Theory and Data.* Potomac, MD: Lawrence Erlbaum Associates.

Murdock, B. B. Jr. (1982). A theory for the storage and retrieval of item and associative information. *Psychological Review, 89,* 609-626.

Murdock, B. B. Jr. (1989). Learning in a distributed memory model. In C. Izawa (Ed.), *Current Issues in Cognitive Processes: The Tulane Flowerree Symposium on Cognition* (pp. 69-106). Hillsdale, NJ: Lawrence Erlbaum Associates.

Murdock, B. B., Jr., & Anderson, R. E. (1975). Encoding, storage, and retrieval of item information. In R. L. Solso (Ed.), *Information Processing and Cognition: The Loyola Symposium* (pp. 145-194). Hillsdale, NJ: Lawrence Erlbaum Associates.

Murdock, B. B., & Kahana, M. J. (1993a). Analysis of the list strength effect. *Journal of Experimental Psychology: Learning, Memory, and Cognition, 19,* 689-697.

Murdock, B. B., & Kahana, M. J. (1993b). List-strength and list-length effects: Reply to Shiffrin, Ratcliff, Murnane, and Nobel (1993). *Journal of Experimental Psychology: Learning, Memory, and Cognition, 19,* 1450-1453.

Murdock, B. B., & Lamon, M. (1988). The replacement effect: Repeating some items while replacing others. *Memory and Cognition, 16,* 91-101.

Murnane, K., & Shiffrin, R. M. (1991). Interference and the representation of events in memory. *Journal of*

Experimental Psychology:Learning, Memory and Cognition, 17, 855-874.

Nairne, J. S. (1991). Positional uncertainty in long-terrm memory. *Memory & Cognition, 19,* 332-340.

Nairne, J. S. (1992). The loss of positional certainty in long-term memory. *Psychological Science, 3,* 199-202.

Newell, A. (1973). Production systems: Models of control structures. In W. C. Chase (Ed.), *Visual Information Processing* (pp. 463-526). New York: Academic Press.

Newell, A. (1990). *Unified Theories of Cognition.* Cambridge, MA: Harvard University Press.

Newell, A., Shaw, J. C., & Simon, H. A. (1958). Elements of a theory of human problem solving. *Psychological Review, 65,* 151-166.

Norman, D. A. (1970). Introduction: Models of human memory. In D. A. Norman (Ed.), *Models of Human Memory* (pp. 1-15). New York: Academic Press.

Norman, D. A., & Rumelhart, D. E. (1970). A system for perception and memory. In D. A. Norman (Ed.), *Models of Human Memory* (pp. 19-64). New York: Academic Press.

Norman, D. A., & Rumelhart, D. E. (1975). *Explorations in Cognition.* San Francisco: Freeman.

Nosofsky, R. M. (1984). Choice, similarity, and the context theory of classification. *Journal of Experimental Psychology:Learning, Memory, and Cognition, 10,* 104-114.

Nosofsky, R. M. (1986). Attention, similarity, and the identification-categorization relationship. *Journal of Experimental Psychology: General, 115,* 39-57.

Nosofsky, R. M. (1988). Exemplar-based acccounts of relations between classification, recognition, and typicality. *Journal of Experimental Psychology: Learning, Memory, and Cognition, 14,* 700-708.

Osgood, C. E. (1949). The similarity paradox in human learning: A resolution. *Psychological Review, 56,* 132-143.

Peterson, L. R. (1966). Short-term memory and verbal learning. *Psychological Review, 73,* 193-207.

Peterson, L. R., & Peterson, M. (1959). Short-term retention of individual verbal items. *Journal of Experimental Psychology, 58,* 193-198.

Phillips, J. L., Shiffrin, R. M., & Atkinson, R. C. (1967). Effects of list length on short-term memory. *Journal of Verbal Learning and Verbal Behavior, 6,* 303-311.

Postman, L. (1961). The present status of interference theory. In C.

N. Cofer (Ed.), *Verbal Learning and Verbal Behavior* (pp. 152-168). New York: McGraw-Hill.

Raaijmakers, J. G. W. (1993). The story of the two-store model of memory: Past criticisms, current status, and future directions. In D. E. Meyer & S. Kornblum (Eds.), *Attention and Performance, XIV* (pp. 467-480). Cambridge, MA: MIT Press.

Raaijmakers, J. G. W., & Shiffrin, R. M. (1980). SAM: A theory of probabilistic search of associative memory. In G. H. Bower (Ed.), *The Psychology of Learning and Motivation: Advances in Research and Theory, Vol. 4* (pp. 207-262). New York: Academic Press.

Raaijmakers, J. G. W., & Shiffrin, R. M. (1981). Search of associative memory. *Psychological Review, 88,* 93-134.

Ratcliff, R. (1978). A theory of memory retrieval. *Psychological Review, 85,* 59-108.

Ratcliff, R. (1981). A theory of order relations in perceptual matching. *Psychological Review, 88,* 552-572.

Ratcliff, R., Clark, S. E., & Shiffrin, R. M. (1990). The list-strength effect: I. Data and discussion. *Journal of Experimental Psychology: Learning, Memory, and Cognition, 16,* 163-78.

Ratcliff, R., & McKoon, G. (1991). Using ROC data and priming results to test global memory models. In W. E. Hockley, & S. Lewandowsky (Eds.), *Relating theory and data: Essays on Human Memory in Honor of Bennet B. Murdock* (pp. 279-296). Hillsdale, NJ: Lawrence Erlbaum Associates.

Ratcliff, R., Van Zandt, T., & McKoon, G. (1995). Process dissociation, single-process theories, and recognition memory. *Journal of Experimental Psychology: General, 24,* 352-374.

Shadmehr, R., & Holcomb, H. H. (1997). Neural correlates of motor memory consolidation. *Science, 277,* 821-825.

Shiffrin, R. M., Huber, D. E., & Marinelli, K. (1995). Effects of category length and strength on familiarity in recognition. *Journal of Experimental Psychology: Learning, Memory, and Cognition, 21,* 267-287.

Shiffrin, R. M., & Raaijmakers, J. (1992). The SAM retrieval model: A retrospective and prospective. In A. F. Healy, S. M. Kosslyn, & R. M. Shiffrin (Eds.), *From Learning Processes to Cognitive Processes: Essays in Honor of William K. Estes* (pp. 69-86). Hillsdale, NJ: Lawrence Erlbaum Associates.

Shiffrin, R. M., Ratcliff, R., & Clark, S. E. (1990). The list-strength effect: Theoretical mechanisms. *Journal of Experimental*

Psychology: Learning, Memory, and Cognition, 16, 179-95.

Shiffrin, R., Ratcliff, R., Murnane, K., & Nobel, P. (1993). TODAM and list-strength and list-length effects: Comment on Murdock and Kahana (1993a). *Journal of Experimental Psychology: Learning, Memory, and Cognition, 19,* 1445-1449.

Sperling, G. (1967). Successive approximations to a model for short-term memory. *Acta Psychologica, 27,* 285-292.

Squire, L. R. (1986). Mechanisms of memory. *Science, 232,* 1612-1619.

Standing, L., Conezio, J., & Haber, R. N. (1970). Perception and memory for pictures: Single-trial learning of 2,500 visual stimuli. *Psychonomic Science, 19,* 73-74.

Sternberg, S. (1966). High-speed scanning in human memory. *Science, 153,* 652-654.

Tulving, E., & Hastie, R. (1972). Inhibition effects of intralist repetition in free recall. *Journal of Experimental Psychology, 92,* 297-304.

Underwood, B. J. (1957). Interference and forgetting. *Psychological Review, 64,* 49-60.

Underwood, B. J. (1969). Attributes of Memory. *Psychological Review, 76,* 559-573.

Underwood, B. J. (1977). *Temporal Codes for Memories: Issues and Problems.* Hillsdale, NJ: Lawrence Erlbaum Associates.

Woodward, A. E. J., Bjork, R. A., & Jongeward, R. N. (1973). Recall and recognition as a function of primary rehearsal. *Journal of Verbal Learning and Verbal Behavior, 12,* 608-617.

Yonelinas, A. P., Hockley, W. E., & Murdock, B. B. Jr. (1992). Tests of the list-strength effect in recognition memory. *Journal of Experimental Psychology: Learning, Memory, and Cognition, 18,* 345-355.

Chapter 5

Part-List Cuing Revisited: Testing the Sampling-Bias Hypothesis

Jeroen G.W. Raaijmakers
R. Hans Phaf
University of Amsterdam, the Netherlands

The SAM (Search of Associative Memory) model was originally developed as a model for free and cued recall during the beginning of 1978. After the initial simulations of a number of standard findings in free recall had shown that the model performed reasonably well (see Raaijmakers & Shiffrin, 1980), the model was applied to the part-list cuing effect, an intriguing finding that was a real puzzle at that time (and perhaps still is, see Nickerson, 1984). This effect refers to the phenomenon in a free recall paradigm that presenting some of the list items as cues for recall does not help subjects in improving their retrieval of the remaining items (the "targets"). This paradigm was devised by Slamecka (1968) as a test of the general assumption that memory is associative and that such associations should aid the retrieval of associated items from memory. Thus, it was assumed that the retrieval of the list items from memory should be facilitated when subjects are given some of them as cues. Hence, the finding that no positive effect was obtained and that often the cues even seemed to have a slight effect was a real puzzle.

In May 1978, the first simulations of this paradigm were run with the SAM model. The results showed that the model predicted the part-list cuing effect, even though the assumptions of the model were such that it made heavy use of interitem associations. Although the model predicted this result, we did not understand very well why. We initially thought that this prediction resulted from the assumption in the model that associations were strengthened ("incremented") following successful recall. However, in November 1978, in a class project at Indiana University, one of Shiffrin's students ran a simulation of the model with all strengthening parameters set to zero. To our surprise, the effect did not disappear.

Given the structure of the SAM model and the observation that the effect (at least within the model) did not depend on the incrementing assumptions, it had to be the case that the prediction was due to the fact that the cues used by the noncued subjects (the cues they generated themselves during the recall process) were somehow better than the randomly selected part-list cues that were used by the cued subjects. One reason for the superiority of self-generated cues might be that these were not sampled randomly but with a probability that was related to their strength. Thus, these items presumably were stronger and hence might also have stronger interitem associations than the experimenter-provided part-list cues.

In order to understand more fully what was going on, we ran a number of simulations with a very simplified version of SAM (Raaijmakers, 1979). In this version, all items were of equal strength and the only process that played a role was the sampling process (i.e., "recovery" was always successful). A very simple associative structure was assumed in which each item was associated to exactly one other item. In these simulations a negative part-list cuing effect was obtained when the cues were drawn at random from all list items, even though the setup was such that strong positive effects would have been obtained if the cues had been selected in concordance with the stored associative structure, that is, one cue per pair (as in regular paired-associate recall). These analyses showed that there was a subtle factor that favored the noncued group. It turned out that the cues used by the cued group were inferior to the self-generated cues used by the noncued group due to a sampling bias: the self-generated cues could provide access to the most "profitable" clusters of interassociated items, those composed of all target items, and the experimenter-provided cue items could not do this (since these were by definition not associated to the items in those clusters).

This explanation was proposed by Raaijmakers and Shiffrin (1981a) as the major explanation for why the SAM model predicted the part-list cuing effect. They (p. 114) pointed out that the prediction was crucially dependent on the fact that the associative strength distribution was not uniform since the effect becomes positive when all strengths are set to the same value (hence the normally existing structure in the matrix of retrieval strengths is eliminated). Additional analyses gave further support for the SAM explanation. In particular, it was shown that the model predicted a positive effect of cuing when the context-to-item associations were very weak. In such a case, the noncued group would no longer be able to self-generate enough cues: Bad cues are still better than no cues at all. Experiments by Blake and Okada (1973) and Basden (1973) indeed showed positive cuing effects when the cues were given following inter-polated study of an interfering list.

Over the years, several other explanations have been provided for the part-list cuing effect. Most of these explanations assume (in one way or another) that subjects do not or cannot make use of interitem associations to aid recall. Other explanations assume that the normal retrieval process in the cued condition is somehow disrupted and hence less effective than that in the control condition. For example, Basden, Basden and Galloway (1977) proposed that the effect is due to the fact that the order of recall in the cued group is suboptimal because it is not compatible with the organization that was stored during study of the list. However, the explanation proposed by Raaijmakers and Shiffrin (1981a) still seems the only one that is capable of explaining not just the basic result, but also a range of variations, including those situations in which a positive effect is obtained. Most importantly, the SAM explanation does not rely on the awkward assumption that in free recall no use is made of interitem associations. On the contrary, the sampling bias explanation is critically dependent on the fact that such associations are effective.

Not everyone was, however, convinced by our analyses. For example, Nickerson (1984) in his review of the literature, criticized our explanation because it made "some assumptions the only justification for which seems to be that they are needed to explain the effect" (p. 550). He was referring to the assumption that both groups sample the same number of clusters. Although he did acknowledge that this was only assumed for the simplified illustration in the Raaijmakers and Shiffrin (1981a) article, Nickerson completely disregarded the fact that in the full SAM model this was not in fact assumed a priori. The simplified illustration served only to explain a rather subtle factor that had been missed in all previous discussions of the part-list cuing phenomenon (i.e., the sampling bias factor). The crucial aspect was not that an equal number of clusters was accessed but that the cue items that were used by the cued group could only give access to clusters of items that had at least one cue in them. The "assumption" that the cued group would access about the same number of clusters was not an a priori assumption, but rather could be derived from the general retrieval assumptions (i.e., the assumption that the efficiency of retrieval decreases with each additional retrieval). Hence, Nickerson's objection seems unfounded.

A more crucial objection was advanced by Roediger and Neely (1982). They described an experiment by Park (1980) that showed that when words were embedded in sentences, part-list cues did aid recall. However, when the same items were embedded in categorized lists, the usual negative part-list cuing effect was observed. A similar reversal was observed when subjects studied sets of word triples either by forming coherent interactive images or separate images. Roediger and Neely proposed a distinction between horizontal (direct interitem) and vertical associations. According to them, only when there are horizontal associations between items (direct item-to-item associations), part-list cuing leads to facilitation. When there are no horizontal associations, the result is inhibition. They pointed out that this result is difficult to reconcile with the SAM explanation since SAM already uses a rich interitem associative structure in its prediction of part-list cuing inhibition.

In addition, the SAM model has been criticized as being overly compli-cated and of using a large number of parameters (see Roediger, 1993), hence making it easy to predict any result. Moreover, "designing independent tests of the model may be difficult, since its ten parameters and numerous countervailing processes make unambiguous predictions hard to come by" (Roediger & Neely, 1982, p. 225). Although this objection seems unfair when a quantitative model like SAM is compared to verbal, descriptive theories (a nonquantitative version of SAM would surely be more powerful in the sense of being consistent with an ever larger set of data patterns since it is less constrained), it does point to the importance of being able to devise proper experimental tests of the model. In this chapter, we will present a series of experiments that were motivated by the SAM explanation for the part-list cuing effect and that may provide a critical test of our explanation against explanations such as the one proposed by Roediger and Neely (1982).

In particular, we wanted to show that even in cases where the normal testing procedure leads to part-list inhibition, a positive effect could be obtained using a different testing procedure. Basically, the idea was to give the recall test either immediately after study or after a delay filled with the learning of an unrelated list. The latter should lead to retroactive interference and hence recall levels should be much lower after the interpolated learning. In SAM, this would be equivalent to the assumption that the context strengths were much lower in the delayed testing case than in immediate testing (see Mensink & Raaijmakers, 1988). As was mentioned above, Raaijmakers and Shiffrin (1981a) showed that SAM predicts a positive part-list cuing effect if the context strengths are low, since in that case the noncued group will not be able to generate a sufficient number of items to use as cues whereas the cued group still has the experimenter-provided cues to use in their retrieval.

A second crucial aspect of the SAM explanation was that the cuing effect would become positive if the cues are not sampled randomly (as is normally the case) but are chosen in such a way that they would give maximum access to the stored clusters. For example, the effect should become positive if the list consists of a number of categories and subjects are given one cue per category. Thus we assumed that if one would let subjects study a list of paired associates and then at test would give half of the items as cues, the part-list cuing effect should be negative if the cue words are sampled randomly and positive if one cue word is chosen from each pair of words. The simplified model that had been used to analyze SAM's prediction of the part-list cuing effect indeed predicted such a result.

In the first experiment, we presented subjects lists of paired associates. There were five test conditions, three immediate and two delayed ones. The three immediate cuing conditions were: no cues (the *control* condition), random half of the words as cues (the *random* condition), or one cue from each pair (the *1Q* condition). The two delayed conditions were: no cues or a random half of the words. Based on the analyses described above, we expected that there would be a negative part-list cuing effect in the immediate condition for randomly chosen cue words but a positive effect for the condition with one cue per pair. On the delayed condition, the part-list cuing effect should reverse, hence the random cue condition should now be superior to the no cue control condition.

Experiment 1

Method

Subjects. Thirty-two volunteer subjects participated in Experiment 1. All subjects were undergraduate psychology students at the University of Nijmegen who participated for course credit. Subjects were tested in groups of 2-5 subjects at a time.

Materials and Design. There were five conditions in the experiment. In all conditions, subjects were asked to study a list of 20 unrelated word pairs (hence 40 words in total). In three conditions, recall was tested immediately, in two conditions recall was tested after a delay filled with three study-test cycles of an unrelated list of 25 word pairs. In the immediate testing conditions, either no cues were given (*control*), or 20 randomly chosen words were given as cues (*random*), or one cue from each pair was given (either the first or the second, *1Q*). In delayed testing, either no cues were given or 20 randomly chosen words were given as cues. All words were common Dutch nouns. Each subject participated in all three immediate testing conditions and in one of the two delayed test conditions. As each subject participated in four conditions, four lists of 20 unrelated word pairs were constructed. The order of the conditions and the assignment of lists to conditions were counterbalanced across subjects.

Procedure. Subjects were seated in front of a monitor. The subjects booths were separated by screens. After a practice list, the four experimental lists plus the three repetitions of the interpolated list were presented. The word pairs were presented for 4 seconds each. After each presentation of a list, a three digit number was presented on the screen followed by 10 single-digit numbers that had to be subtracted from the three-digit number. Each number was presented for 2 seconds, hence this task (that was used to eliminate recall from STS) took about 20 seconds. At the end, they wrote down the answer on their answer sheet.

After the arithmetic task, subjects were either tested immediately or they were given the interpolated learning task. At test, they were asked to recall in writing (answer sheets were provided) as many words as possible from the list presented last, in any order. They were given two minutes to recall. After each test, the answer sheets were collected by the experimenter. The instructions

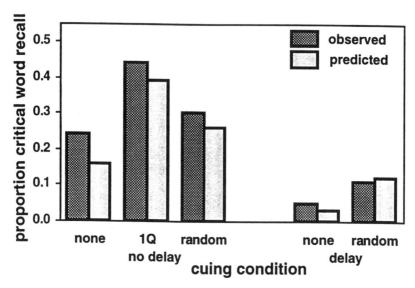

FIG. 5.1: Observed and predicted proportions of
critical word recall for each cuing condition in
Experiment 1. Predictions were obtained from the
SAM Model (adapted to study of word pairs) with $R =$
2, $A = 0.3$, $B = 0.8$, $C = 0.3$, $D = 0.02$, $E = F = G = 2$,
$K_{MAX} = 50$ and $L_{MAX} = 2$. For delayed testing, the
context strength was decreased to $A = 0.05$.

explained that on some tests a number of words from the list would be presented
on the screen and that these could be used to recall other words that they had
been associated with. The interpolated list consisted of 25 unrelated word pairs.
Each pair was presented during study for 3 seconds. After all pairs had been
presented, a test was given of the interpolated list in which the first member of
the pair was given for subjects to write down the second member. Response
time was six seconds per tested item. The whole session lasted about one hour.

Results and Discussion

In Fig. 5.1 the proportions of noncue words (targets) recalled in each condition
are shown. Two repeated-measures analyses of variance were performed on
these data, one for the immediate testing conditions and one for the delayed
testing conditions. All differences between conditions were significant at $\alpha =$
0.05. As expected, in immediate testing performance in the 1Q condition was

superior to the other two conditions. However, the random cue condition was also superior to the no-cue control condition. We had expected to find a standard negative part-list cuing effect based on the simulation results with the simplified version of SAM. In delayed testing, the cuing effect was positive, as expected. However, since the effect was also positive in immediate testing, we obviously did not obtain the reversal of the effect as we had expected.

These results replicate the positive cuing effects obtained by Park (1980, see Roediger & Neely, 1982) when during study subsets of words are strongly interassociated, such as by forming interactive images. These results seem to be inconsistent with the explanation given by SAM for the part-list cuing effect since SAM has been shown to predict a negative effect in free recall even when the interitem associations are strong. However, these simulation results were obtained with the normal simulation program for free recall in which items are presented one at a time. In such a case, the clusters formed during study will be overlapping. In the present case, however, the items are presented in pairs. If it is assumed that interitem associations will only be formed between the two members of a pair, the resulting clusters will be non-overlapping. In previous analyses of SAM (see Raaijmakers & Shiffrin, 1981b) we did indeed assume that when paired-associates are studied, the buffer would contain only the two members of the pair being studied and hence words belonging to different pairs would not become associated. On the other hand, simulations with the simplified model had led us to expect a negative part-list cuing effect even for lists of pairwise associated items.

The results of this experiment prompted us to take a closer look at the predictions of the full SAM model, adapted to this experimental design. We ran a number of simulations, assuming that items were studied in pairs. As in Raaijmakers and Shiffrin (1981b), the amount of information stored on a trial is assumed to be a function of the number of items in the buffer. Thus, if there are 2 items in the buffer, the increase in contextual associative strength will be $a/2$ for each second of study. Otherwise, the simulation program was exactly the same as that used in the original analyses of the part-list cuing paradigm.

To our surprise, the results of these simulations showed that the SAM model did in fact predict a positive cuing effect when the items are studied in pairs. In Fig. 5.1 the results are shown based on 500 simulation runs with the following parameter values (no attempt was made to search the parameter space exhaustively in order to optimize the fit of the predictions): $r = 2$, $a = 0.3$ (immediate testing) or $a = 0.05$ (delayed testing), $b = 0.75$, $c = 0.25$, $d = 0.02$, $e = f = g = 2$, $K_{MAX} = 50$ and $L_{MAX} = 2$ (see Raaijmakers & Shiffrin, 1981a, p. 97, for an explanation of the parameters of the SAM model). Hence, it was assumed that delayed testing leads to a decrease in the context-to-image strengths but leaves all other aspects unchanged. The SAM model predicts all of the effects that were obtained in this experiment: It shows a huge advantage for the 1Q condition and a slightly superior performance in the random cue condition compared to the no cue control condition, both in immediate and delayed testing.

Hence, despite the fact that the experiment was in some sense not successful because it did not produce the expected reversal of the cuing effect, it did lead to the surprising discovery that the SAM model predicts positive cuing effects if the list consists of a number of small and non-overlapping clusters. The reader will probably wonder (just as we did) why the simplified model did not predict this. Further analyses showed that this was due to the fact that in the simplified model the recovery process was eliminated. If in the full model one sets the probability of successful recovery to 1 (irrespective of the cues used), the predicted part-list cuing effect will always be negative. This is probably due to the fact that such an assumption eliminates one of the few factors in the model that favors the cued condition, relative to the control condition. In the control condition relatively more searches are made using only the context cue, whereas in the cued condition almost all searches are made using both context and item cues. In the latter case, the probability of successful recovery will be greater than when only the context cue is used.

In sum, we have shown that, contrary to what we and others had originally assumed, the full SAM model predicts a positive cuing effect if the list consists of a number of highly interassociated and non-overlapping clusters of items. This is, of course, a highly interesting result, but it also implies that the present experimental setup will not make it possible to test the SAM model against the Roediger-Neely hypothesis that assumes a direct relationship between the stored associative structure and the direction of the part-list effect. In order to decide between these two theories, we need a design in which the part-list cuing effect is negative in immediate testing. Therefore, in the next experiment we gave subjects regular free recall lists (lists of words presented one at a time). Otherwise, the experimental procedures were the same as the previous ones. Subjects were tested either immediately or after a delay filled with study of an unrelated list of paired-associates. One obvious problem with the normal free recall procedure is that one has no control over the clusters that will be formed by a subjects. Hence, it will not be possible to give subjects one cue from each cluster at test. However, on the assumption that consecutive items might be more likely to become interassociated, we included a condition that resembled the one cue per cluster condition of Experiment 1. In this case, we gave subjects either all the items in the even positions as cues or all the uneven items. Obviously, there was no guarantee that this would coincide with the stored associative structure.

Experiment 2

Method

Subjects. Thirty paid subjects from the subject pool of the TNO Research Institute for Human Factors participated in the experiment. Subjects were tested individually.

Materials and Design. There were six conditions in the experiment. In all conditions, subjects were asked to study a list of 40 words. In three conditions, recall was tested immediately, in the other three conditions recall was tested after a delay filled with three study-test cycles of an unrelated list of 25 word pairs (which lasted about 15 min). In both immediate and delayed testing, either no cues were given (*control*), or 20 randomly chosen words were given as cues (*random*), or the 20 words that had been presented in either the even serial positions or the uneven positions (we will still refer to this as the *1Q* condition). All words were common Dutch nouns. Each subject participated in all conditions. Six lists of 40 words were constructed, and the assignment of lists to conditions as well as the order of the conditions were counterbalanced across subjects.

Procedure. The procedure was similar to that of Experiment 1, except that now the words were presented one at a time, for 2 seconds each. The whole session lasted about two hours. There was a break about halfway during the session.

Results and Discussion

For each subject, the number of target words recalled was determined for each condition with cues. Two scores were computed for each of the two conditions without cues, one score as a control for the random cues condition and one as a control for the 1Q condition (two scores are needed since the target items are different depending on the cues that are actually given). A 6 x 2 x 2 x 2 repeated-measures analysis of variance with groups as between-subjects factor and delay, cue type (random vs. 1Q) and cuing (with or without cues) was performed. As expected, there was a large effect of delay: $F(1, 24) = 110.9, p < .001$. None of the other main effects was significant. Thus, the cue type factor neither generated any effect nor interacted with any of the other factors. Hence, there was no advantage for the 1Q condition relative to the random cue condition. Apparently, the associative structure cannot be characterized as one of pairwise associations between consecutive items. There was, however, a significant interaction between delay and cuing: $F(1, 24) = 10.8, p < .005$. Figure 5.2 shows the nature of this interaction: the effect of cuing is negative in immediate testing, but positive in delayed testing. We have, here, confirmed the

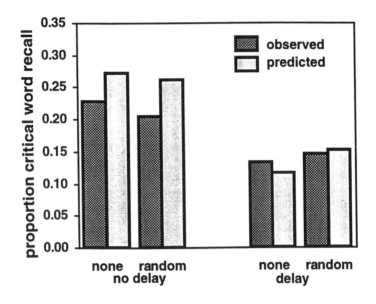

cuing condition

FIG. 5.2: Observed and predicted proportions of critical word recall for the cued and noncued conditions in Experiment 2. Predictions were obtained from the SAM Model with $R = 4$, $A = 0.3$, $B = 0.1$, $C = 0.1$, $D = 0.02$, $E = F = G = 2$, $K_{MAX} = 50$ and $L_{MAX} = 2$. For delayed testing, the context strength was decreased to $A = 0.10$.

prediction of SAM that the part-list cuing effect reverses when unaided retrieval (as in the control condition) becomes difficult.

In Fig. 5.2 we also present the predictions from SAM. These predictions are based on 500 simulation runs with the same model as was used to generate the predictions for Experiment 1, but now adapted to regular free recall. Thus, the traditional buffer model was used, but the amount of information stored on a trial is a function of the number of items in the buffer. The following parameter values were used: $r = 4$, $a = 0.3$ (immediate testing) or $a = 0.10$ (delayed testing), $b = 0.10$, $c = 0.10$, $d = 0.02$, $e = f = g = 2$, $K_{MAX} = 50$ and $L_{MAX} = 2$. Again, these predictions are representative and are not based on any elaborate search of the parameter space. These simulation results demonstrate that the SAM model indeed predicts the observed reversal of the cuing effect in delayed testing.

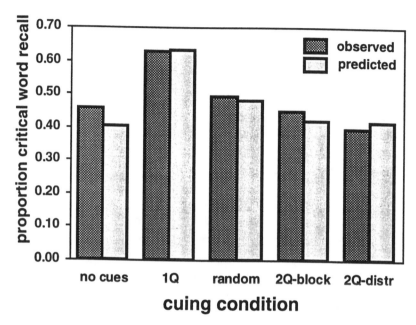

cuing condition

FIG. 5.3: Observed and predicted proportions of critical word recall for the cued and noncued conditions in Experiment 3. Predictions were obtained from the SAM Model for categorized lists with $R = 4$, $PCS = 1.30$, $A = 0.1$, $B = 0.0$, $C = 0.1$, $D = 0.02$, $E = F = G = .7$, $K_{MAX} = 50$ and $L_{MAX} = 3$ (see text for explanation).

number of words recalled from cued and noncued categories separately (see Table 5.1). Whereas cuing has a positive effect on the recall performance for items belonging to the cued categories, the effect on recall of the members of the noncued categories is clearly negative. The proportion items recalled from non-cued categories declines with the number of items recalled from the cued categories. Since recall from cued categories precedes recall from noncued categories, this may be interpreted as an indication that recall of an item reduces the probability of recall of a further item.

This is further illustrated by the data in Table 5.2 in which the proportion of categories from which at least one item is retrieved and the proportion of critical items recalled from these 'retrieved' categories are given. It is evident that the probability of retrieving a category increases with the number of cues provided from that category. However, the probability of retrieving a noncued

Table 5.2
Proportion of Categories Retrieved and Proportion of Critical Words Recalled from Retrieved Categories For Cued and Noncued Categories Separately in Experiment 3.

		no cues	*1Q*	*random*	*2Q block.*	*2Q distr.*
categories retrieved	*cued*	--	0.83	0.80	0.87	0.89
	noncued	0.53	--	0.25	0.39	0.30
critical items recalled	*cued*	--	0.76	0.81	0.83	0.82
	noncued	0.86	--	0.78	0.78	0.76

category decreases with the number of retrieved cued categories. When no categories are cued, 53% of the noncued categories are retrieved, while in the random cue condition (in which on the average 7.4 categories were cued), only 25% of the noncued categories were retrieved. However, once a category is retrieved, the proportion of recalled critical items from that category is approximately constant. Such effects can be explained by the assumption that as more and more categories are retrieved, there is increasing output interference, making it more and more difficult to retrieve other categories (or items from other categories).

Thus, in the present experiment both positive and negative cuing effects were observed. These results support the hypothesis that the critical factor in the sign of the part-list cuing effect is not the use of horizontal or vertical associations but the selection of the cues relative to the stored associative structure.

We also analyzed whether the SAM model could account for these effects. In order to maximize the contrast of the SAM model with theories assuming vertical associations, it was assumed that category information was completely captured by the interitem associations between items belonging to the same category. Thus, all associations between items belonging to the same category were given a relatively high pre-experimental associative strength (*PCS*, pre-experimental category strength). The association strengths resulting from the study of the items were added to these pre-experimental strengths. However, for the present experiment the pre-experimental strengths are indistinguishable from the experimental interitem strengths because all members of a category were always studied together. In the simulations we have, therefore, set PCS to a relatively high value and the normal interitem strength parameter (b) to zero. Otherwise, the standard SAM assumptions and parameter definitions were used (e.g., a gives the amount of contextual strength added per second of study). Figure 5.3 gives representative predictions based on 100 simulation runs with the parameter values $r = 4$, $PCS = 1.30$, $a = 0.1$, $b = 0.0$, $c = 0.1$, $d = 0.02$, $e = f = g = .7$, $K_{MAX} = 50$ and $L_{MAX} = 3$. SAM correctly predicts strong positive effects of cuing with one cue per category, either small negative or small positive effects in the random cuing condition and larger negative effects in the two cues per category conditions. The simulation model that was used has no mechanism to predict a difference depending on how the categories from which the two cues are given, are distributed across the list. In order to explain such a difference, the model had to be adjusted by introducing different contexts for different parts of the list (i.e., different contexts for the beginning, middle, and end of the list). Simulations with such an adjusted model indeed produced the observed pattern. However, we will not pursue this second-order effect further since it is not important for the central issue of this chapter, namely the issue of whether the part-list cuing effect can be explained by a model that relies on horizontal associations.

General Discussion

One of the most intriguing findings obtained in the present experiments was the unexpected (small) positive effect of cuing when the study list consists of either paired-associates or a number of small-sized categories. In the past, positive part-list cuing effects have been interpreted as being due to the formation of horizontal associations during study of the list (Roediger & Neely, 1982). The direction and size of the effect, however, were shown here to depend critically on two factors that only affect the retrieval process rather than the stored associative structure. In Experiments 1 and 3, the effect depended, to a large degree, on whether the cues were chosen randomly or in such a way that they were distributed evenly across the associative clusters formed during study. In Experiment 3, moreover, there was a strong positive cuing effect if one cue was chosen from each category but the effect was negative if two cues were chosen from each of five categories and no cues from the remaining five categories.

In addition, we experimentally verified the prediction of SAM that the direction of the part-list cuing effect may reverse if it becomes difficult to retrieve items without any experimenter-provided cues. In Experiment 2, the effect was negative in immediate testing, but positive when the test was given after a delay filled with the study of another, unrelated list.

We have also shown that the SAM model correctly predicts the main results of these experiments. The prediction of the positive effect with randomly chosen cues, in particular, was surprising since we had originally assumed that the model would predict a negative effect. This clearly shows that in the case of a complicated phenomenon such as the part-list cuing effect, one should not rely on intuitive speculation or (as we did) on simplified assumptions. Rather, the lesson that we learned is that one should always run simulations of the actual model to verify one's intuitions. This may sound trivial, but the history of the theoretical analysis of the part-list cuing effect shows that it is often disregarded. Thus, in his review of the literature, Nickerson (1984) incorrectly ascribes a number of assumptions to the SAM model, assumptions that are in fact not made, as would have been clear had the actual model been examined in more detail. For example, Nickerson (1984, p. 549-550) argues that the SAM model makes the assumption that both groups sample the same number of clusters and that the only justification for this assumption is the fact that it is needed to explain the effect. However, the SAM model does not *assume* a priori that both groups sample the same number of clusters. Rather, this may, in practice, often be the result of a much more basic assumption in SAM, namely that there are "costs" involved in retrieving items, and that retrieving items that were already retrieved in prior retrieval cycles increases the likelihood that subjects will stop the retrieval process for these items or those in the same category.

Finally, we have also shown (once again) that, contrary to what is often said, the SAM model does not have so many degrees freedom that it may predict any result. As Raaijmakers and Shiffrin (1981a) already demonstrated, the prediction of a negative part-list cuing effect in regular free recall holds for almost all reasonable values of the parameters and is a consequence of the basic structure of the model. In this study, we also found that the prediction of a positive cuing effect for random cuing of lists of paired-associates is obtained for almost all values of the parameters. Moreover, in those cases, where the effect does depend on the value of a parameter (as was the case for the contextual strength parameter), it is possible to set up experiments to test such a dependency (as we did with the delay manipulation).

All in all, the present results demonstrate that the SAM model is still the only viable explanation for the part-list cuing effect and that results that were thought to be inconsistent with the model, can in fact be shown to follow from its assumptions. It is also clear, however, that, even though the part-list cuing effect itself may not be a puzzle anymore, analyzing why the SAM model predicts this effect remains a puzzling affair due to the fact the phenomenon is dependent on many details of the experimental procedure, making it impossible to use one's intuition to generate predictions. Rather, one should always run the actual simulations. This also shows why quantitative modeling is essential and should not just be considered a personal hobby of a some mathematical enthusiasts.

Summary

The SAM model proposed by Raaijmakers and Shiffrin (1981a) provides an explanation for the part-list cuing effect first observed by Slamecka (1968). In this chapter we present experimental evidence that supports some of the crucial predictions of the SAM model, namely that the part-list cuing effect depends on the relation of the cue items to the stored associative structure and the ability of subjects in the noncued condition to self-generate cues. In Experiment 1 an unexpected positive effect was obtained when the study list consisted of paired-associates rather than single words. This result was replicated in Experiment 3 for a list composed of small-sized categories. This experiment also showed a negative part-list cuing effect when two items from each of five categories were given as cues, whereas a large positive effect was obtained when one cue from each of ten categories was given. In addition, Experiment 2 showed a reversal of the cuing effect depending on whether the recall test was given immediately or after a delay with study of an unrelated list.

Simulation results showed that the SAM model could handle this pattern of results quite well. Other explanations (Roediger & Neely, 1982) that have been given for the positive cuing effects that are sometimes obtained (and were replicated in the present experiments) do not seem to be able to explain the change of the effect from negative to positive, depending on the overall level of recall. Thus, the present results provide strong support for the sampling-bias hypothesis that has been proposed by Raaijmakers and Shiffrin (1981a) as an explanation for the part-list cuing phenomenon.

References

Basden, D.R. (1973). Cued and uncued free recall of unrelated words following interpolated learning. *Journal of Experimental Psychology, 98*, 429-431.

Basden, D.R., Basden, B.H., & Galloway, B.C. (1977). Inhibition with part-list cuing: Some tests of the item strength hypothesis. *Journal of Experimental Psychology: Human Learning and Memory, 3*, 100-108.

Blake, M., & Okada, R. (1973). Intralist cuing following retroactive inhibition of well-learned items. *Journal of Experimental Psychology, 101*, 386-388.

Hudson, P.T.W. (1982). *Preliminary category norms for verbal items in 51 categories in Dutch.* Technical Report 82FU05, Department of Psychology, University of Nijmegen, Nijmegen, the Netherlands.

Mensink, G.J., & Raaijmakers, J.G.W. (1988). A model for interference and forgetting. *Psychological Review, 95*, 434-455.

Nickerson, R.S. (1984). Retrieval inhibition from part-set cuing: A persisting enigma in memory research. *Memory & Cognition,* 1984, *12,* 531-552.

Park, N.W. (1980). *Superadditivity of retrieval cues as a function of encoding operations.* Unpublished doctoral dissertation, University of Toronto.

Raaijmakers, J.G.W. (1979). *Retrieval from long-term store: A general theory and mathematical models.* Unpublished doctoral dissertation, University of Nijmegen, Nijmegen, the Netherlands.

Raaijmakers, J.G.W., & Shiffrin, R.M. (1980). SAM: A theory of probabilistic search of associative memory. In G.H. Bower (Ed.), *The psychology of learning and motivation: Advances in research and theory. (Vol. 14).* (pp. 207-262). New York: Academic Press.

Raaijmakers, J.G.W., & Shiffrin, R.M. (1981a). Search of associative memory. *Psychological Review, 88,* 93-134.

Raaijmakers, J.G.W., & Shiffrin, R.M. (1981b). Order effects in recall. In J.B. Long & A.D. Baddeley (Eds.), *Attention and Performance IX.* (p. 403-415). Hillsdale, NJ: Lawrence Erlbaum Associates.

Roediger, H.L. (1993). Learning and memory: Progress and challenge. In Meyer, D.E. & Kornblum, S. (Eds.), *Attention and Performance XIV: Synergies in experimental psychology, artificial intelligence, and cognitive neuroscience.* (pp. 509-528). Cambridge, MA: The MIT Press.

Roediger, H.L., & Neely, J.H. (1982). Retrieval blocks in episodic and semantic memory. *Canadian Journal of Psychology, 36,* 231-242.

Slamecka, N.J. (1968). An examination of trace storage in free recall. *Journal of Experimental Psychology, 76,* 504-513.

Chapter 6

List-length Effect and Continuous Memory: Confounds and Solutions

Daryl D. Ohrt
Scott D. Gronlund
University of Oklahoma, U. S. A.

"Clearly the information relevant to the current list of items being tested must be kept separate from the great mass of other information *in long term store* ... How this is managed is a real mystery" (Atkinson & Shiffrin, 1968, p. 82, italics added). Although a solution regarding how to manage this mystery has been offered (see Raaijmakers & Shiffrin, 1981—changes in context from one list to the next), most models of memory, including the Atkinson-Shiffrin model, make the same simplifying assumption ("without real justification," p. 82), that each list is isolated from the next in a list-learning experiment. Murdock and Kahana (1993a) recently challenged this assumption and proposed a *continuous memory* in which items from the current list were added to a memory which already included the previous lists (as well as pre-experimental information).

The challenge arose out of attempts by Murdock and Kahana (1993a) to modify the Theory of Distributed Associative Memory or TODAM model (Murdock, 1982) to account for the absence of a list-strength effect (LSE) in recognition (Ratcliff, Clark, & Shiffrin, 1990). A LSE was said to have occurred when after some items on a list were strengthened (either by lengthening study time or through repeated study), retrieval of the nonstrengthened items was harmed. Although Ratcliff et al. (1990) found that a LSE occurred in free and cued recall, standard recognition failed to produce a LSE. In other words, strengthening some items did not adversely affect the probability of recognizing the nonstrengthened items. This was troubling as the global memory models (Search of Associative Memory or SAM—Gillund & Shiffrin, 1984; MINERVA 2—Hintzman, 1984; the Matrix model—Pike, 1984; Humphreys, Bain, & Pike, 1989; and TODAM—Murdock, 1982) predicted that a LSE would occur in both recognition and recall. Of these models, Shiffrin, Ratcliff, and Clark (1990) were able to modify only the SAM model to account for the differing effects of list strength on recognition and recall.

Murdock and Kahana (1993a) showed that through the addition of a continuous memory to the TODAM model, it could predict a null LSE in recognition. However, the large number of competing items from prior lists made the length of the *current* list a nonsalient feature. This resulted in the predicted absence of a list-length effect (LLE) (Shiffrin, Ratcliff, Murnane, & Nobel, 1993). It has been known for many years that the proportion of items recalled or recognized decreases as the number of items to be learned increases.

This finding was first reported by Strong (1912) but has since been demonstrated to be a robust and general finding (for example, Gugerty, 1997; Richard, Richard, & Wells, 1991; Steele & Rawlins, 1989). This led Murdock and Kahana (1993b) to challenge the veracity of the LLE on empirical grounds (see also Anderson, Bjork, & Bjork, 1994). Specifically, they claimed that all previous experiments that had resulted in a LLE had confounded list length with, among other things, the number of test items and the number of items intervening between study and test.

Some support for this challenge comes from the finding of a smaller, although still robust, LLE in recognition when the retention interval and serial study position of test items were controlled (Gronlund & Elam, 1994; see also Murnane & Shiffrin, 1991). It is possible that the removal of all the confounds identified by Murdock and Kahana (1993b) would further reduce or even eliminate the LLE. Experiment 1 tested for this possibility by controlling for the number of items intervening between study and test (Murdock & Kahana, 1993b, called this the study-test lag), equating the retention interval (the time between when an item was studied and when it was tested) and the number of tests scored, and controlling the study position of tested items.

Experiment 1

We presented participants with a short or a long study list, followed by an arithmetic task, and then either 'yes/no' recognition tests or a free-recall test.

Method

Participants, Materials, and Apparatus. Fifteen volunteers paid $5 per hour were recruited from the University of Oklahoma campus community. Target and distractor words were selected from Kucera and Francis (1967). The 1650 words were all one or two syllables, four to eight letters in length, with a frequency greater than six per million. Timing and response collection for all experiments was under microcomputer control using the CogSys software of Ratcliff, Pino, and Burns (1986; see also Greene, Ratcliff, & McKoon, 1988).

Procedure. We tested participants individually for four 50-min sessions, one session per day. A session consisted of 16 blocks with each block consisting of a study phase, an arithmetic phase, and a test phase. The short list contained 12 words and the long list contained 82 words. The presentation rate was 1500-ms per word. The words were randomly selected without replacement from the word pool for each session. Words were repeated across but not within sessions.

Immediately following the study phase, the arithmetic phase consisted of the serial presentation of six digits at a rate of 1500-ms per digit. Participants added these digits cumulatively. The length of this phase was the same for both the long and short lists.

On half of the blocks, participants were given a "yes/no" recognition test and on the other half participants performed a free-recall test. Participants did not know until after study which type of test they would perform. For recall tests, participants had 2.5 minutes to recall as many words as possible from the list they had just studied. Participants were instructed by the computer to begin recall as soon as the arithmetic task was complete and were signaled by the computer to stop recall when time was up.

On recognition tests, only performance on words from the end of a study list were of interest. We selected target words from study positions 73 through 80 for long lists, and from study positions 3 through 10 for short lists (see Fig. 6.1). This equated the retention interval between lists. We controlled the assignment of study positions to recognition test positions in the following way: In the short list, the critical targets studied in positions 3-6 were randomly assigned to test positions 3-11 and the critical targets studied in positions 7-10 were randomly assigned to test positions 12-22. In the long list, the critical targets studied in positions 73-76 were randomly assigned to test positions 3-11 and the critical targets studied in positions 77-80 were randomly assigned to test positions 12-22. Those positions not filled by critical targets were filled with distractors (selected from the same word pool but not previously studied). Two tests preceded (and in the short list, followed) these tests of interest. In the long list, 16 filler tests followed; 8 were targets randomly selected from study positions 3-72 and 8 were distractors (in a random order). The inclusion of words from study positions 3-72 was done to keep participants from unduly focusing on the end of the long list.

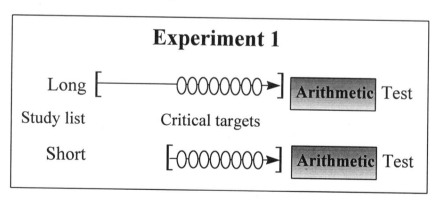

FIG. 6.1. A graphical depiction of the three phases of Experiment 1 (study, arithmetic, test) for long and short lists. The duration of each phase is denoted by its horizontal length. The ellipses embedded in the study list represent the critical targets.

Results and Discussion

In recognition, only those tests that fell between test positions 3-22 were analyzed because they addressed Murdock and Kahana's (1993b) contention and satisfied the constraints of equal retention intervals and controlled study-test lags for long and short lists. The participants' hit and false alarm rates collapsed across days were converted to d'. These individual d's were used to compute an overall mean d'. For the critical items from the long and short lists, d' was 1.88 and 2.83, respectively. A dependent t-test showed a reliable LLE in recognition, $t(14) = 2.59$, $S_e = 0.367$. All p-values are less than .05 unless otherwise indicated. The mean d' for the long list filler items was quite good (1.70), showing that participants did not unduly focus on the end of the long list. The probabilities of recall for all items on the long and short lists were .10 and .34, respectively. A dependent t-test revealed this to be a reliable LLE: $t = 10.87$, $S_e = 0.021$. The results were similar when we looked at the recall of critical targets only (long list—13%, short list—30%). Contrary to Murdock and Kahana's (1993b) prediction, the LLE did not disappear when we controlled the study-test lag, the number of items scored, and the study positions of the tested items, and equated the retention interval.

One potential shortcoming of Experiment 1 was that we used what Murdock and Kahana (1993b) termed a scoring window to control for the number of tested items. A scoring window involves the analyzing of only a subset of the items actually tested (that is, 16 words tested in the long list condition were not scored). Murdock and Kahana contended that if one assumed the continuous accumulation of items in memory, the use of a scoring window confounded the number of items tested with list length. Consequently, when long lists were tested, more items were stored (the additional test items), resulting in poorer performance on subsequent lists. Therefore, we eliminated the use of a scoring window in Experiments 2a and 2b. In addition, we again controlled for serial study position effects, the number of intervening items, and retention interval.

Experiment 2

Experiments 2a and 2b varied list length by manipulating category length (see Shiffrin, Huber, & Marinelli, 1995, for evidence of parallel effects of the number of items on a list and category length). All study lists had a total of 50 words; 10 were members of one semantic category and 40 were members of another. In this case, because all categories had approximately the same number of exemplars, category length referred to the episodically-defined size of the category, not its semantic size.

Method

Participants, Materials, and Apparatus. Experiments 2a and 2b had 30 and 32 participants, respectively.   All participated to fulfill a requirement in an introductory psychology course.   The study words were taken from 18 categories normed by Battig and Montague (1969).   All categories had at least 48 single-word members.   In two cases, this required the addition of a category member or two that had recently come into the language (for example, racquetball).

Procedure. Participants completed one 50-min session consisting of 9 study-test blocks.   At study, 50 words were presented sequentially at a rate of 1500-ms per word.   Ten of these words were members of one semantic category and 40 were members of another.   Only one of these categories was tested, but participants did not know which one until after the study phase was complete. Between the study and test phases, participants performed the same arithmetic task used in Experiment 1.

Pairs of participants were yoked to control for possible semantic category size effects (that is, the decrease in memory performance as the size of the category increases; see Johns, 1985) and possible items effects.   The assignment of a category to the long or short condition and the order in which long or short categories were tested was randomly determined for each yoked pair.   A yoked pair was tested on the same category (for example, trees); for one of these participants, "trees" was the long category, for the other it was the short category.   In Experiment 2a (the recognition experiment), items were randomly selected to be targets or distractors for each yoked pair, but once selected, served as targets and distractors for both yoked participants.   In Experiment 2b (the recall experiment), the same category served as the to-be-recalled category in the long condition for one participant and in the short condition for the yoked participant.

Experiment 2a.   Participants were given "yes/no" recognition tests. Critical targets were always those studied in positions 4, 10, 16, 22, 28, 34, 40, and 46 (see Fig. 6.2).   For one yoked participant, short category items were assigned to these positions, for the other, long category items were assigned Words from study positions 4, 10, 16, and 22 were tested in positions 1 through 8 and words studied in positions 28, 34, 40, and 46 were tested in positions 9 through 16.   Within these constraints, test position was determined randomly. Distractors were nonstudied members from the same category as the targets.

Experiment 2b.   Participants were given free-recall tests in which they were instructed to write down all members from a specified category that they could recall from the list.   Participants were allowed 4 minutes to recall long categories and 2 minutes to recall short categories.   At the end of the recall period, a series of computer-emitted beeps signaled the participants to stop recalling and to prepare for the next list.

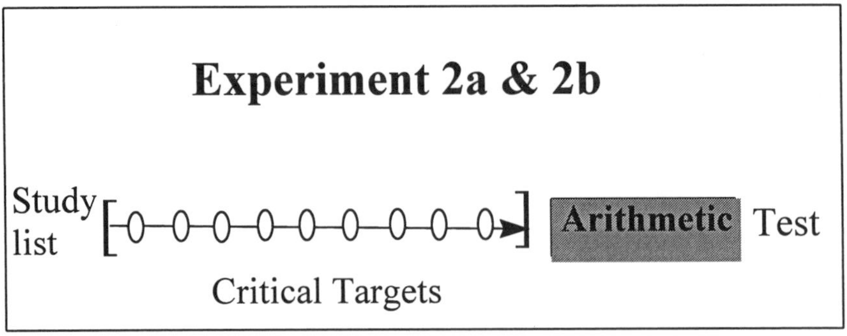

FIG. 6.2. Graphical depiction of the three phases of Experiment 2a (study, arithmetic, test). Ellipses embedded in the study list represent critical targets.

Results and Discussion

In Experiment 2a, the mean d's for the long and short categories were 1.64 and 2.41. A dependent t-test showed that this LLE was reliable: $t(29) = 3.26$, $S_e = 0.243$. In Experiment 2b, the mean probability of recall for the long and short categories were .36 and .60. A dependent t-test showed that this was a reliable LLE: $t(31) = 11.35$, $S_e = 0.021$. The intrusion rates were .07 (short) and .10 (long); both greater than zero; $t(31) = 11.19$, $S_e = 0.006$ and $t(31) = 6.06$, $S_e = 0.015$, but not different from each other: $t(31) =1.68, p > .05, S_e = 0.014$.

We reject Murdock and Kahana's contention that the adoption of a continuous memory can explain the null LSE in recognition; the LLE is not an experimental artifact (see also Shiffrin et al., 1993). Experiments 2a and 2b controlled for all confounds proposed by Murdock and Kahana (1993b) as well as those controlled for by Gronlund and Elam (1994). This was accomplished without the use of a scoring window and without limiting target selection to the primacy or recency portions of the list. Although semantic categories were used, the use of categories of similar length and the yoking of participants controlled for semantic category size and item effects.

How do the global memory models fare when applied to these data? We focused our theoretical exploration on the SAM model, although we believe that the difficulties we encountered and the solution we offer could be extended to any of the global models. Specifically, we will show that the SAM model either over-predicts the size of the LLE or utilizes implausible parameter values to fit the data. Subsequently, we will explore the impact on the size of the LLE of relaxing the continuous memory assumption to determine whether the competition from prior lists could be partial (as opposed to complete in the case of continuous memory, or nonexistent—the simplifying assumption made by Atkinson & Shiffrin, 1968).

In attempting to modify the SAM model to account for these data, we shall also question a second commonly held assumption: Testing has no impact on memory (see also Kim & Glanzer, 1995; Murdock & Kahana, 1993b). We will show that the incorporation of tested items into memory can account for the present data and that it also has other interesting theoretical implications. We begin by reviewing the SAM model as originally formulated. This review is followed by two modified versions of the model that explore the partial memory assumption and the effect of adding test items to memory.

Search of Associative Memory (SAM) Model Overview

Retrieval Matrix. The SAM model stores studied items as distinct episodes called images. An image contains the event itself (that is, the item) and some proportion of the information rehearsed with this event in short-term memory (that is, the overall context and other studied items). Remembering is a function of the strength of connection between retrieval cues and these images.

The strength of connection between retrieval cues and images is a function of four parameters: a, b, c, and d. Context as a cue is connected to an image on the list with strength a. By assuming that items *not* on the list have a negligible context strength and can thus be ignored, this parameter serves to isolate the current study list from other things in memory. An item used as a cue is connected to its own image with strength c (the self strength) and to other items with which it was rehearsed with strength b (the inter-item strength). An item cue is connected to all other items on the list with which it was *not* rehearsed with strength d (the residual strength). A variability function is assumed to operate on these strengths in the following way: A given strength has an equal probability of being strengthened by 50%, weakened by 50%, or retaining its original strength (see Gillund & Shiffrin, 1984, for details). The present experiments do not require Shiffrin et al.'s (1990) differentiation process (as an item is studied longer it will become more connected to context and to items with which it was rehearsed and less connected to items with which it was not rehearsed) because we did not vary study time or number of repetitions.

Fig. 6.3 shows the retrieval matrix resulting from the study of a list of five singly presented words (A, B, C, D, and E). The images A, B, C, D, and E are listed horizontally; the retrieval cues (A, B, C, D, E, X, and Context) are listed vertically (X represents a distractor). It was assumed that an item was rehearsed with the item presented prior to and just following its presentation. The effect of variability is not shown.

Single-Item Recognition. In general, the familiarity of any image i (I_i) given cues Q_1 to Q_N is given by the cues' strength of connection (S) to all of the LL images in memory (see Equation 6.1), weighted by the amount of attention given to each cue (w_j). The attention weights typically sum to 1.0 (see Gronlund & Shiffrin, 1986).

$$F(I_i|Q_1,Q_2...Q_N) = \sum_{i=1}^{LL} \prod_{j=1}^{N} S(Q_j,I_i)^{w_j} \qquad (6.1)$$

An "old/new" decision is based on the familiarity value that results when a test probe is matched against memory. If the familiarity exceeds a response criterion, the test probe is labeled "old", otherwise it is labeled "new."

		Images				
		A	B	C	D	E
	A	c	b	d	d	d
	B	b	c	b	d	d
	C	d	b	c	b	d
Cues	D	d	d	b	c	b
	E	d	d	d	b	c
	X	d	d	d	d	d
	Context	a	a	a	a	a

FIG. 6.3. The retrieval structure of the SAM model following the study of a list of single items.

Forced-Choice-Recognition. In forced-choice recognition, participants are simultaneously presented with a number of items at test. The participants must then select the one target from amongst the many distractors. In the SAM model, "old/new" decisions are made by computing the familiarity for all choices (see Equation 6.1) and selecting the one with the greatest familiarity.

Recall. In the SAM model, recall is a series of search cycles (Raaijmakers & Shiffrin, 1981). On each cycle, cues are assembled, attention weights are selected, and a sample is made of an image in memory. Information is recovered from the image in an attempt to recall the item encoded in the image. If recovery is successful, the item is recalled; if not, the same cues could be used to sample another image, a new cue might be tried, or the search could be terminated.

The probability of sampling any image i (I_i) given cues Q_1 to Q_N is given by the ratio of the cues' strength of connection to I_i divided by the cues' strength of connection to all the images in memory (see Equation 6.2).

$$P_s(I_i|Q_1,Q_2...Q_N) = \frac{\prod_{j=1}^{N} S(Q_j,I_i)^{w_j}}{\sum_{i=1}^{LL} \prod_{j=1}^{N} S(Q_j,I_i)^{w_j}} \qquad (6.2)$$

The probability of recovering sufficient information from the sampled image to recall the encoded item is given by Equation 6.3:

$$P_R(I_i | Q_1, Q_2 \ldots Q_N) = 1 - \exp\{-w_j \sum_{j=1}^{N} S(Q_j, I_i)\} \qquad (6.3)$$

Additional parameters are needed to govern the control processes in recall, L_{MAX} and K_{MAX}. A set of cues is used for L_{MAX} failures before search changes to a new cue set. Search terminates after K_{MAX} search failures (a search failure is a failure to recover an item from a sampled image).

The SAM model produces a LLE in recognition because as list length increases, the variability of the familiarity of targets and distractors increases. However, the distance between the two distributions (the mean familiarities) remains constant (that is, both distributions increase by the same amount). Increasing variability with no change in the relative positions of the means results in greater overlap of the distractor and target distributions, which reduces their discriminability and decreases memory performance.

In recall, a LLE arises due to the increasing likelihood of resampling an already recalled image (a failure) as list length increases. The longer the list, the faster the rate at which failures accumulate. Given that K_{MAX} does not change with list length, this results in a lower proportion of the images being sampled in a long list at the time the search is terminated.

Fits to Empirical Data

Applications of the model to Experiment 2 would require two additional parameters, one to reflect the strength of connection of the category cue to its members, and a second to reflect the category cue's connection to members of other categories. Furthermore, all the parameters could vary with category length. As a result, the model as applied to Experiment 2 was so over-parameterized that it was theoretically uninformative (although it was nonetheless the most informative empirically). As a consequence, we fit only the data from Experiment 1.

Group d's and recall probabilities collapsed across participants for the long and short lists were used for all data fitting. We chose these measures because the SAM model was designed to fit group data (that is, treating the data as one super-participant) rather than the mean of individual participants required for statistical tests. The group d's for the long and short lists for Experiment 1 were 1.56 and 2.17. The recall probabilities were unchanged.

We initially fit the most restricted version of SAM with all parameters held constant with list length (see SAM$_R$ in Table 6.1). The formulas used for the d' predictions are listed in the Appendix. We used the minimization routine from Mathematica© (Wolfram, 1996) to find the best fit to the recognition data. These parameter values (given in Table 6.1) were maintained in the simulations used to produce the recall predictions. SAM_R predicted a LLE over twice the size of the observed LLE in recognition. In recall, the discrepancy is less than in recognition and can be eliminated if L_{MAX} and/or K_{MAX} vary with list length. We focused on the recognition mispredictions.

TABLE 6.1
Model Fits to Experiment 1 Data

	Short List		Long List	
	d'	Pr(Recall)	d'	Pr(Recall)
Observed	2.17	.33	1.56	.10
SAM_R[a]	2.42	.33	.92	.19
SAM_{CM}[b]	2.18	.33	1.56	.21
SAM_T[c]	2.14	.34	1.55	.13

[a] $a = 0.39$ $b = 0.245$, $c = 0.26$, $d = 0.07$.
[b] short $LL = 52$, long $LL = 100$, common: $a = 0.6$, b, $c = 0.5$, $d = 0.073$.
[c] $a = 0.378$, $a_T = 2.27$, b, $c = 1$, $d = 0.121$.
$L_{MAX} = 4$ and $K_{MAX} = 60$ for all simulations reported in the table.

In Gronlund and Elam (1994, Experiment 1), SAM similarly failed to fit the recognition data. However, the design of that experiment was such that the critical targets were among the first 12 items studied in both short and long lists. Consequently, participants would not know what the eventual list length was until after the critical targets were presented, which meant that it was not reasonable for parameter values to change with list length. However, in the current Experiment 1, critical targets were presented for study at the end of the long list, by which time participants knew that the list was long. Consequently, we next fit the SAM model allowing the a, b, c, and d parameters to vary with list length. Not surprisingly, this produced a better fit to the data. However, the parameter values were not plausible. For instance, the b and c parameters were greater for the long list than the short list (short list b, $c = 0.316$, long list b, $c = 0.6$). This indicated that the items in the long list were encoded better than items in the short list; a difficult proposition to justify given that there was no evidence that participants focused solely on the end of the long list. The original version of the SAM model seemed unable to account for these data.

Modifications to SAM

The model fits just described assumed that each list was completely isolated from every other list ($LL = 12$ or 82). If we completely eliminate this assumption, all lists would be the same regardless of length and we would see no LLE in recognition or recall. This is essentially the continuous memory assumption that Murdock and Kahana (1993a) added to the TODAM model. Another option is to relax this assumption such that there is some, but not complete, blending of successive lists. This would result in two types of list length. The objective list length (that is, the experimenter-controlled number of items in the list) is what SAM and other global memory models use; the subjective list length (the number of items in memory that are more than negligibly connected to the study context) would be the length of the current list plus the additional items already in episodic memory.

To explore the possibility that use of subjective list lengths would improve the ability of the model to fit the data, we treated LL as a free parameter. We found that any pair of list lengths that produced a short list length to long list length ratio of .52 would fit the recognition data (for example, $LL_{short} = 52$, $LL_{long} = 100$, the objective ratio was 12/82 or .15). The fit is listed in Table 6.1 (see SAM_{CM}). However, when these same parameter values were used to fit the recall data, the model predicted recall probability in the short list twice as great as what was observed. Relaxing the continuous memory assumption does not appear to be a fruitful direction to pursue. Choosing LL's that fit the recognition data will not fit the recall data, and vice versa.

We next tried relaxing the null impact of test items on memory, much as Raaijmakers and Shiffrin (1981) did for recall (they referred to this as incrementing). We assumed that tested items are added to memory in much the same way that studied items are added to memory. A decline in memory performance with test position would be a consequence of this modification, a finding that is often observed (for example, Atkinson & Shiffrin, 1968; Kim & Glanzer, 1995; Ratcliff & Murdock, 1976; Shulman, 1974).

Adding test items to memory should decrease the size of the LLE produced by the model because of the proportionally greater effect additional test items have on a short list compared to a long list. For example, if an 12- and an 82-item list were studied and followed by 16 test words, it would result in only a 20% increase in length for the long list, but a 160% increase for the short list. Thus, adding test items to memory will have a larger impact on performance in the short list than the long list.

The details of this modified model (SAM_T) are as follows. Items are added to memory as an image after the item is used as a memory probe (in recognition) or after it is produced as a response (in recall). In recognition, the new image is connected by strength c to the matching cue and is connected residually (d) to other cues. In recall, the new image is connected by strength c to the matching cue, strength b to the retrieval cue, and residually (d) to other cues. The strength of connection between a test image and context at the time of test is a_T (true for both recognition and recall). This was the only new parameter introduced (although it is plausible that interitem strengths at retrieval should be distinguished from interitem strengths at study). Fig. 6.4 illustrates the changes to the retrieval matrix after recognition of a distractor (Y) and a target (C).

		Images						
		A	B	C	D	E	T_{1Y}	T_{2C}
	A	c	b	d	d	d	d	d
	B	b	c	b	d	d	d	d
	C	d	b	c	b	d	d	c
Cues	D	d	d	b	c	b	d	d
	E	d	d	d	b	c	d	d
	X	d	d	d	d	d	d	d
	Context	a	a	a	a	a	a_T	a_T

FIG. 6.4. **The retrieval structure of the SAM$_T$ model following the study of a list of single items and recognition of two test words (T_{1Y} denotes that the first test was a distractor item (Y) and T_{2C} denotes that the second test was the test of a target, C).**

We now have a model of recognition with parameters: a, b, c, d, and a_T, plus L_{MAX} and K_{MAX} for recall. To reduce the degrees of freedom of the model, we set $b = c$ and held parameter values constant between list lengths (set to 12 and 82). The fits to Experiment 1 are shown in Table 6.1 (denoted as SAM$_T$). Clearly, this modification brings the model in line with the data. As with the unmodified SAM model, a reduction in the K_{MAX} parameter for the short list (simulating the earlier cutoff of recall) produced an even better fit to the recall data. The Appendix lists the equations for mean familiarity and variance of targets and distractors for SAM$_T$ for three different methods of combining a and a_T.

While we view SAM$_T$ as step forward, the need for seven parameters to fit four data points is not a strong statement for the global memory models as a whole or the SAM$_T$ model in particular (although there were only two degrees of freedom to fit the recognition data: the ratio of b/d and a_T). However, in the following sections, we identify and discuss the additional capabilities of SAM$_T$. Specifically, SAM$_T$ predicts equal ROC function slopes for lists of different lengths (Gronlund & Elam, 1994). It also offers an alternative explanation of the performance advantage for a target amongst nonoverlapping distractors compared to a target amongst overlapping distractors in forced-choice recognition (Clark, Hori, & Callan, 1993). Both have previously been cited as problems for the global memory models (Clark & Gronlund, 1996).

Additional Benefits of SAM$_T$

Variance Ratios. According to the SAM and MINERVA 2 models, increasing list length increases the variance of both distractor and target familiarity distributions. In effect, each additional item adds a constant to the variance of both distractors and targets (see Gronlund & Elam, 1994, for a computational demonstration). As a consequence, the longer the list length, the closer the distractor and target variances will be to equal (their ratio will approach 1.0). For example, assume that the variance contributed by a target is 6 and the variance contributed by each distractor is 1. For a five-item list, the ratio (variance of five distractors /[variance of four distractors + one target]) is 5/10 or 0.5. If the *LL* increases to 50, the ratio becomes 50/55 or 0.91. This prediction was tested by Gronlund and Elam (1994) using receiver operating characteristic (ROC) analyses (Egan, 1958; Ratcliff, Sheu, & Gronlund, 1992).

Participants made recognition decisions based on a six-point confidence scale ranging from "sure yes" to "sure no." Plotting the cumulative proportion of hits versus the cumulative proportion of false alarms at each confidence level produced an ROC function. When this function was subjected to a *z*-transform, the slope of the function provided an estimate of the ratio of the standard deviation of distractors to targets (assuming that the underlying distributions are normal). Gronlund and Elam (1994, Experiment 1) found that the standard deviation ratio was unaffected by list length and was close to 1.0 (ratios of 1.04 and 1.05 for the long and short lists, respectively). The original SAM model predicted ratios of 0.93 and 0.63 for the long and short lists, respectively.

We fit the *d'* data from Gronlund and Elam's (1994) Experiment 1 using the SAM$_T$ model, keeping all parameters constant across list lengths (as required by their experimental design). SAM$_T$ was able to fit the *d'* data exactly (in contrast to the original SAM model). Furthermore, SAM$_T$'s predicted standard deviation ratios were 0.94 for the short list and 0.96 for the long list, statistically undifferentiable from the Gronlund and Elam findings. The addition of test items in SAM$_T$ increased the standard deviation for the short list much more than for the long list and thereby equated the standard deviation ratio.

Forced-Choice Recognition. In the global memory models, discrimination of targets from distractors in forced-choice recognition is a function of the mean familiarity advantage of targets over distractors as well as the variability amongst the target and distractors. If the mean differences are equivalent in two conditions, better recognition performance will be observed in the condition where the variability amongst the targets and distractors is lowest.

Clark et al. (1993) examined this prediction. Participants studied word pairs denoted AB, CD, EF, GH, IJ, etc. They were then given two types of forced-choice recognition tests. In one type, participants had to choose among choices that shared a word (for example, participants simultaneously viewed

AB, AD, or AF). Clark et al. called these overlapping tests. In the other type of test, participants had to choose among choices that shared no words (for example, AB, CF, or GJ). These were called nonoverlapping tests. For both types of tests, the mean difference amongst the targets and distractors was equivalent; however, because overlapping tests resulted in less variability amongst target and distractors than did the nonoverlapping tests, the global models predicted better performance for the overlapping tests (see Clark et al. for the derivations).

Clark et al. (1993) found that performance was better for the nonoverlapping tests. They hypothesized that the nonoverlapping performance advantage was due to the greater number of cues from the nonoverlapping tests (6 versus 4) that could be utilized by a recall process (see also Nobel & Huber, 1993). However, the SAM_T model offers a different explanation for the nonoverlapping test advantage.

In the SAM_T model, familiarity, not variance, is the important factor. As each test pair in the trio is evaluated, we assume that the constituent items are added as images to memory before the next pair is evaluated. Items added to memory at test are connected with strength c to themselves, b to their test partner, d to other items, and a_T to the test context. In the overlap condition, as the familiarity of each pair is evaluated, the shared member of the pairs (A) is associated not only with its study partner (B) but also with the other test partners (D and F). The result is that the familiarity of the distractor pairs increase, and because there are two distractor pairs to one target pair, the former increases more than the latter, making discrimination among them more difficult. The same thing happens in the nonoverlapping case, but because no items are shared, the increase in distractor strength is less than in the overlapping case. The net result is that the difference in familiarity between target and distractors in the nonoverlapping condition is greater than in the overlapping condition, producing better performance in the nonoverlapping condition (see Fig. 6.5).

General Discussion

We found no support for Murdock and Kahana's (1993b) contention that the LLE is largely the result of experimental confounds. Experiment 1 equated the retention interval and the number of items scored, and controlled the number of intervening study items. Experiment 2a eliminated the use of a scoring window. A significant LLE remained in both recognition and recall. Memory models must simultaneously account for the effect of list length on performance in both recognition and recall, as well as the lack of an effect of list strength on recognition performance (Shiffrin et al., 1993). This pattern of results is very problematic for the continuous memory assumption.

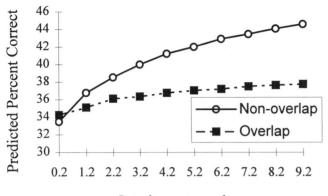

Interitem strength

FIG. 6.5. **Predictions of the SAM$_T$ model for overlapping and nonoverlapping tests as $b = c$ increases from 0.2 to 9.2 ($a = 0.5$, $d = 0.1$, $a_T = 0.5$).**

At this time, only the SAM model can predict a LLE (in recall and recognition) and a null LSE in recognition with a positive LSE in recall. However, when we fit the original SAM model to the data from Experiment 1 and fixed the parameter values across list lengths, the model produced a LLE twice the observed size. If the parameter values were allowed to vary with list length, the model could fit the data, but only with untenable parameter values.

Our first attempt to improve the ability of the SAM model to fit the data was to relax the assumption that current lists are completely isolated from prior lists. We did this by estimating *LL* as a parameter. The result was that a short-to-long list length ratio of .52 fit the recognition data, however, the model mispredicted recall. Relaxing the list-isolation assumption did not improve the fit of the model to the data.

We next revised the SAM model to allow items to be added to memory during testing (retaining the list-isolation assumption). This revised model (SAM$_T$) predicted the correct magnitude of the LLE for recognition and recall, declining performance with test position (Atkinson & Shiffrin, 1968; Kim & Glanzer, 1995; Ratcliff & Murdock, 1976; Shulman, 1974), equivalent distractor to target standard deviation ratios as a function of list length (Gronlund & Elam, 1994), and produced a nonoverlapping distractor advantage in forced-choice recognition (Clark et al., 1993). These phenomena were all previously unexplained by the global memory models.

Prior to this research, we viewed these and other challenges to the global models (see review by Clark & Gronlund, 1996) as sufficient to warrant modifications to the existing models (for example, the addition of a search process to recognition, Clark, 1992; Gronlund, & Ratcliff, 1989; Hintzman,

Curran, & Oppy, 1992; Jacoby, 1991; Yonelinas, 1994) or the development of new theoretical approaches (McClelland & Chappell, 1995; Murdock, 1993; Shiffrin & Steyvers, 1997). However, our work suggests that much can still be learned about how memory works by revisiting prior theoretical efforts and their assumptions, including the list-isolation assumption of the modal model of Atkinson and Shiffrin (1968).

Summary

Atkinson and Shiffrin (1968) made the simplifying assumption that each list of studied items was isolated from prior lists. This assumption was recently challenged by Murdock and Kahana (1993a). Removing this assumption allowed the TODAM model to predict null list-strength effects in recognition (see Ratcliff, Clark & Shiffrin, 1990). However, it eliminated the prediction that memory performance decreased as the number of studied items in a list increased (the list-length effect—LLE). Murdock and Kahana (1993b) argued that a null LLE prediction was plausible because previous experiments confounded list length with other factors making it unclear whether the LLE was a "real" effect or an artifact. We conducted two experiments that demonstrated robust LLE's despite the elimination of confounding factors. The original SAM memory model was unable to fit these data; however, a modified version, in which test items were added to memory and the list-isolation assumption was retained, was successful. This modification also offered possible solutions to two other empirical challenges facing the global memory models.

Acknowledgments

This work was conducted in partial fulfillment of the Master's degree requirements of the University of Oklahoma by the first author under the supervision of the second author. We thank Shelia Kennison for her helpful comments on this chapter. Correspondence concerning this chapter should be addressed to Scott D. Gronlund, Department of Psychology, University of Oklahoma, Norman, OK 73019. E-mail: sgronlund@ou.edu.

Appendix

Equations 6.A1 through 6.A5 were used to derive d' predictions for the original SAM model. The parameters a, b, c, and d reflect the context, inter-item, self, and residual strengths. We assumed that context and item cues share attention equally, therefore each had an attention weight of 0.5. The constant LL was set equal to the list length. The constant k was used in the variability function (see Gillund & Shiffrin, 1984); its value was equal to 0.9772. We give the expressions for the familiarity of a target—F(T), and a distractor—F(D), and the variance (Var) for each.

$$F(T) = k^2(2a^{.5}b^{.5} + a^{.5}c^{.5} + (LL - 3)a^{.5}d^{.5}) \tag{6.A1}$$

$$F(D) = k^2(LL \cdot a^{.5}d^{.5}) \tag{6.A2}$$

$$Var(T) = (1 - k^4)(2ab + ac + (LL - 3)ad) \tag{6.A3}$$

$$Var(D) = (1 - k^4)(LL \cdot ad) \tag{6.A4}$$

$$d' = \frac{(F(T) - F(D))}{\sqrt{Var(D)}} \tag{6.A5}$$

There are three versions of the SAM_T model that differ as a function of the relationship of a to a_T (the context strength at test). The model given in equations 6.A6 through 6.A9 assumed no relationship between these two parameters. The $\bar{T}$ constant is the mean number of test words presented prior to a given test item. Equations 6.A10 through 6.A13 assumed that a_T was a multiplicative combination of study context (a) and test context (a_T). This resulted in the study context parameter dropping out of the d' calculations, as it does in the original SAM model, resulting in context-independent recognition (for example, Godden & Baddeley, 1980). Equations 6.A14 through 6.A17 assume that a_T is an additive combination of a and a_T. All three variations were equally capable of fitting the data from Experiment 1, as well as producing a nonoverlap advantage and equal ROC ratios.

$$F(T) = k^2(2a^{.5}b^{.5} + a^{.5}c^{.5} + (LL - 3)a^{.5}d^{.5} + \bar{T} \cdot a_T^{.5}d^{.5}) \tag{6.A6}$$

$$F(D) = k^2(LL \cdot a^{.5}d^{.5} + \bar{T} \cdot a_T^{.5}d^{.5}) \tag{6.A7}$$

$$Var(T) = (1 - k^4)(2 \cdot ab + ac + (LL - 3)ad + \bar{T} \cdot a_Td) \tag{6.A8}$$

$$Var(D) = (1 - k^4)(LL \cdot ad + \bar{T} \cdot a_Td) \tag{6.A9}$$

$$F(T) = k^2(2 \cdot a^{.5}b^{.5} + a^{.5}c^{.5} + (LL - 3)a^{.5}d^{.5} + \bar{T}(a \cdot a_T)^{.5}d^{.5}) \tag{6.A10}$$

$$F(D) = k^2(LL \cdot a^{.5}d^{.5} + \bar{T}(a \cdot a_T)^{.5}d^{.5}) \tag{6.A11}$$

$$Var(T) = (1 - k^4)(2 \cdot ab + ac + (LL - 3)ad + \bar{T}(a \cdot a_T)d) \tag{6.A12}$$

$$Var(D) = (1 - k^4)(LL \cdot ad + \bar{T} \cdot (a \cdot a_T)d) \tag{6.A13}$$

$$F(T) = k^2(2 \cdot a^{.5}b^{.5} + a^{.5}c^{.5} + (LL - 3)a^{.5}d^{.5} + \bar{T}(a + a_T)^{.5}d^{.5}) \tag{6.A14}$$

$$F(D) = k^2 (LL \cdot a^{-5} d^{.5} + \bar{T}(a + a_T)^{.5} d^{.5})$$ (6.A15)

$$\text{Var(T)} = (1 - k^4)(2 \cdot ab + ac + (LL - 3)ad + \bar{T}(a + a_T)d)$$ (6.A16)

$$\text{Var(D)} = (1 - k^4)(LL \cdot ad + \bar{T}(a + a_T)d)$$ (6.A17)

References

Anderson, M. C., Bjork, R. A., & Bjork, E. L. (1994). Remembering can cause forgetting: Retrieval dynamics in long-term memory. *Journal of Experimental Psychology: Learning, Memory, and Cognition, 20,* 1063-1087.

Atkinson, R. C., & Shiffrin, R. M. (1968). Human memory: A proposed system and its control processes. In K. W. Spence & J. T. Spence (Eds.), *The Psychology of Learning and Motivation: Advances in Research and Theory: Vol. 2* (pp. 89-195). New York: Academic Press.

Battig, W. F., & Montague, W. E. (1969). Category norms for verbal items in 56 categories: A replication and extension of the Connecticut category norms. *Journal of Experimental Monographs, 80 (3).*

Clark, S. E. (1992). Word frequency effects in associative and item recognition, *Memory & Cognition, 20,* 231-243.

Clark, S. E., & Gronlund, S. D. (1996). Global matching models of recognition memory: How the models match the data. *Psychonomic Bulletin & Review, 3,* 37-60.

Clark, S. E., Hori, A., & Callan, D. E. (1993). Forced-choice associative recognition: Implications for global-memory models. *Journal of Experimental Psychology: Learning, Memory, and Cognition, 19,* 871-881.

Egan, J. P. (1958). *Recognition memory and the operating characteristic* (Tech. Note. # AD-152650). Bloomington: Indiana University Hearing and Communication Laboratory.

Gillund, G., & Shiffrin, R. M. (1984). A retrieval model for both recognition and recall. *Psychological Review, 91,* 1-65.

Godden, D. R., & Baddeley, A. D. (1980). When does context influence recognition memory? *British Journal of Psychology, 71,* 99-104.

Greene, S., Ratcliff, R., & McKoon, G. (1988). A flexible programming language for generating stimulus lists for cognitive psychology experiments. *Behavior Research Methods, Instruments, & Computers, 20,* 119-128.

Gronlund, S. D., & Elam, L. E. (1994). List-length effect: Recognition accuracy and the variance of underlying distributions. *Journal of Experimental Psychology: Learning, Memory, and Cognition, 20,* 1355-1369.

Gronlund, S. D., & Ratcliff, R. (1989). Time course of item and associative information: Implications for global memory models. *Journal of Experimental Psychology: Learning, Memory, and Cognition, 15*, 846-858.

Gronlund, S. D., & Shiffrin, R. M. (1986). Retrieval strategies in recall of natural categories and categorized lists. *Journal of Experimental Psychology: Learning, Memory, and Cognition, 12*, 550-561.

Gugerty, L. J. (1997). Situation awareness during driving: Explicit and implicit knowledge in dynamic spatial memory. *Journal of Experimental Psychology: Applied, 3*, 42-66.

Hintzman, D. L. (1984). MINERVA 2: A simulation model of human memory. *Behavior Research Methods, Instruments, & Computers, 16*, 96-101.

Hintzman, D. L., Curran, T., & Oppy, B. (1992). Effects of similarity and repetition on memory: Registration without learning? *Journal of Experimental Psychology: Learning, Memory, and Cognition, 18*, 667-680.

Humphreys, M. S., & Bain, J. D., & Pike, R. (1989). Different ways to cue a coherent memory system: A theory for episodic, semantic, and procedural tasks. *Psychological Review, 96*, 208-233.

Jacoby, L. L. (1991). A process dissociation framework: Separating automatic and intentional uses of memory. *Journal of Memory and Language, 30*, 513-541.

Johns, E. E. (1985). Effects of list organization on item recognition. *Journal of Experimental Psychology: Learning, Memory, and Cognition, 11*, 605-620.

Kim, K., & Glanzer, M. (1995). Intralist interference in recognition memory. *Journal of Experimental Psychology: Learning, Memory, and Cognition, 21*, 1096-1107.

Kucera, H., & Francis, W. N. (1967). *Computational analysis of present-day American English*, Providence, RI: Brown University.

McClelland, J. L., & Chappell, M. (1995). *Familiarity breeds differentiation: A Bayesian approach to the effects of experience in recognition memory* (Technical Report PDP.CNS.95.2). Pittsburgh: Carnegie Mellon University Center for the Neural Basis of Cognition.

Murdock, B. B. (1982). A theory for the storage and retrieval of item and associative information. *Psychological Review, 89*, 609-626.

Murdock, B. B. (1993). TODAM2: A model for the storage and retrieval of item, associative, and serial-order information. *Psychological Review, 100*, 183-203.

Murdock, B. B., & Kahana, M. J. (1993a). Analysis of the list-strength effect. *Journal of Experimental Psychology: Learning, Memory, and Cognition, 19*, 689-697.

Murdock, B., B., & Kahana, M. J. (1993b). List-strength and list-length effects: Reply to Shiffrin, Ratcliff, Murnane, and Nobel (1993).

Journal of Experimental Psychology: Learning, Memory, and Cognition, 19, 1450-1453.

Murnane, K., & Shiffrin, R. M. (1991). Interference and the representation of events in memory. *Journal of Experimental Psychology: Learning, Memory, and Cognition, 17*, 855-874.

Nobel, P. A., & Huber, D. E. (1993). Modeling forced-choice associative recognition through a hybrid of global recognition and cued recall. *Proceedings of the 15th Annual Conference of the Cognitive Science Society*, Boulder, CO, 783-788.

Pike, R. (1984). A comparison of convolution and matrix distributed memory systems. *Psychological Review, 91*, 281-294.

Raaijmakers, J. G. W., & Shiffrin, R. M. (1981). Search of associative memory. *Psychological Review, 88*, 93-134.

Ratcliff, R., Clark, S. E., & Shiffrin, R. M. (1990). List- strength effect: I Data and discussion. *Journal of Experimental Psychology: Learning, Memory, and Cognition, 16*, 163-178.

Ratcliff, R., & Murdock, B. B. (1976). Retrieval processes in recognition memory. *Psychological Review, 83*, 190-214.

Ratcliff, R., Pino, C., & Burns, W. T. (1986). An inexpensive real-time microcomputer-based cognitive laboratory system. *Behavior Research Methods, Instruments, & Computers, 18*, 214-221.

Ratcliff, R., Sheu, C.-F., & Gronlund, S. D. (1992). Testing global memory models using ROC curves. *Psychological Review, 99*, 518-535.

Richard, J. D., Richard, R. D., & Wells, G. L. (1991). Outcome trees and baseball: A study of expertise and list length effects. *Organizational Behavior and Human Decision Processes, 50*, 324-340.

Shiffrin, R. M., Huber, D. E., & Marinelli, K. (1995). Effect of category length and strength on familiarity in recognition. *Journal of Experimental Psychology: Learning, Memory, and Cognition, 21*, 267-287.

Shiffrin, R. M., Ratcliff, R., & Clark, S. E. (1990). List-strength effect: II Theoretical mechanisms. *Journal of Experimental Psychology: Learning, Memory, and Cognition, 16*, 179-185.

Shiffrin, R. M., Ratcliff, R., Murnane, K., & Nobel, P. A. (1993). TODAM and the list-strength and list-length effects: Comment on Murdock and Kahana (1993). *Journal of Experimental Psychology: Learning, Memory and Cognition, 19*, 1445-1449.

Shiffrin, R. M., & Steyvers, M. (1997). A model for recognition memory: REM—Retrieving effectively from memory. *Psychonomic Bulletin & Review, 4*, 145-166.

Shulman, A. I. (1974). The declining course of recognition memory. *Memory & Cognition, 2*, 14-18.

Steele, K., & Rawlins, J. N. (1989). Rats remember long lists of non-spatial items. *Psychobiology, 17*, 438-452.

Strong, E. K., Jr. (1912). The effect of length of series upon recognition memory. *Psychological Review, 19*, 447-462.

Yonelinas, A. P. (1994). Receiver-operating characteristics in recognition memory: Evidence for a dual-process model. *Journal of Experimental Psychology: Learning, Memory, and Cognition, 20,* 1341-1354.

Wolfram, S. (1996). *The Mathematica Book.* (3rd ed., p. 120). New York: Cambridge University Press.

Chapter 7

Cues and Codes in Working Memory Tasks

Michael S. Humphreys
University of Queensland, Australia

Gerald Tehan
University of Southern Queensland, Australia

In a recent symposium on short-term memory Richard Shiffrin had the task of providing a commentary upon the papers in the symposium. He made two comments in that summary that set the scene for the research that we describe in the following chapter.

"There is presently a rather nonspecific *modal* view of short-term memory. This view contains three components: *temporary activation, control processes* and *capacity limitations.*" (Shiffrin, 1993, p. 195).

"In comparison with models of long-term retrieval, however, . . . models for short-term memory are still at an early stage of development" (Shiffrin, 1993, p. 196).

The first comment would suggest to us that there has been no radical change in focus in the study of short-term memory over the 30 years since the seminal paper of Atkinson and Shiffrin (1968), that centered around these three attributes. Probably the most influential development in that period has been the fractionation of Atkinson and Shiffrin's short-term store into a multicomponent working memory system (Baddeley, 1986; Baddeley & Hitch, 1974). However, for all components of Baddeley's working memory system, temporary activation of particular types of representations, control processes, and capacity limitations remain central issues.

The second comment suggests to us that while there has been substantial progress in understanding some features of some short-term memory tasks, there are other aspects that have received very little attention. For example, we know a considerable amount about the serial recall of span length lists. Speech based variables such as modality of presentation, phonemic similarity, articulatory suppression, irrelevant speech and word length all affect span performance (see Baddeley, 1986 for a review). We know that lexical access is an important determinant of span (Hulme, Maughan & Brown, 1991;

Schweickert, 1993) and we know that order errors are both lawful and complex (Estes, 1972; Henson et al., 1996). However, as Shiffrin points out, we know very little about what cues are used in immediate serial recall or how they function. In fact, there is very little current discussion of what cues are used to access item information; how cues elicit phonemic, semantic or lexical representation of list items; or how cues differentiate the most recent list (set of items) from earlier lists. In order to examine these cuing issues we developed a short-term cued recall paradigm.

Short-Term Cued Recall

In our task, subjects receive a series of trails consisting of one or two four-word blocks. In advance of a trial, subjects never know whether that trial will be a one- or a two-block trial. Each word in a block is presented in lower case at a one-second rate. For one-block trials, subjects are tested immediately after the fourth word, usually with serial recall but in some experiments with cued recall. On two-block trials the two blocks are separated by the presentation of a place-holding symbol (!). Subjects are instructed that if the second block is presented they are to concentrate on learning the second block because they will never be tested on the first block. In many of the experiments we sometimes tested the second block for serial recall. This was done because we wanted our subjects to study the lists as they would for a standard span test. On most occasions, however, the second block was tested by presenting a cue for one of the words in the second block. The single cue was presented in upper case either immediately after the last word in Block 2 or after a two second delay filled with the articulation of two four-digit numbers. In various experiments both category labels, pre-existing associates, and part words (stems and endings) have been used as cues. With a category label subjects are instructed that an instance of that category was presented in Block 2 and they are asked to use the cue to help them recall that instance. In this paradigm proactive interference (PI) is manipulated by including a foil in Block 1 that is also subsumed under the cue. For example, if the cue is *ANIMAL* the Block-1 foil might be *dog* and the Block-2 target *cat*. Because subjects are never tested on Block 1, they have every reason to forget or stop rehearsing the words in Block 1 as soon as they see the place-holding symbol. The sequence of events in a typical two-block trial is depicted in Fig. 7.1.

We used the short-term cued recall paradigm in order to establish that:

1) PI occurred at sufficiently short retention intervals to be a potential factor in working memory paradigms.
2) Phonological memory codes are involved in short-term cued recall just as they are in short-term serial recall.

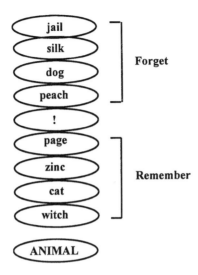

FIG. 7.1. Sequence of events in a typical two-block trial with an immediate test. The foil in Block 1 is *dog*, the target in Block 2 is *cat* and the cue is ANIMAL. The remaining words are fillers and ! is the signal to the subject that Block 2 will be presented.

3) The cue is involved in the retrieval process and is critical to PI. Subjects are not searching the list to find an item that is related to the cue.

PI at Short Intervals

In two of our earliest experiments (published as Experiments 3 and 4 in Tehan and Humphreys, 1995) we used the short-term cued recall paradigm to look at PI with category and ending cues. With a category cue there was almost no sign of PI on an immediate test (probability correct with and without interference equals .85 and .87, respectively). In contrast, there was a substantial amount of interference on a test that was delayed by two seconds of shadowing (probability correct with and without interference equals .58 and .79, respectively). With ending cues interference was again found on a delayed test (probability correct with and without interference equals .62 and .79, respectively). However, with ending cues there was also interference on an immediate test (probability correct with and without interference equals .85 and .92, respectively). We have replicated these findings several times. On an immediate test with category cues evidence for a small amount of PI can be found if one examines the intrusions of the Block-1 foil. In addition, recall in the Interference condition is almost always slightly less than is recall in the No-Interference condition. In contrast to the weak evidence for interference on an immediate test with category cues, we almost always find a significant interference effect on an immediate test with ending cues.   With both types of cues we almost always find a significant interference effect on a delayed test. In this chapter all references to significant effects refer to $p < .05$.

In these experiments the retention interval is 1-2 seconds on an immediate test (measured from the end of the presentation of the target to the start of the presentation of the cue) and the interval between the foil and the target is 4 seconds.   On a delayed test where PI is a large factor for both category and ending cues, the retention interval is 3-4 seconds.   These retention intervals are comparable to the retention intervals found in many working memory paradigms.

Phonological Memory Codes

We also felt that we could explain the observed PI effects by assuming that phonological memory codes were involved in short-term cued recall just as they are in short-term serial recall.   This explanation required us to make a few assumptions about the duration of these codes.   Very briefly we assumed that on an immediate test there would be a phonological code for the Block-2 target but not for the Block-1 foil.   We also assumed that two seconds of shadowing activity would be sufficient to largely eliminate the phonological code for the Block-2 target and that semantic codes would be present for the Block-1 foil and the Block-2 target for both the immediate and delayed test.   With these assumptions we explain the relative immunity to PI on an immediate test with category cues, to the discriminability produced by the phonological code.   That is, there is a phonological code for the target but not the foil and this code provides a basis for discriminating between them.   The relative lack of immunity with ending cues is explained by assuming that there is still a phonological code for the target but this code doesn't provide a good means for discriminating between the target and the phonologically similar foil.   The assumption that semantic codes are relatively long lasting and are thus still present for the foil as well as the target on the delayed test explains why PI is found with both kinds of cues on the delayed test.

An obvious way to test the phonological code hypothesis was to select category instances that rhyme.   Unfortunately, with the exception of *cat* and *rat* from the animal category there are not very many good examples of rhyming category instances.   Nevertheless, enough examples were found to conduct the experiment (Experiment 5 of Tehan & Humphreys, 1995).   There were three conditions.   In the No-Interference condition there was a target in Block 2 and no foil in Block 1.   In the Interference-Nonrhyme condition there was a target in Block 2 and a nonrhyming foil (a member of the same taxonomic category as the target) in Block 1. In the Interference-Rhyme condition there was a target in Block 2 and a rhyming foil (the foil rhymed with the target and was a member of the same taxonomic category) in Block 1. On an immediate test the probability of recall was .87, .82, and .74 for the No-Interference, Interference-Nonrhyme, and Interference-Rhyme conditions, respectively. The results were as expected with more interference produced by rhyming members of the category than by nonrhyming members.

We have provided converging evidence for the role of transient phonemic codes in producing immunity to PI by showing that with spoken presentation of the first block and visual presentation of the second block, the phonemic code of a nonrhyming Block-1 foil can be strengthened to the extent that PI will be observed on an immediate test (Experiment 6 of Tehan & Humphreys, 1995). Furthermore, using serial recall, we have demonstrated (Experiments 1 & 2 of Tehan & Humphreys, 1995) that the time frame that sees the emergence of PI also sees the disappearance of phonemic similarity effects (Baddeley, 1966; Conrad, 1965).

Up until now our explanation of the early emergence of PI with rhyming targets has been based on a very general metaphor of discrimination. That is we have assumed that phonological codes will not serve to discriminate the target from a phonologically similar foil. In advancing this explanation we were not thinking of a discrimination process that followed on from the memory retrieval process. Instead our conception of the discrimination process was based on the connectionist model proposed by Chappell and Humphreys (1994). We will briefly describe how this model can be applied to short-term cued recall and then describe how we tested the model and provided additional evidence for the involvement of phonological memory codes in short-term cued recall.

In order to apply the Chappell and Humphreys model to short-term cued recall we assume that there are pre-existing associations between the cue and the cue's associates. We also assume that at the time of study an association is learned between a rapidly changing contextual cue and the items in a block. Items are represented as distributed patterns and we assume that some of the elements in these distributed patterns represent semantic information and some represent phonological information. We also assume that the phonological information lasts for a shorter time (it may be learned rapidly and unlearned or interfered with rapidly) than does the semantic information. When a subject is asked to use an extralist cue to recall an item from Block 2, we assume that the contextual cue to activates the semantic and phonological elements of the items studied in Block 2 but only the semantic elements of those items studied in Block 1. The contextual cue is also assumed to suppress all other elements. Likewise, the extralist cue is assumed to activate all of the semantic and phonological elements in each of its associates and suppress all other elements. The result of this pattern of activation and suppression is to leave active the semantic elements of those items that are associated with the cue and which occurred in either Block 1 or 2. The phonological elements of those items associated with the cue and which occurred in Block 2 are also left active.   The effect is to approximate the intersection between the items in the blocks and the associates of the cue (Humphreys, Wiles, & Bain, 1993; Humphreys, Wiles, & Dennis, 1994).   The final step in the memory recovery process is to use the intraitem information stored in the Chappell and Humphreys autoassociator to converge to a particular output.   That is, the patterns representing particular words are stored in the autoassociator prior to learning the contextual associations.   The autoassociator uses this preexisting information to clean up the information that remains after the "intersection" is computed.   To accomplish this clean up process the autoassociator turns on elements that are strongly supported by the active elements and turns off elements that are only weakly supported by the other active elements.   After a series of iterations the autoassociator tends to converge to one of the prelearned patterns.

When a target and foil rhyme (e.g., *cat* and *rat*) we assume that they share some of their phonological elements.   The result is that the phonological elements in the target tend to support (turn on) the semantic elements in both the target and foil.   This support for the semantic elements in the foil tends to reduce the probability of recalling the target and to increase the probability of producing the foil as an intrusion.   However, in this model the Block-2 phonological elements that overlap with the foil's phonological elements do not have to come from the target.   That is, they could come from a rhyme of the foil that is unrelated to the target or they could even be distributed across different Block-2 filler items.

In order to test these ideas we compared a No-Interference condition, a Standard Interference condition, and an Interference Plus Rhyme condition (Experiment 1 of Tehan & Humphreys, 1998).   In the later condition, a rhyme of the foil was included amongst the Block-2 fillers.   For example, the Block-1 foil might be *dog*, the Block-2 target *cat*, the rhyming word *log* and the cue *ANIMAL*.   An immediate test was used and as usual the probability of recalling the target was about the same in the No-Interference and Standard Interference conditions.   There was, however, a small probability ($< .05$) that the Block-1 foil would intrude in the Standard Interference conditions.   When a word that rhymed with the Block-1 foil was included in Block 2, there was a decrease in the recall of the target and an increase in the number of times the Block-1 foil intruded

After determining that we could enhance PI by including a rhyme of the Block-1 foil in Block 2, we attempted to replicate this effect when the foil's phonemes were distributed across three different fillers.   For example, in Experiments 2 and 3 of Tehan et al. (1998) the Block-1 foil might be *dog*, the Block-2 target *cat*, the Block-2 fillers *dart*, *mop*, and *fig* and the cue *ANIMAL*.   As in the example given, the phonemes in the filler items occurred in the same position within the filler word as did the corresponding phoneme in the foil.   In both Experiments 2 and 3, in comparison to a Standard Interference condition, there was a significant increase in the probability that the Block-1 foil would intrude.

The finding that we could enhance Block-1 intrusions by distributing the foil's phonemes across three different Block-2 fillers supported some of the principle assumptions in the Chappell and Humphreys (1994) model. In particular, the assumptions that words have distributed representations and that all of the items in the list are activated at the time of retrieval.

The Involvement of the Cue in the Retrieval Process

In long-term memory paradigms there is substantial support for the assumption that a cue directly accesses the memory for the occurrence of an item in a list (Humphreys et al., 1993). In short-term memory paradigms, however, it has been a standard assumption that items are recalled from something like the Atkinson and Shiffrin buffer. Thus, it becomes very important in the short-term memory context to show that when we provide a cue, recall starts with the cue and not with a search of a buffer or short-term memory store.

In order to demonstrate that the cue was involved we borrowed a method used by Gardiner, Craik, and Birtwistle (1972) and Dillon and Bitner (1975). The basic idea was to equate for storage and then show that PI would vary with the cue provided. In Experiment 2 of Tehan and Humphreys (1996) subjects studied a foil in Block 1 and a target in Block 2. Then they were given a cue which subsumed both the Block-1 foil and the Block-2 target or a cue which just subsumed the Block-2 target. For example, the Block-1 foil might be *hydrogen* and the Block-2 target *aluminum*. A cue which subsumes both foil and target is *CHEMICAL ELEMENT*. A cue which subsumes only the target is *METAL*. There were three conditions: No-Interference (a target in Block 2 but no foil in Block 1), Different Category (a foil in Block 1 and a target in Block 2 with a cue which only subsumes the target), and Same Category (a foil in Block 1 and a target in Block 2 with a cue which subsumes both the target and foil). Only a delayed test was used. The probability of recalling the target was .41, .39, and .30 in the No-Interference, Different Category, and Same Category conditions, respectively. The difference between the No-Interference and Different Category conditions was not significant whereas the difference between the No-Interference and Same Category conditions was significant.

In their Experiment 3, Tehan and Humphreys (1996) replicated the No-Interference and Different Category conditions using a stem cue. That is, subjects would study *wrench* in Block 1 and *bench* in Block 2 of the Different Category condition whereas they would only study *bench* in Block 2 of the No-Interference condition. In both conditions the stem cue *BEN___* was used and subjects received both immediate and delayed tests. They did not use a Same Category condition (e.g., cuing with *___ENCH*) because previous work (Tehan & Humphreys, 1995) had shown that a Same Category condition produced PI relative to a No-Interference condition on both an immediate and a delayed test.

As we expected there was no significant difference between the No-Interference and Different Category conditions on both the immediate and delayed tests. The previous two experiments indicate that interference effects are dependent on the cue; not just confusion in storage. In order to provide converging evidence on the role of the cue in providing access to these short-term memories we turned to the category dominance effect; a well known long-term memory phenomenon (Nelson, Schreiber, & McEvoy, 1992). That is, in long term memory the probability of recalling a target given a part word, extralist associate, or category label as a cue is an increasing function of the probability that the cue will elicit the target in free or controlled association.

In our short-term cued recall paradigm we predicted that with category cues there would be a category dominance effect on a delayed test, but not on an immediate test: Because the target is unlikely to be phonologically similar to the other members of the category, the phonological information available on an immediate test would make it possible to discriminate between the target in Block 2 and all other associates of the cue. However, with ending categories we expected to find category dominance effects on both immediate and delayed tests because the phonological information about the target is not helpful in discriminating the target from its rhymes. If these predictions could be confirmed, we would provide additional, albeit indirect, evidence on the role of phonological memory codes and direct evidence on the involvement of the cue's associates in the retrieval process.

These predictions about category dominance effects were tested in Experiments 4 and 5 of Tehan and Humphreys (1996). In these experiments a slight modification of the standard paradigm was used: Instead of studying two blocks of four words each, subjects studied one block of six words. A single target word, either high dominance or low dominance, was embedded amongst five filler words and both immediate and delayed tests were used. In Experiment 4, category cues were used and retention intervals were varied both between and within subjects. When retention intervals were varied between subjects, the probabilities of recalling the target on an immediate test were .83 and .81 for high and low dominance instances, respectively. The same probabilities on a delayed test were .73 and .60, respectively. The effect of dominance was significant for the delayed test, but not for the immediate test. When retention intervals were varied within subjects, the probabilities of recalling the target on an immediate test were .77 and .71 for high and low dominance instances, respectively. The same probabilities on a delayed test were .73 and .50, respectively. Again the effect of dominance was significant on a delayed test, but not on an immediate test.

When ending categories were used (Experiment 5), the probabilities of recalling the target word on an immediate test were .88 and .79 for high and low dominance instances, respectively. The same probabilities on a delayed test were .76 and .63, respectively. As predicted, the effects of dominance were significant on both the delayed and immediate test.

In sum, PI and category dominance effects are cue dependent. Furthermore, transient phonemic codes appear to be involved in category dominance effects, another cuing phenomenon, as they are in PI effects.

Temporary Activation, Control Processes, and Limited Capacity

As we noted in the introduction the three characteristics of short-term memory (temporary activation, control processes, and limited capacity) that featured so prominently in Atkinson and Shiffrin (1968) are still a feature of current approaches to short-term memory. The present approach with its emphasis on cues and codes is no exception. Temporary activation is part of the concept of a short-lasting phonological memory code though this may not be the entire story; it is possible that we will also have to postulate a rapidly changing contextual cue which permits subjects to retrieve items from the last block, especially when there is a separation between the last block and earlier blocks. Although not emphasized in our discussion, control processes are implicated not only in rehearsal but in the retrieval of information from the recent past; there has to be a decision about the relevant episode (e.g., the last block, an earlier block, or the experiment) and the appropriate cues have to be assembled and used (e.g., using the most recent or current context as opposed to an experiment wide context, using a cue that has a pre-existing relationship with a word presented earlier or a cue that was studied with a word that was presented earlier, etc.). Limited capacity comes from the inability to protect more than a small number of items from the interfering effects of prior learning. That is, the other items in an experiment interfere whenever we attempt to retrieve an item that had occurred in that experiment. This interference can be overcome if we can focus on a subset of the items in an experiment. For example, when the items in an experiment belong to different conceptual categories, category labels allow us to isolate the members of that category from the other items in the experiment. Short-lasting phonological codes and rapidly changing contextual cues permit us to focus on the last list or block in an experiment. However, this ability to focus on the last list or block begins to break down when the last list or block becomes longer or if a retention interval (especially a retention interval filled with acoustic/articulatory activity) is introduced.

Although we have addressed the issues of temporary activation, control processes, and limited capacity, our approach to short-term memory differs from the Atkinson and Shiffrin approach and most of the recent work in this area. We believe that these differences have implications for working memory (how recent information is used to comprehend passages and solve problems) and for the measurement of individual differences in working memory. We address these implications in the remainder of the chapter.

Experiment 1

The current experiment examines the possibility that PI can be observed in working memory tasks. Given our work on short-term PI effects, we think that at the point of attempting recall, the characteristics of working memory tasks have more in common with the conditions that produce PI than those that produce immunity to PI.

The prototypical working memory task is the reading span task developed by Daneman and Carpenter (1980), in which subjects read a series of sentences and are required to remember the last item of each sentence. Reading span is measured by the number of final words that can be recalled in order. This task involves both processing and memory components, but at the point of recall, only the memory component is critical. The early words in each sentence are of no importance in the task. The final word in each sentence is the sole focus of attention. From this perspective the working memory task looks quite similar to our short-term PI task, in that at the point of recall, the items in the first block are of no importance and the items in the second block are the sole focus of attention. In both tasks, there are aspects of the current trial that are irrelevant and should be ignored and there are a small number of items that have to be remembered. The only real difference between the two tasks is that in the working memory task, the to-be-forgotten and the to-be-remembered parts of the task are occurring at roughly the same time. In the PI task they are occurring sequentially, probably making retrieval in this task easier than in the working memory task. Given that PI can be observed in the easier task, it seems plausible that interference would also be observed in the harder task.

The conditions that produce PI for nonrhyming items depend primarily on list length, retention interval and retrieval cue. Thus, first and foremost, PI is observed only if both the target and interfering items are subsumed by the cue (Humphreys & Tehan, 1996). Second, subspan lists are immune to PI on an immediate test, but are prone to PI after a brief retention interval (Humphreys & Tehan, 1992; Tehan & Humphreys, 1995; Wickens, Moody & Dow, 1981). Third, PI can be observed on an immediate test if list length is supraspan (Dempster & Cooney, 1982; Halford, Maybery & Bain, 1988). We think that considerations about retention intervals make the working memory task a prime candidate for observing PI or interference effects. Take a three sentence sequence in the Daneman and Carpenter task for example. At the point of recall, the final item of the third sequence will have just been studied. The final item from the first sentence may have been rehearsed along with the final item from the second sentence after processing the second sentence, but rehearsal of the final item from both first and second sentences will have been followed by the processing of the third sentence. Thus, memory for the final word from the third sentence might be immune to interference by virtue of the very short retention interval, but memory for the final words in the first two sentences could well be prone to interference because of the retention interval introduced by the processing of the third sentence.

There are some data relevant to this issue. Turner and Engle (1989) developed four different measures of working memory capacity, all of which involved processing a number of sequences followed by recall of the final item in each sequence. In two of these measures, the processing part involved determining the legitimacy of a sentence as quickly as possible. For the recall component, subjects in one condition had to recall the final word of each sentence. In the other condition subjects had to recall a final digit that had been presented at the end of each sentence. In the remaining two conditions, subjects first determined the legitimacy of a series of arithmetic problems and then had to recall either the word that followed each of the arithmetic problems or the digit that followed each of the problems. The results indicated that following sentence verification, digit recall was better than word recall, but following arithmetic verification word recall was better than digit recall. Although the significance of this interaction was not tested, this finding along with the basic similarities between the working memory task and our short-term PI task warranted a direct examination of PI effects in working memory.

In the current experiment we have used Oakhill, Yuille, and Parkin's (1988) procedure to produce the equivalent of a working memory digit span. Subjects processed sequences of items that ended with a digit. Following the presentation of multiple sequences, subjects attempted to recall the final digit from each sequence in order. What varies across conditions is the material in the processing stage. In two conditions, the processing material is also digits. However, in the other condition the processing material is letters, with the final item on each sequence being a digit. Given that PI occurs when the cue subsumes both the target(s) and the interfering material, the expectation is that processing letters is going to interfere less with memory for digits than will the processing of digits.

On some digit processing trials, we have also attempted to reduce interference by presenting the digits in an ascending sequence, the final digit being a deviation from that sequence. For example, subjects might have the following two sequences 23456782 and 91234569. The final type of sequence involved a random sequence of the digits 1 to 9 followed by the TBR digit, e.g. 84937627. We thought it possible for subjects to encode the ascending string into a format that would produce less interference than would be produced by a random string of digits. Our intuitions about reducing interference by changing the encoding format are based on observations about when Block-1 intrusions occur. That is, we know that in a two-block trial where the second block is tested for serial recall, intrusions from Block 1 tend to occur in position. Thus a word in position 2 of Block 1 will tend to intrude in position 2 of Block 2. We assume that this pattern of intrusions represents a tendency for the cues used in recalling the words in the serial structure of Block 2 to activate the words in the corresponding positions of the structure in which the Block 1 words were stored. It followed that if the structure or format in which the words in Block 1 were stored was different from the structure or format with which the words in Block 2 were stored there might be a reduction in PI.

Method

Subjects. Twenty-four psychology students from the University of Southern Queensland participated to fulfil course requirements or for a ticket in a small cash lottery.

Procedure and Materials. On each trial subjects were presented from three to five sequences of items which were read aloud, with the additional requirement that the final item in the sequence be remembered. The terminal item of each sequence was a digit. As with most span procedures, the number of sequences per trial increased throughout the course of the experiment. Initially, there were three sequences per trial, and there were three such trials before the number of sequences increased to four. The experiment ended with the presentation of five sequences per trial. Each sequence was 8 items long. The items were presented individually at a one second rate. After the TBR digit had been presented, a question mark appeared on the screen for 1 second to indicate the end of that sequence and that the previous digit was the target digit. A half second pause then preceded the presentation of the next sequence. The end of a trial was signified by a row of X's (XXXXXX), signalling the subjects that they had 5 seconds to recall the final digit from each sequence.

While the final item in each sequence across the experiment was always a digit, the items presented before the terminal digit varied. In one condition, the processing items were 7 consonants. These consonants were randomly determined for each sequence and then a terminal digit was randomly assigned to each sequence. In the ordered digit condition, the items were 7 digits that were presented in ascending strings. The starting value for each string was randomly determined, and 1 always followed 9 in the sequence, for example, 7891234. Once the digit strings had been determined for each sequence, a terminal digit was then randomly assigned to each sequence. In the final condition, the processing items were again digits, but the order of the digits was randomized for each sequence. Again, each terminal digit was randomly assigned.

All subjects studied the same set of sequences in each condition. The order of conditions, however, was counterbalanced across subjects.

Results

For each subject, three span measures were derived, one for each type of processing material. While trials of two sequences were not tested, we assumed that all subjects could recall two digits under the current experimental procedure.

Thus, with a base span of 2, full span was calculated by adding another .33 for each trial on which the terminal digits were correctly recalled in presentation order. Given this methodology, mean spans were 4.16, 3.71, and 3.55, for letters, ordered digits and random digits, respectively. A one-way repeated measures ANOVA indicated that there were reliable differences between the means, $F(2, 46) = 11.61$, $MSE = .210$. Two planned comparisons indicated that span when processing letters was significantly higher than for span when processing random digits, $t(23) = 4.65$, Cohen's d = .95. Sixteen subjects demonstrated a letter span advantage, 2 had a digits advantage, and there were 6 tied scores. Ordering the digits in an ascending sequence did not appear to have the desired effect; there was no reliable difference in span between the ordered and random digits conditions, $t(23) = 1.04$, Cohen's d = .21. Twelve subjects demonstrated an ordering advantage, 8 had a digits advantage, and there were 4 tied scores.

Discussion

The current experiment sought to test the idea that PI could be observed in a standard working memory task. There were clear differences in digit recall as a function of the processing material. Remembering digits was much easier when subjects had processed letters than when they had processed other digits. We attribute this difference in span to the fact that, at retrieval, the preterminal digits in each sequence served as a source of interference for the TBR terminal digits. This explanation would also apply to the Turner and Engle data in which digit and word span varied as a function of the processing material; recalling digits was easier against a background of words and recalling words was easier against a background of arithmetic problems.

The cuing explanation of the above PI effects, was also tested by looking at the difference between ordered sequences and random sequences of pre-terminal digits. The expectation was that subjects could store the organized sequence in a format that would reduce interference. Only a marginal decrease in the amount of interference was observed.

To explain the results from a working memory perspective (as a simultaneous competition between storage and processing), one would have to argue that processing digits is more difficult than processing consonants. However, reading digits and letters should be highly automated for university students. In addition, in other tasks digits are processed more quickly than letters; digits are read more quickly than letters (Schweickert & Boruff, 1986; Standing, Bond, Smith & Isley, 1980) and span is correspondingly higher for digits (Crannell & Parrish, 1957; Schweickert & Boruff, 1986; Standing, Bond, Smith & Isley, 1980).

If we are correct in assuming that PI effects are operating in the working memory task, then some of the findings attributable to differences in working memory capacity could possibly be understood as being due to PI effects. For example, differences in the comprehension of simple versus complex sentences has been attributed to differences in processing demands associated with the two types of sentences (Just & Carpenter, 1992) or with individual differences in working memory capacity (Waters & Caplan, 1996). Given that at recall subjects have to recall a serial list of unrelated words, it is possible that a well-formed, easily read sentence might be stored in a format that produces less interference with serial recall than would the storage of another serial list of words. Our prediction here is predicated on the assumption that cues (chaining, position, etc.) are used in the recall of a serial list but that different cues or cue combinations are used in the recall of a well formed easily understood sentence. This idea is tested in the next experiment.

Experiment 2

In Experiment 2 we return to a PI task in which items are presented in two the TBR items. In the first Block, 12 words were presented individually and subjects were asked to simply read each word aloud as it appeared on the screen. An exclamation mark followed as a block separator and then five unrelated words were presented as the TBR targets. The subjects were required to read the Block-2 words silently and then recall them in order. Given that five words is a little above span for most subjects and that subjects had read the sentence aloud and the TBR words silently, we expected that performance would be off ceiling and that PI effects might be observed.

Four different types of sentences were read during Block-1 presentation. The first two types involved easy to comprehend, well formed sentences: Either the first two lines of well known nursery rhymes, or simple subject-verb-object sentences. The other two sentence types were more difficult to comprehend. They were either legitimate but complex, center-embedded sentences, or simple sentences in which the order of the words had been randomized. We assumed that the first two types might be stored in a format that would produce relatively little interference with the recall of a serial list. We also assumed that there would be no alternative but to store the last type of sequence (the randomly ordered sentence) as a serial list and as a consequence it might produce the most interference with the recall of another serial list. To the extent that the third type of sequence (the center-embedded sentence) is hard to understand, it could be stored in a format that is more like the format of a serial list than the format of a well understood sentence. As a consequence, the center-embedded sentence might produce a level of interference with the recall of a serial list that was intermediate to the level produced by the serial string and the well formed sentences.

Method

Subjects. Twenty people who were studying introductory psychology units at the University of Southern Queensland participated for course credit or for a ticket in a small cash lottery.

Procedure. The subjects studied forty trials that were based upon the Tehan and Humphreys (1995) short-term cued recall task. Each trial consisted of two blocks separated by an exclamation mark (!). The first block consisted of 12 words and subjects were instructed that they were simply to read each word aloud as it appeared on the computer screen. These twelve items were presented at the rate of one item per second. The second block consisted of five unrelated words, each of which were again presented individually at a one second rate. Subjects were instructed to read them silently but to try and remember them because they would be tested on these items. Immediately following the final word in the second block, subjects attempted to verbally recall the five items that they had just seen in serial order. They were instructed to substitute the word "blank" for any word that they could not remember.

Materials. The key materials in this experiment were the items in the first block. The twelve words in each trial made an English sentence, but varied in pre-existing familiarity and the way they conformed to simple structure. Ten of the trials involved the first two lines of well known nursery rhymes, for example, *"Humpty Dumpty sat on a wall, Humpty Dumpty had a great fall"*. Another ten trials consisted of simple, well formed sentences, for example, *"A little dog with long curly ears came running into the room"*. The third type involved center embedded English sentences, for example, *"The small boy that the girl that the man saw met slept"*. The final type of sentence was like the second type described above, however, the order of the words was randomized, for example, *"Poor the outskirts very of village a the lived there on farmer"*.

The TBR words that appeared in the second block were designed to be similar to those appearing in the above sentences. That is, they were one syllable nouns, adjectives, verbs and function words. Two hundred such words were obtained and to create the trials these words were randomly assigned to the 40 trials for each subject, five to each trial. Thus, while the sentences that formed the first block did not vary across subjects, the TBR words that were paired with each sentence did differ for each subject. Furthermore, the order of the forty trials was randomized for each subject.

Results

Collapsed across serial position, the mean probability of recalling the Block-2 target items in correct serial position was .59 for the nursery rhyme sentences, .57 for the simple sentences, .50 for the center embedded sentences, and .54 for the randomized sentences. An initial 4 (sentence type) x 5 (serial position) repeated measures ANOVA indicated that there were reliable differences between the sentence types, F (3, 54) = 6.34, MSE = .025; there were serial position effects, F (4, 72) = 41.98, MSE = .062, but the interaction was not significant.

While sentence type does have an impact on Block-2 recall, we assumed that the differences would be most sensitive to the well-formed, ill-formed distinction. Thus, our planned comparison involved differences between the average of the rhyme and well-formed sentences and the average of the center embedded and randomized sentences. The data on which the comparison was made are presented in Fig. 7.2. Block-2 recall was better when the sentences were well formed than when they were ill-formed, F (1, 18) = 14.09, MSE = .014, serial position effects were obviously present, F (4, 72) = 41.98, MSE = .031, and the interaction was not reliable.

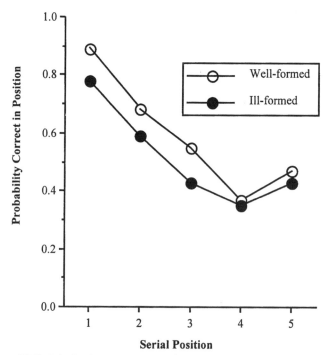

FIG. 7.2. Serial position curves for the recall of the Block-2 words as a function of whether well formed and poorly formed sequences were read in Block 1. To be scored as correct a word had to be recalled in position.

Discussion

In Experiment 1 we showed that category specific interference could be obtained in a working memory span task. In Experiment 2 we used a PI task and showed that sentence complexity has an effect on PI, by showing that sentence complexity has an influence on memory for words, even when subjects had every reason to have stopped processing the sentences while they were processing the TBR words. These results must cast some doubt on the standard interpretation of working memory span tasks as reflecting differences in working memory span capacity (to simultaneously perform a task while storing information). However, the confounding of complexity with the actual words used in the sentences casts some doubts on this conclusion. To overcome this problem we decided to replicate Experiment 2 using only the materials used in the center-embedded sentence condition and sentences composed of the same words but reformatted into right-branching sentences. For example, the center-embedded sentence, *"The boy that the girl that the man saw met slept"* becomes *"The man saw the girl that met the boy that slept"*. (from Andrews, 1997). To the extent that the right-branching version can be comprehended and stored in an appropriate format and the center-embedded sentence cannot, we would expect that recall of the Block-2 targets would be better following the study of the right-branching sentences than following the study of the center-embedded sentences.

Experiment 3

Method

Subjects. Another group of 20 students from the University of Southern Queensland participated for course credit or for a ticket in a small cash lottery.

Procedure and Materials. The basic procedure was identical to that in Experiment 1. However, in the current study the participants only studied 16 trials in which they read a sentence and then studied a list of five words. After studying the list of five words, subjects were required to recall the list in serial order. What differed was whether the sentences were center embedded or right branching. Subjects studied 8 trials of each type with center embedded and right branching versions of each sentence being counterbalanced across subjects. Each sentence in this experiment was 11 items long.

Results

Recall of the items in the second block is summarized in Fig. 7.3. A 2 x 5 repeated measures ANOVA confirmed that recall was sensitive to sentence type with performance being better in the easy to comprehend, right branching condition than in the hard to comprehend, left branching condition, $F(1, 19) = 6.09$, $MSE = .015$; serial position effects were also reliable, $F(4, 74) = 60.80$, $MSE = .033$; but the interaction was not.

Discussion

Again Block-2 recall differs as a function of the type of sentence that had to be read in the first block, even though instructions stressed that this material was to be ignored while processing the Block-2 words. The differences in the current experiment cannot be attributed to materials differences since the materials were counterbalanced across subjects. All that varied was the word order and the consequent ease of comprehension. When the items in Block-1 were arranged in a center-embedded sequence, recall of the target items in Block-2 deteriorated relative to when the items in the first block were arranged in a right-branching structure. This pattern suggests that hard to comprehend sentences are stored in

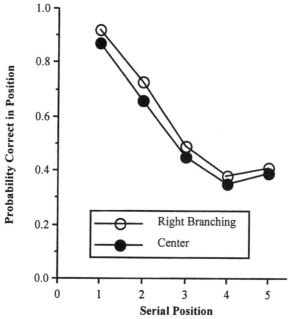

FIG. 7.3. Serial position curves for the recall of the Block-2 words as a function of whether well formed and poorly formed sequences were read in Block 1. To be scored as correct a word had to be recalled in position.

a format that produces more interference with the recall of a serial list than are easy to comprehend sentences.   It also raises the possibility that part of the correlation between sentence span tasks and measures of verbal ability result from failures to comprehend some sentences with the concomitant in the interference produced on serial recall by the way in which an uncomprehended sentence is stored.

PI and Individual Differences in Working Memory

Short-term PI effects have, for the most part, been explored within the framework of the Brown-Peterson task. By comparison little work has been done with respect to other short-term memory tasks. The fact that PI effects in short-term memory have remained a non-issue can be attributed to the fact that buffer models like Atkinson and Shiffrin (1968) or the phonological loop of Baddeley (1986) strongly implicate immunity to PI. That is, the limited capacity buffer serves as a simple mechanism for isolating current learning from prior learning. This same basic mechanism for the isolation of current learning from previous learning also appears as a feature of multicomponent working memory systems (cf. Just & Carpenter, 1992, p. 123.). However, our work has suggested that short-term PI effects are best understood as an emergent characteristic of the interaction between cues and codes.   Furthermore, the three experiments presented in this chapter support the assumption that PI effects will be found in working memory paradigms.   More generally we would suggest that the conditions that do and do not produce PI need to be considered in analyses of working memory, including individual differences in working memory.

In many circumstances, such as comprehending a passage or performing mental arithmetic, we would expect a phonological memory code to protect the current passage or problem from the interfering effects of previous passages or problems. There may also be conditions where semantic cues serve to isolate the relevant information from other information. In addition, we need to consider the possibility that rapidly changing contextual cues may help to isolate recent information. For example, Loess and Waugh (1967) showed that in the Brown-Peterson paradigm the interfering effects of a prior list could be reduced if the separation between the prior list and the current list were increased.   This reduction in interference could occur either because the preceding list was forgotten or because the last list was more readily isolated from the preceding list by a rapidly changing contextual cue.   For the present purposes it does not matter just why interference was reduced.   The important point is that a short lasting phonological code, or an appropriate discriminative cue that subsumes the information in the last list but not the information in earlier lists, are not the only mechanisms that can protect current learning from previous learning.

The relevance of our analysis of how current learning is protected from previous learning to the study of individual differences in working memory can be illustrated by a study reported by Martin (1993). Martin was concerned with the question of whether the articulatory loop (phonological memory code) had a role in sentence comprehension. In addressing this question, Martin carried out a series of studies on a brain damaged patient (E. A.) who had no apparent phonological code. For example, Martin reports E. A. has a span of about two words for auditory presentation and three words for visual presentation. In one study E. A. was required to determine whether the gender of the subject of a sentence matched a pronoun that was used at the end (e.g., "The girl fell down the stairs at least once a week and often hurt himself."). The performance of E. A. in detecting these mismatches was comparable to the performance of a control group.

In testing E. A. on these sentences Martin used procedures which are standard in working memory research: Each sentence is presented in isolation, allowing time for the subject to respond, followed by a brief interval of at least several seconds prior to the beginning of the next sentence. According to our analysis, this interval between sentences will reduce the amount of PI from previous sentences which reduces the need for a phonological code. In order to maximize the need for a phonological code, it is necessary to maximize PI. For example, PI can be increased by using a two-block design; present a sentence and either test that sentence, or immediately present a second sentence. PI can also be increased by having a specific source of interference in the previous sentence. To return to the gender match example, the sentence "The boy frequently fell off his bicycle and sometimes hurt himself" might be followed by the test sentence "The girl fell down the stairs at least once a week and often hurt himself". Finally, PI can also be manipulated by an appropriate pattern of reading aloud and reading silently. That is, in a two-block paradigm normal subjects, but not subjects deficient in a phonological code, should be affected by whether the first sentence is read aloud and the second silently or vice versa.

Conclusion

We have presented an approach to short-term memory that emphasizes cues and codes. In particular we showed that PI could be found at very short (2 to 4 second) retention intervals, that PI depends on the cue that was used, and that short-lasting phonological memory codes are involved in short-term cued recall just as they are in short-term serial recall

We then applied our ideas about cues and codes to working memory paradigms. In Experiment 1 we showed that working memory span performance depended on the match between the kind of materials being recalled and the kind of materials that were processed. In Experiments 2 and 3 we showed that in a PI paradigm hard to comprehend sentences produced more interference than easier sentences. The later finding implies that the format of stored sequences (e.g., sentence versus serial list) may determine the extent of interference in the recall of a serial list.   Finally, we considered the issue of where a deficit in phonological encoding might show up in working memory performance (e.g., sentence comprehension).   Our answer was that the conditions which maximize PI are the ones which are most likely to show a performance difference. More generally, we think that one of the primary roles served by the phonological code is to protect recent learning from the interfering effects of prior learning.

Summary

A short-term cued recall paradigm is described and results using this paradigm are reviewed.   These results show that proactive interference (PI) can be obtained at very short retention intervals (2 to 4 seconds), that PI depends on the cue used, and that short-lasting phonological memory codes serve to protect current learning from prior learning. This approach with its emphasis on cues and codes is then applied to working memory.

Acknowledgments

This research was supported by Australian Research Council grant No. A79531860.   We would like to thank Rose Woodward for her help in testing subjects.

References

Andrews, G. (1997). *Relational Complexity as a capacity construct in cognitive development.* Unpublished doctoral dissertation, University of Queensland, Australia.

Atkinson, R. C., & Shiffrin, R. M. (1968). Human memory: a proposed system and its control processes. In K. W. Spence & J. T. Spence (Eds.), *The Psychology of learning and motivation: Vol. 2* (pp. 89-195). New York: Academic Press.

Baddeley, A. D. (1966). Short-term memory for word sequences as a function of acoustic, semantic and formal similarity. *Quarterly Journal of Experimental Psychology, 18A*, 362-365.

Baddeley, A. D. (1986). *Working Memory.* Oxford: Oxford University Press.

Baddeley, A. D., & Hitch, G. (1974). Working memory. In K. W. Spence & J. T. Spence (Eds.), *The Psychology of learning and motivation: Vol. 8* (pp. 67-89). New York: Academic Press.

Chappell, M., & Humphreys, M. S. (1994). An auto-associative neural network for sparse representations: Analysis and application to models of recognition and cued recall. *Psychological Review, 101*, 103-128.

Conrad, R. (1965). Order errors in immediate recall of sequences. *Journal of Verbal Learning and Verbal Behavior, 4*, 161-169.

Crannell, C. W., & Parrish, J. M. (1957). A comparison of immediate memory span for digits, letters, and words. *Journal of Psychology, 44*, 319-327.

Daneman, M., & Carpenter, P. A. (1980). Individual differences in working memory and reading. *Journal of Verbal Learning and Verbal Behavior, 19*, 450-466.

Dempster, F. N., & Cooney, J. B. (1982). Individual differences in digit span, susceptibility to proactive interference, and aptitude/achievement test scores. *Intelligence, 6*, 399-416.

Dillon, R. F., & Bittner, L .A. (1975). Analysis of retrieval cues and release from proactive inhibition. *Journal of Verbal Learning and Verbal Behavior, 14*, 616-622.

Estes, W. K. (1972). An associative basis for coding and organization in memory. In A. W. Melton & E. Martin (Eds.), *Coding processes in human memory.* (pp. 161-190.) Washington, DC:Winston.

Gardiner, J. M., Craik, F. I. M., & Birtwistle, J. (1972). Retrieval cues and release from proactive inhibition. *Journal of Verbal Learning and Verbal Behavior, 11*, 778-783.

Halford, G. S., Maybery, M. T., & Bain, J. D. (1988). Set-size effects in primary memory: An age-related capacity limitation? *Memory and Cognition, 16*, 480-487.

Henson, R. N. A., Norris, D. G., Page, M. P. A., & Baddeley, A. D. (1996). Unchained memory: Error patterns rule out chaining models of immediate serial recall. *Quarterly Journal of Experimental Psychology, 49A*, 80-115.

Hulme, C., Maughan, S., & Brown, G. D. A. (1991). Memory for familiar and unfamiliar words: Evidence for a long-term memory contribution to short-term memory span. *Journal of Memory and Language, 30*, 685-701.

Humphreys, M. S., & Tehan, G. (1992). A simultaneous examination of recency and cueing effects. In A. Healy, S. Kosslyn & R. M. Shiffrin (Eds.), *From learning theory to cognitive processes: Essays in honor of William K. Estes. Vol. 2* (pp. 143-159). Hillsdale NJ: Lawrence Erlbaum Associates.

Humphreys, M. S., Wiles, J., & Bain, J. D. (1993) Memory retrieval with two cues: Think of intersecting sets. In D. E. Meyer & S. Kornblum (Eds.), *Attention and performance XIV: Synergies in experimental psychology, artificial intelligence, and cognitive neuropsychology—A silver jubilee* (pp 489-508) Cambridge, MA: MIT Press.

Humphreys, M. S., Wiles, J., & Dennis, S. (1994). Toward a theory of human memory: Data structures and access processes: *Behavioral and Brain*

Sciences, 17, 655-667.

Just, M. A., & Carpenter, P. A. (1992). A capacity theory of comprehension: Individual differences in working memory. *Psychological Review, 99*, 122-149.

Loess, H., & Waugh, N. (1967). Short-term memory and intertrial interval. *Journal of Verbal Learning and Verbal Behavior, 6*, 455-460.

Martin, R. C. (1993). Short-term memory and sentence processing: Evidence from neuropsychology. *Memory & Cognition, 2*, 176-183.

Nelson, D. L., Schreiber, T. A., & McEvoy, C. L. (1992). Processing implicit and explicit representations. *Psychological Review, 99*, 322-348.

Oakhill, J., Yuille, N., & Parkin, A. (1988). Memory and inference in skilled and less skilled comprehenders. In M. M. Gruneberg, P. E. Morris, & R. N. Sykes (Eds.), *Practical aspects of memory: Current research and issues: Vol. 2* (pp. 315-320). Chichester, England: John Wiley & Sons.

Schweickert, R. (1993). A multinomial processing tree model for degradation and redintegration in immediate recall. *Memory and Cognition, 21*, 168-175.

Schweickert, R., & Boruff, B. (1986). Short-term memory capacity: Magic number or magic spell? *Journal of Experimental Psychology: Learning Memory and Cognition, 12*, 419-425.

Shiffrin, R. (1993). Short-term memory: A brief commentary. *Memory and Cognition, 21*, 193-197.

Standing, L., Bond, B., Smith, P., & Isley, C. (1980). Is the immediate memory span determined by subvocalization rate? *British Journal of Psychology, 71*, 525-539.

Tehan, G., & Humphreys, M. S. (1995). Transient phonemic codes and immunity to proactive interference. *Memory and Cognition, 23*, 181-191.

Tehan, G., & Humphreys, M. S. (1996). Cuing effects in short-term recall. *Memory and Cognition, 24*, 719-732.

Tehan, G., & Humphreys, M. S. (1998). Creating proactive interference in immediate recall: Building a dog from a dart, a mop, and a fig. *Memory and Cognition, 26*, 477-489.

Turner, M., & Engle, R. W. (1989). Is working memory capacity task dependent? *Journal of Memory and Language, 28*, 127-154.

Waters, G. S., & Caplan, D. (1996). The measurement of verbal working memory and its relation to reading comprehension. *Quarterly Journal of Experimental Psychology, 49A*, 51-79.

Wickens, D. D., Moody, M. J., & Dow, R. (1981). The nature of timing of the retrieval process and of interference effects. *Journal of Experimental Psychology: General, 110*, 1-20.

Chapter 8

Recall of Order Information:
Evidence Requiring a Dual-Storage Memory Model

Alice F. Healy
University of Colorado, U. S. A.

Thomas F. Cunningham
St. Lawrence University, U. S. A.

Although we have not been working with Atkinson and Shiffrin's (1968) buffer model, our research addressed a fundamental distinction raised by their model, namely the distinction between short-term store (STS) and long-term store (LTS). Likewise, our research has addressed the control process that played a central role in the buffer model, namely the rehearsal process. Unlike Atkinson and Shiffrin, we distinguish between an active rehearsal process, which brings information into LTS, and a passive rehearsal process, which maintains information in STS. Our guiding theoretical framework has been the perturbation model of immediate memory originally proposed by Estes (1972; see Estes, 1997, for the most recent version of this model and see Lee, 1992, for a helpful summary). As originally proposed, this mathematical model included only a single memory store comparable to STS and a single passive rehearsal process. However, the findings of our research document and underline the need to add to the model a second memory store comparable to LTS, which allows for a distinction between active and passive rehearsal processes.

Background

During the past 15 years, our program of research has focused on the immediate recall (i.e., the recall over retention intervals up to 30 s) of serial order information. We have used a constant methodology (e.g., Cunningham, Healy, Till, Fendrich, & Dimitry, 1993; Cunningham, Healy, & Williams, 1984; Cunningham, Marmie, & Healy, 1998; Healy, Fendrich, Cunningham, & Till, 1987). Specifically, we have made use of the distractor paradigm introduced by Brown (1958) and Peterson and Peterson (1959), employing the specific version of it developed by Conrad (1967), in which the to-be-recalled items consist of letters and the distractor task occurring during the retention interval consists of reading aloud a variable length list of interpolated digits. To ensure that we tested for order information only, we have used a reconstruction method, in which participants always have information about the identity of the letters available during stimulus presentation and at the time of recall so that their task has been limited to reproducing the order in which the letters had appeared (see, e.g., Healy, 1974). Our methodology has also been characterized by the use of a partial report procedure, such that the sequence of to-be-remembered letters presented on a trial is divided into two four-letter segments and only one of the segments is cued for recall at the time of test (see, e.g., Anderson, 1960; Brown, 1954; Lee & Estes, 1981). Segment boundaries are marked by an exclamation point (!) between the fourth and fifth letters of the eight-letter sequence. At the end of a digit-filled retention interval, a recall cue (. or :) is presented indicating to the participant to write down either the first or second segment of letters. For example, a sample trial requesting recall of the second letter segment following a retention interval of four digits might be composed of the following characters: -- FBHK!RLMQ6841:

Our research using this methodology has corroborated three primary findings that emerged in an earlier, seminal study by Lee and Estes (1981). First, there is a steep drop in performance as retention interval increases. Second, there is a marked advantage for the second, or most recently presented, segment of letters relative to the first. Third, the serial position functions are bow-shaped and nearly symmetrical at each retention interval. These three findings served as the basis for the development of the perturbation model.

According to the perturbation model, as outlined by Lee and Estes (1981), STS codes are organized in a hierarchical arrangement. At the lowest level of the hierarchy are codes containing information concerning the position of an individual item within a segment; at the next level of the hierarchy are codes revealing which one of the segments within a trial contains the individual item; at the highest level are codes indicating the particular trial of the item in question. The basis for immediate recall in this model is a recurrent reactivation of the hierarchical code structure. At each reactivation, the information at each of the three levels is recoded but with some probability (*theta*) that the relative position of adjacent items, segments, or trials is perturbed so that an interchange in positions occurs between two neighbors.

We have used this methodology and theoretical framework to explore the influence of several important variables on the immediate recall of order information, including the effects of segment repetition over a session (Cunningham et al., 1984), the effects of segment cuing (Healy et al., 1987), the effects of segment importance and expectancy (Cunningham et al., 1993; Healy & Cunningham, 1995), and, most recently, the effects of item distinctiveness (Cunningham et al., 1998).

Segment Repetition

In Experiment 1 of our first study (Cunningham et al., 1984), we investigated the facilitative effects of repetition on the immediate recall of order information. In effect, we reexamined a classic study by Hebb (1961), which resulted in his rejecting a major assumption of his theory (Hebb, 1949), namely, that STS is represented by transient, reverberatory activity traces corresponding to to-be-remembered items, whereas LTS traces occur as a result of a distinct process of consolidation. Hebb's (1961) study was designed to test the "notion that memory span performance ("immediate" memory) is based on activity traces and should, therefore, have no long-term effects if consolidation of the activity traces was disrupted by subsequent incompatible activities" (Melton, 1967, p. 34). A basic trial in Hebb's study involved the oral presentation of a nine-digit number and a request of immediate serial recall following the last digit of the number. A sequence of 24 trials of this type was conducted with repetitions of the same nine-digit number introduced on every third trial. Although Hebb predicted no advantage for the repeated number, he found that participants showed dramatic improvement in recalling the nine-digit number that had been repeated. On the basis of this finding, which has since been termed the "Hebb repetition effect," Hebb concluded that his original (Hebb, 1949) position that STS was simply reverberatory was in error. Murdock (1974, p. 164) noted a similarity between the Estes (1972) perturbation model and Hebb's (1949) theory. Hence, the Hebb (1961) repetition effect could be viewed as a challenge to the perturbation model as well as to the fundamental distinction made by the buffer model between STS and LTS.

Was Hebb's (1961) study an adequate test of his theory? Should we conclude that an LTS trace for order information is established as a result of repetition per se? Evidence from Cohen and Johansson (1967) suggests that mere stimulus repetition is not sufficient to set up a permanent structural trace but that overt responding is necessary for producing a Hebb repetition effect. Using this background as a point of departure, we (Cunningham et al., 1984) emphasized different rehearsal processes—passive and active, and proposed that it is not responding per se (i.e., identifying an item when it is presented) that is crucial for promoting transfer from STS to LTS but rather the active, purposeful rehearsal processes that are a natural concomitant of producing recall responses at the time of testing. Our reasoning was consistent with Shiffrin's (1975) position that active processes of rehearsal and coding are required for placement in LTS. Thus, the fact that an item is registered and passively rehearsed in STS does not guarantee its transfer to LTS.

We compared two conditions that differed in the opportunity they provided for active, purposeful rehearsal of the critical stimuli. In both conditions the critical stimuli (i.e., the letters from a given segment occurring in a particular order) were repeated on successive trials; in one condition, these stimuli were identified during presentation but not tested, whereas in the other condition, participants not only identified the stimuli during presentation but also were tested on them after each of their repetitions. We assumed that a comparison of these two conditions would provide an indication of the importance of active rehearsal in obtaining the facilitative effects of repetition, and it would also allow us to determine the relative contributions of stimulus repetition and test repetition in producing the repetition effect. Specifically, we employed one condition (same segment) in which the same segment (either the first or the second) was tested with recall on all four presentations and another condition (switched segment) in which one segment from the pair was tested on the first three presentations, and the other segment was tested on the fourth. We compared these conditions to determine if repeating only the stimulus presentation (switched segment) had the same beneficial effect on recall levels as repeating both the stimulus presentation and its test (same segment). In the switched-segment condition, we assume that only passive rehearsal was occurring over the first three presentations of that segment that was subsequently tested on its fourth presentation. In contrast, in the same-segment condition, we assume that in addition to passive rehearsal, active rehearsal was taking place during the three tests of that segment subsequently tested again on the fourth presentation.

We found no evidence of a repetition effect in the switched segment condition. However, correct recall on the fourth presentation was high for the same-segment condition, in which the segment had been previously tested three times. We interpreted the facilitative effect of repeated testing as due to an active (rather than passive) rehearsal process.

Segment Cuing

In Experiment 2 of Cunningham et al. (1984), we examined the influence of another variable that was expected to affect the extent of active rehearsal. We arranged matters so that active rehearsal would be increased during presentation of the stimuli and during the retention interval, rather than during the test period alone. In the standard partial report task, participants cannot anticipate which segment will be tested because the recall cue (postcue) occurs only after the presentation of the letter segments. However, in a variant of that procedure, we provided participants in advance of item and postcue presentation with a warning signal (precue) indicating which segment would be tested later. We found that such precuing led to superior performance on an immediate recall test. We successfully applied the perturbation model to our procedure and were able to provide an account within that framework for the effects of precuing. Specifically, we fit the data from our condition with no precues using the same probability for memory perturbations ($theta$ = .04) as Lee and Estes (1981) had used earlier to fit their data from a related experiment. Then we found that the elevated levels of recall from the precuing condition could be accommodated by reducing the perturbation probability ($theta$ = .02). Because the probability of a perturbation applies at each reactivation (or each time interval between the input and test of a segment), a reduction in perturbation probability can be interpreted as an improvement in the passive rehearsal process that is used to maintain the information about the segment in STS until it is tested.

In response to our work, Estes (1983) showed that the perturbation model could be fit to our data in another manner. Rather than allowing the perturbation probability *theta* to change (especially because the same probability value was found to fit the data from different experiments in different laboratories), he added a parameter *alpha* for the probability that the code for an item's position would continue to be subject to the perturbation process. Thus, 1 - *alpha* is equal to the probability of storing the initial encoding of the item's position in LTS, where the code would no longer be subject to the perturbation process. By increasing the LTS probability (1 - *alpha*) but keeping constant the

STS perturbation probability (*theta*), Estes was able to fit the data from the precuing situation as well as we had when we changed only the perturbation probability. Because the probability of storage in LTS was applied to the initial representation, an increase in LTS probability can be interpreted as an improvement in initial coding. From this finding, then, it can be concluded that precuing may have its effect by facilitating item encoding rather than passive rehearsal. Because both fits to the data (that obtained by varying the STS perturbation probability and that obtained by varying the LTS probability) were equally good, it could not be determined at this point whether the precuing effect was due to improved passive rehearsal or improved encoding processes.

Estes (1983) went on to show, however, that the two alternative accounts could be distinguished if the retention interval separating the presentation of the to-be-remembered information and its test were to be increased. After relatively long delays, the dual-storage model with the elevated LTS probability predicts that performance will remain above the chance level, but the original single-storage model with the reduced STS perturbation probability and no LTS component predicts chance-level performance.

In Healy et al. (1987, Experiment 1), we conducted an investigation along the lines suggested by Estes (1983). Specifically, we compared precue and postcue conditions across retention intervals ranging from 0 to 60 digits (or from 0 to 30 s). Whereas the original perturbation model with no LTS component would lead to the prediction that performance in the precue and postcue conditions would converge at the longest retention interval, we found consistently superior recall with the precue relative to that with the postcue across all retention intervals. Further, performance in neither the postcue nor precue condition reached the chance level at the longest retention interval, in accordance with the predictions derived from the modified dual-storage version of the perturbation model suggested by Estes (1983). We specifically compared the original perturbation model with the modified dual-storage version in their ability to account for performance under precue and postcue conditions. The original model included only one parameter *theta* representing the STS perturbation probability, whereas the modified model added a second parameter *alpha*, with 1 - *alpha* representing the LTS encoding probability. The results revealed superior fits for the dual-storage model in both conditions, thus implicating LTS processes in this task. Further, encoding, rather than rehearsal, processes were implicated as the basis for the advantage due to precuing. The best fits to both precue and postcue conditions were obtained by changing the value of only the LTS encoding parameter *alpha*, not the STS perturbation parameter *theta*, which was held constant at the value .04 found to yield the best fits in previous studies.

The locus of the precuing advantage was also addressed in an empirical test to determine whether rehearsal processes or encoding processes were responsible for the precuing advantage (Experiment 2, Healy et al., 1987). Specifically, the major question in this experiment was whether precuing has its effect by enhancing encoding at the initial presentation of the segment or by facilitating rehearsal during the period between the presentation of the segment and its test. An encoding effect would be attributable to LTS, whereas a rehearsal effect would be attributable to STS. Our empirical test involved a comparison of the postcue and precue conditions with a new intermediate cue condition, in which the warning signal cue occurred between the presentation of the letters and digits. Because the intermediate cue was presented after the to-be-remembered letters, it could only influence rehearsal, not encoding, processes. As previously, we found superior performance for the precue relative to the postcue, but we found no facilitating effect of the intermediate cue. The absence of an advantage for the intermediate cue implied that there was no enhanced rehearsal of the cued segment during the digit-filled retention interval.

Thus, the combined results of both the theoretical test (Experiment 1) and the empirical test (Experiment 2) indicated that the locus of the precuing advantage is in the initial encoding of the to-be-remembered material. More generally, our combined findings provided strong support for a dual-storage memory model that distinguishes between STS and LTS processes.

Segment Importance and Expectancy

The enhanced performance in the precue condition raises the question of the fate of the uncued segment. Assuming the precued segment receives more extensive LTS encoding, the uncued segment may receive less extensive LTS encoding relative to that normally given to segments in the postcue condition. Hence, examining performance on the uncued segment in the precue condition should provide an excellent opportunity in which to reduce the operation of LTS encoding processes and thereby assess the operation of STS processes. We would, thus, be in an optimal position to examine the rate of forgetting from STS. The two experiments in our next series (Cunningham et al., 1993) used two different methods that allowed us to examine the rate of forgetting from STS relatively uncontaminated by LTS encoding processes. The first method manipulated participants' expectancy concerning the segment to be recalled, and the second manipulated the importance of the segment to be recalled. Specifically, in Experiment 1 we varied the participants' expectancy for which one of two segments would be cued for recall. In the crucial experimental condition, participants were led by a precue to expect to recall one of the to-be-remembered segments of letters but then on 25% of the trials were forced by a postcue to switch recall to the other segment instead. Experiment 2 was conducted in the context of a game with the object to recall the important (cued) segment for game points. However, the participants were informed that an added challenge in playing the game was that they were required to recall first the other, unimportant (uncued) segment before recalling the important segment. Hence, Experiment 2 involved a whole report procedure in which only one segment, the important segment, was cued but both segments were recalled, with the uncued segment recalled first and the cued segment recalled second. In the crucial experimental condition, a precue was used so that at the time of encoding (not just at the time of test) participants were led to believe that the critical uncued segment was less important to recall than the segment that was cued. Thus, in the crucial precue condition of Experiment 2, LTS encoding processes were minimized for the critical uncued segment by reducing the participant's assessment of its importance. The manipulations of encoding processes used in both experiments were successful. In Experiment 1, there was a large effect of the switch manipulation and in Experiment 2, performance was better on the cued segment than on the uncued segment even though the uncued segment was recalled first.

A question of primary interest in this study was whether the modified dual-storage version of the perturbation model could account for performance when LTS encoding processes were minimized and, hence, STS processes were isolated as much as possible. These conditions were realized in the crucial switch-trials condition of Experiment 1 and in the uncued segment of the crucial precue condition of Experiment 2. The precuing in both of these conditions encouraged the participants to attend maximally to the cued segment and, thus, ignore maximally the uncued segment. Because the two experiments yielded analogous patterns of results for these critical conditions, we chose to fit the modified perturbation model only to the data from Experiment 2, which included a 0-s-retention interval and more trials per participant in the crucial test condition. It is of most importance to determine whether the STS passive rehearsal parameter *theta* or the LTS encoding parameter *alpha* required adjustment in order to account for memory performance. We found that the perturbation model had no problems predicting the level of performance if we provided for an extra set of eight reactivations, or opportunities for perturbations in STS, occurring at the time of the final recall cue, when the participants had to shift their attention from the cued segment to the uncued segment, which was to be recalled first. With this provision, we were able to account for the levels of performance in the crucial test condition which reduced elaborative encoding processes when we kept the STS perturbation probability *theta* constant at .04 (the value used in previous studies) and decreased only the LTS probability 1 - *alpha*. This finding implies that we were successful in isolating STS passive rehearsal processes and reducing the influence of LTS elaborative encoding. Indeed, we found that the value of 1 - *alpha* that yielded the best fit was .005, which is very close to the minimum value (zero) which eliminates the LTS component. The fact that we did not need to raise the value of *theta* (the perturbation rate or rate of forgetting from STS) suggests that there was no evidence in our study for any more rapid forgetting rate from STS when LTS processes were minimized.

Our conclusion that there is a constant rate of forgetting from STS that is not influenced by the participants' expectancy to recall contrasts sharply with an earlier study by Muter (1980; see also Sebrechts, Marsh, & Seamon, 1989), who reported very rapid forgetting from STS when participants' expectancy to recall after a distractor task was minimized. Muter (1980) developed a variant of the distractor paradigm in which participants recalled target trigrams following a distractor task on a small subset of critical trials. To examine the rate of forgetting from STS, Muter compared critical trials with a 0-s-retention interval to critical trials after a longer interval (e.g., 2 s or 4 s) filled with the distractor task.

Muter (1980) attempted to reduce the effect of LTS processing by leading the participants to expect that they would not be tested for recall of the target trigrams following the distractor task. Participants were led to this expectation in two ways: First, 9-17% of the experimental trials in Muter's study were ones in which participants received practice on the distractor task without a subsequent recall test of the target trigram. These trials with no recall test after distractor activity presumably discouraged LTS active rehearsal processes of the target trigram on any trials in which the distractor task appeared. Second, 78-84% of the experimental trials in his study were "maintenance trials" in which the participants received a trigram, followed by a blank screen, followed by a word prompt which cued recall of the trigram presented at the start of the trial. Because there was no distractor activity, Muter implied that participants were led to use essentially only STS passive rehearsal processes on these trials.

However, we (Healy & Cunningham, 1995) argued that the maintenance trials in Muter's (1980) study led his participants to have an initial high overall expectancy that recall would be requested on a given trial, although they should have a low expectancy to recall on those trials having a distractor task. This high overall recall expectancy by the participants can explain why Muter (1980) found very high performance both on his maintenance trials and on his critical trials occurring after a 0-s-retention interval (which were essentially equivalent to the maintenance trials). We therefore argued that the very rapid rate of forgetting reported by Muter (1980) was an artifact produced by differences in recall expectancy between the critical trials at the 0-s-retention interval and those at the longer intervals having a distractor task. In other words, participants in Muter's (1980) study expected to recall the letters at the 0-s-retention interval but not after the longer intervals of distracting activity so that "delay interval was confounded with expectancy to recall" (Cunningham et al., 1993, p. 683). In a commentary, Muter (1995) himself acknowledged that "Even in Muter's experiments, there was no evidence of very rapid forgetting beyond a two-second retention interval" (p. 9). However, 2 s was in fact the shortest nonzero retention interval used by Muter on the critical trials. Thus, the evidence of very rapid forgetting found by Muter came entirely from the comparison of the 0-s-retention interval critical trials with the 2-s- or longer retention interval critical trials. Hence, Muter's (1980) results are consistent with our conclusion that manipulating recall expectancy influences strength of initial encoding and LTS active rehearsal processes but does not lead to a change in the STS passive rehearsal processes or in the rate of forgetting from STS, which is well described by the *theta* parameter in the perturbation model.

Item Distinctiveness

Although our past research emphasized the manipulation of whole segment information, our most recent research (Cunningham et al., 1998) focused on the manipulation of individual item characteristics within a segment by employing two item manipulations of distinctiveness. These manipulations made an item more distinctive either by highlighting it in red or by deleting it and replacing it with an uninformative red dash. We had been able to explain the full set of findings from our previous studies in terms of the dual-storage version of the perturbation model. However, that version of the perturbation model has no mechanism to account for any facilitation or inhibition of the encoding or rehearsal of an item that has been made distinctive within a segment of known items. Hence, our most recent experiments were intended in part as challenges to the perturbation model. Towards that end and to determine the relative magnitude of any effects of distinctiveness, we also included in these new experiments all the major variables that were present in our past research and that showed robust effects that are well explained by the perturbation model. Specifically, we varied the retention interval separating stimulus presentation from recall; we presented the participants with two four-letter segments of items on each trial with one of the two segments precued for recall; and we used both a fast and a slow rate of stimulus presentation. As in previous studies, the identity of the letters in each segment was kept constant and known in advance by the participants, who had only to learn the order of the letters.

Our first experiment investigated the role of distinctiveness in short-term recall of order information by making one letter of a to-be-recalled four-letter segment more distinctive by highlighting it in red. We compared trials that contained a distinctive letter with those containing no distinctive letter, and we found no overall advantage for the recall of the distinct trials relative to that of the nondistinct trials. In fact, we found that for the first of the two segments, there was depressed performance for distinct trials relative to trials with no distinct letter. When we examined recall performance for the distinct trials only, however, we did find enhanced recall for the distinct letter relative to the other letters on those trials, which were recalled with somewhat less accuracy than were the letters on nondistinct trials. Although the advantage for the distinct letter relative to the other letters on the distinct trials was statistically significant, the proportion of correct recall responses for the distinct letter was only slightly greater than that for the other letters. The manipulation of distinctiveness that we used in this experiment was a standard one. Nevertheless, it is noteworthy that in this experiment involving short-term memory of order information, the size of the effect due to the difference between distinct and nondistinct letters was quite small. To determine whether the small magnitude of the distinctiveness effect was due to the particular manipulation of distinctiveness that we employed, in our next experiment we employed an extreme manipulation of distinctiveness.

In our second experiment, an item from a known list of items was made distinctive by its absence, that is, by deleting it from the list of to-be-recalled items and replacing it with a red dash. Our procedure for testing distinctiveness can be viewed as a hybrid of two previous procedures used frequently in the literature. One of these previous procedures is the missing scan technique developed by Buschke (1963). In the standard missing scan procedure, participants are given a known list of items with one of the items missing. The participants' task is to respond with the item missing from the list. The second previous procedure is found in the literature on the generation effect (see, e.g., Slamecka & Graf, 1978). Generation refers to an operation that a participant performs to complete missing stimulus information from an item in a list. A generation condition, in which participants are provided with a fragment that must be completed (or generated) by the participant, is usually contrasted with a control (read) condition, in which participants are provided with list items that are complete.

In design, our second experiment was analogous to our first, except that the to-be-recalled distinctive letter never appeared during stimulus presentation but was replaced by a red dash. Two types of trials were, thus, included: missing letter and no-missing letter. On a missing letter trial, one of the four to-be-remembered letters was absent. The absent letter was replaced by a red dash. A new procedure was added to assess whether the recall order of a segment was affected by the presence of a symbol, the red dash, signifying a missing letter in the segment. Participants typically write down the letters in the same temporal sequence in which they occur, even though they are not explicitly instructed to do so. In this experiment, the experimenter monitored the participants' responses and recorded the order in which the letters were placed onto the response card.

In agreement with previous studies of the analogous generation effect in long-term serial recall (e.g., Nairne, Riegler, & Serra, 1991), we found an overall disadvantage in serial recall for the segments containing a missing letter. This disadvantage was found for the present letters as well as for the absent letter on missing-letter trials although the disadvantage for the absent letter was greater than that for the present letters. However, performance was significantly depressed for the absent letter only when it occurred in the first segment and only when it occurred in the fourth position. Further, as in our first experiment, the significant effects of distinctiveness which we found on the proportion of correct responses were small in magnitude. There was, though, a significant and large effect of distinctiveness on the output order in which participants recalled the letters. Participants were much more likely to recall the letters in the regular order on trials with no missing letters than on missing letter trials.

Despite its large effect on output order, distinctiveness had only small effects on the proportion of correct recall responses in our two experiments, even in the second experiment in which we used an extreme manipulation of distinctiveness. In contrast, the other variables we tested, which we had also examined in our earlier studies, had the same large effects we found previously. Specifically, participants were much more accurate at the slow presentation rate than at the fast rate; they showed decreasing recall accuracy as retention interval increased; they showed an advantage for the most recent of the two segments they were shown; and they revealed a symmetrical bow-shaped serial position function with advantages for the first and last letter in each segment. All of these findings are consistent with predictions derived from the dual-storage version of the perturbation model.

The perturbation model has no mechanism to single out a specific letter in a segment for either enhanced or decreased encoding or rehearsal. How then can the perturbation model accommodate our findings of enhanced performance for a distinctive letter when stimulus information was augmented in our first experiment and depressed performance for a distinctive letter when stimulus information was severely reduced in our second experiment? The findings concerning output order in our second experiment provide insight that allow us to resolve this question. It is evident that the participants adopted a different response strategy when there was a missing letter because the regular response order was used much less often when there was a missing letter. This observation suggests that during recall output, rather than during stimulus encoding or rehearsal, participants generate the missing letter. Because the encoding and rehearsal of the missing letter are not affected, the perturbation model could easily account for the encoding and rehearsal processes in this situation without any changes. The reduced recall performance for the missing letter and the segment containing it could be due simply to the fact that the missing letter must be generated at the time of the recall test. Can this account also explain the results in the first experiment? Although we did not monitor output order in our first experiment, it seems likely that participants deviated from the regular order on distinct trials at least in some cases by writing down first the distinct letter. Hence, output processes seem to provide a basis for explaining the effects caused by the distinctiveness manipulations used in both experiments. Therefore, some mechanism for the effects of output order is needed in the perturbation model. Indeed, in his newest version of the perturbation model, Estes (1997) has included such a mechanism. In this newest version, perturbations occur during response output as well as during stimulus input. Thus, the perturbation model provides a framework in which we can understand the full range of results that we found in these new experiments, even though it includes no mechanism for any enhancement or disruption of the encoding or rehearsal of a distinctive item.

Conclusions

In our studies, we have shown that the dual-storage version of the perturbation model can account for a wide range of results in studies of immediate memory for order information. The question arises whether the same model can also account for studies involving longer retention intervals. Although the perturbation model was developed to account for immediate memory processes, Nairne (1991) argued that the model can also be applied to situations involving longer delays. In particular, Nairne showed that the single-storage version of the model with just the single parameter *theta* for the perturbation rate could account for the results of his experiments involving the reconstruction of order information about lists of words after a 2 min delay interval filled with a distractor task. The model predicted the observed symmetrical bowed serial position functions as well as the gradually declining positional uncertainty curves for both list selection and placement of a word in a list.

In a subsequent study, Nairne (1992) examined the retention of position information over delay intervals ranging from 30 s to 24 hr, and he compared his observations to predictions based on the perturbation model. In applying the perturbation model to this situation, which spanned both short and long delays, Nairne again used the single-storage version of the model with only the single parameter *theta* for the perturbation rate. However, in effect, he added a second parameter, because he assumed that there was an opportunity for a perturbation once every 6 s in the first 30-s interval but after that interval had elapsed only once every 24 min. In other words, the forgetting rate was very rapid over the interval corresponding to immediate retention but was considerably slower over longer delays. This observation suggests instead that a two-parameter dual-storage model (one parameter for STS and one parameter for LTS) is in fact necessary, as we have argued.

In conclusion, our research has supported the important distinction underlying the buffer model between STS and LTS. Further, it has established that there is a passive rehearsal process maintaining information in STS, which is fixed across a wide range of experimental variables and can be simply described using a single constant parameter value (*theta* = .04) from the perturbation model.

Summary

We review our research on recall of order information, which has addressed the fundamental distinction of Atkinson and Shiffrin's (1968) buffer model between short-term store (STS) and long-term store (LTS). Our guiding theoretical framework has been the perturbation model of immediate memory originally proposed by Estes (1972). In its original form, this model included only a single memory store comparable to STS. However, our findings have documented the need to add a second memory store comparable to LTS and have established a fixed rate of forgetting from STS across changes in LTS, with the forgetting rate described using a single constant parameter value from the perturbation model.

Acknowledgments

This research was supported in part by several faculty research awards from St. Lawrence University to Thomas F. Cunningham and by Army Research Institute Contracts MDA903-86-K-0155, MDA903-90-K-0066, MDA903-93-K-0010, and DASW01-96-K-0010 to the University of Colorado (Alice F. Healy, Principal Investigator).

References

Anderson, N. S. (1960). Poststimulus cuing in immediate memory. *Journal of Experimental Psychology, 60*, 216-221.

Atkinson, R. C., & Shiffrin, R. M. (1968). Human memory: A proposed system and its control processes. In K. W. Spence & J. T. Spence (Eds.), *The psychology of learning and motivation: Advances in research and theory* (Vol. 2, pp. 89-195). New York: Academic Press.

Brown, J. (1954). The nature of set-to-learn and of intramaterial interference in immediate memory. *Quarterly Journal of Experimental Psychology, 6*, 141-148.

Brown, J. (1958). Some tests of the decay theory of immediate memory. *Quarterly Journal of Experimental Psychology, 6*, 12-21.

Buschke, H. (1963). Retention in immediate memory estimated without retrieval. *Science, 140*, 56-57.

Cohen, R. L., & Johansson, B. S. (1967). The activity trace in immediate memory: A re-evaluation. *Journal of Verbal Learning and Verbal Behavior, 6*, 139-143.

Conrad, R. (1967). Interference or decay over short retention intervals? *Journal of Verbal Learning and Verbal Behavior, 6*, 49-54.

Cunningham, T. F., Healy, A. F., Till, R. E., Fendrich, D. W., & Dimitry, C. Z. (1993). Is there really very rapid forgetting from primary memory? The role of expectancy and item importance in short-term recall. *Memory & Cognition, 21*, 671-688.

Cunningham, T. F., Healy, A. F., & Williams, D. M. (1984). Effects of repetition on short-term retention of order information. *Journal of Experimental Psychology: Learning, Memory, and Cognition, 10*, 575-597.

Cunningham, T. F., Marmie, W. R., & Healy, A. F. (1998). The role of item distinctiveness in short-term recall of order information. *Memory & Cognition, 26*, 463-476.

Estes, W. K. (1972). An associative basis for coding and organization in memory. In A. W. Melton & E. Martin (Eds.), *Coding processes in human memory* (pp. 161-190). New York: Halsted Press.

Estes, W. K. (1983, August). *Discussion of papers in the Symposium on Quantitative Models of Memory.* Paper presented at the 16th Annual Mathematical Psychology Meeting, Boulder, CO.

Estes, W. K. (1997). Processes of memory loss, recovery, and distortion. *Psychological Review, 104*, 148-169.

Healy, A. F. (1974). Separating item from order information in short-term memory. *Journal of Verbal Learning and Verbal Behavior, 13*, 644-655.

Healy, A. F., & Cunningham, T. F. (1995). Very rapid forgetting: Reply to Muter. *Memory & Cognition, 23*, 387-392.

Healy, A. F., Fendrich, D. W., Cunningham, T. F., & Till, R. E. (1987). Effects of cuing on short-term retention of order information. *Journal of Experimental Psychology: Learning, Memory, and Cognition, 13*, 413-425.

Hebb, D. O. (1949). *Organization of behavior.* New York: Wiley.

Hebb, D. O. (1961). Distinctive features of learning in the higher animal. In J. F. Delafresnaye (Ed.), *Brain mechanisms and learning* (pp. 37-46). New York: Oxford University Press.

Lee, C. L. (1992). The perturbation model of short-term memory: A review and some further developments. In A. F. Healy, S. M. Kosslyn, & R. M. Shiffrin (Eds.), *From learning processes to cognitive processes: Essays in honor of William K. Estes* (Vol. 2., pp. 119-141). Hillsdale, NJ: Lawrence Erlbaum Associates.

Lee, C. L., & Estes, W. K. (1981). Item and order information in short-term memory: Evidence for multilevel perturbation processes. *Journal of Experimental Psychology: Human Learning and Memory, 7*, 149-169.

Melton, A. W. (1967). Relations between short-term memory, long-term memory and learning. In D. P. Kimble (Ed.), *The organization of recall* (pp. 24-62). New York: The New York Academy of Sciences.

Murdock, B. B. (1974). *Human memory: Theory and data.* New York: Wiley.

Muter, P. (1980). Very rapid forgetting. *Memory & Cognition, 8,* 174-179.

Muter, P. (1995). Very rapid forgetting: Reply to Cunningham, Healy, Till, Fendrich, and Dimitry. *Memory & Cognition, 23,* 383-386.

Nairne, J. S. (1991). Positional uncertainty in long-term memory. *Memory & Cognition, 19,* 332-340.

Nairne, J. S. (1992). The loss of positional certainty in long-term memory. *Psychological Science, 3,* 199-202.

Nairne, J. S., Riegler, G. L., & Serra, M. (1991). Dissociative effects of generation on item and order retention. *Journal of Experimental Psychology: Learning, Memory and Cognition, 17,* 702-709.

Peterson, L. R., & Peterson, M. J. (1959). Short-term retention of individual verbal items. *Journal of Experimental Psychology, 58,* 193-198.

Sebrechts, M. M., Marsh, R. L., & Seamon, J. G. (1989). Secondary memory and very rapid forgetting. *Memory & Cognition, 17,* 693-700.

Shiffrin, R. M. (1975). Short-term store: The basis for a memory system. In F. Restle, R. M. Shiffrin, N. J. Castellan, H. R. Lindman, & D. B. Pisoni (Eds.), *Cognitive theory* (Vol. 1, pp. 193-218). Hillsdale, NJ: Lawrence Erlbaum Associates.

Slamecka, N. J., & Graf, P. (1978). The generation effect: Delineation of a phenomenon. *Journal of Experimental Psychology: Human Learning and Memory, 4,* 592-604.

Chapter 9

Efficiency in Acquisition and Short-Term Memory: Study-Test-rest Presentation Programs and Learning Difficulty

Chizuko Izawa
Tulane University, U. S. A.

On the 30th anniversary of the Atkinson-Shiffrin Model, which signaled the greatest advancement in our understanding of short-term memory (STM) processes since Ebbinghaus' (1885) *Ueber das Gedaechtnis*, it seems fitting to consider the efficient use of time in achieving optimal acquisition and retention. Learning efficiency requires the effective use of time.

"Time is of the essence" (Stephen Acre, 1941). For many centuries, scholars, literary figures, statesmen, and even folk wisdom have articulated their views of "time." According to Seneca, "*Omnia aliena sunt, tempus tantum nostrum est* [Nothing is ours except time]" (A.D. 64*)*. Likewise, Eastern civilization highly values time. A Chinese proverb, for example, asserts, "*Cuen jin nan mai cuen guang yin* [An inch of gold will not buy an inch of time]!"

Yet, the concept of time has been often elusive, back in the 5th century, for example, St. Augustine was at a loss about defining time. The total time hypothesis (TTH; e.g., Bugelski, 1962; Murdock, 1960) seems similarly elusive, as are the interactions of time factors in many learning and memory processes.

The Original Total Time Hypothesis (TTH)

While the cognitive revolution promoted research in the areas of information processing, mental representations, structures, types, and categories of memory systems (*cf.* Estes, 1991; Eysenck, 1990; Hoffman & Deffenbacher, 1992), it propelled research on acquisition and relevant processes to the periphery. Thus, the time is more than ripe to fill this hiatus and to revisit TTH (total time hypothesis) in an effort to assess its boundaries: When does it hold, and when does it break down? We must evaluate these issues in view of the numerous studies that either support (e.g., Newman, 1964; Postman & Goggin, 1966,

165

Slamecka, 1969) or contradict it (e.g., Hintzman, 1970; Underwood, 1970). For a comprehensive review of the literature, see, for example, Izawa and Hayden (1993).

According to TTH, total time X (e.g., minutes) is required to learn list Y (e.g., words/concepts), irrespective of how time X is used or programmed. Therefore, TTH directly challenges the fundamental premise of increasing efficiency in learning and retention, that is, achieving more than Y (Y+) within a given time X, or requiring less time X (X-) to learn list Y.

In contrast, Izawa's study-test-rest (S-T-r[1]) presentation program hypothesis, based on a growing body of evidence gleaned over the past three decades, maintains that acquisition and retention are functions of the scheduling of study (S, a presentation of both cue and target terms of Pair v (A_v-B_v) in instances of cued-recall/paired-associate learning, PAL), test (unreinforced T, a presentation of the cue term alone, A_v-? without feedback), and rest (r) item/event presentation programs. According to this hypothesis, an investment of time X may produce varied degrees of learning, depending on the programming of S, T, and r presentations. Optimal programming presents an opportunity for more efficient learning!

The difference between these opposing theories is clear: The quantity, and not the quality, of time matters to TTH, whereas quality is the critical issue for the S-T-r presentation program hypothesis. In addition, alternative hypotheses exist to TTH and the S-T-r presentation program hypothesis: They include the frequency and duration hypotheses (Izawa, 1993a, 1993b, in press). At this point, however, we need to examine the elusive nature of total time, a key issue for TTH.

Total Time Effects Are Pervasive

Clarification of the "time" factor in TTH (total time hypothesis), as well as other relevant psychological phenomena, is necessary. Total time effects have frequently been misinterpreted: Time elements are often tacitly involved, or go unnoticed, which leads to incorrect assessments and erroneous conclusions. For example, Cooper and Pantle's (1967) extensive review of the total time hypothesis was no exception (e.g., see Izawa, 1993a).

The "total time" in TTH is explicitly defined as "learning" or study (S) time (e.g., Bugelski, 1962), nothing more, nothing less. Thus, Bugelski's total time hypothesis can be restated as the total study-time hypothesis (TSTH, *cf.*

---

[1] A lower case r indicates rest, because r events are nonspecific, and are not Experimenter-controlled, as, for example, S and T, and differ distinctively from a clearly defined event, notwithstanding that some rest activities are Experimenter-determined.

Izawa, 1993a, 1993b, in press; Izawa & Hayden, 1993). All uses of time which do not constitute S (study) time are, therefore, irrelevant to TTH.

In addressing the use of inappropriate total time effects, it should be noted that the S (S time) effect has attracted a variety of labels in various learning and memory processes. A few examples below will suffice. There is a critical need here for clear distinctions among Study (S), unreinforced Test (T) (with no feedback), and rest (r) effects.

Frequency/Repetition/Familiarity/Rehearsal/Priming Effects and the Total Time Effects

Centuries before the founding of experimental psychology, people recognized the dictum, *"Usus promptum facit"* [Practice makes perfect] (e. g., Christopher, 1766; Crabbe, 1810; Dickens, 1870). Surely, Ebbinghaus (1885), the first empirical investigator of human learning, experimentally demonstrated this long-recognized fact: the more S trials, the better the performance. This finding has been replicated numerous times since. Greater practice forges greater familiarity with the study materials, thereby generating the frequency or repetition effect.

For example, compare the following two conditions: In one, Presentation Program 9.1, learners studied the material during one S cycle, in which each item of the n paired-associates in list Y was presented one at a time (say, at a 2 sec rate) before the T (test) cycle, whereas in the second, Program 9.2, learners studied five times. The independent variable here is the frequency of S:

$$S\ T \tag{9.1}$$
$$SSSSS\ T \tag{9.2}$$

In general, findings reveal that learning in Presentation Program 9.2 exceeds learning in Program 9.1, thereby demonstrating the S frequency/repetition effect. However, this interpretation is only partially correct, in that the same results can easily be interpreted as supporting TTH at an indirect and relaxed level[2]: since Program 9.2 had five times as much S time vis-à-vis Program 1 ($2n$ vs. $10n$ sec), one might argue the greater the total S time, the greater the learning!

Exactly the same line of reasoning applies to the familiarity, rehearsal, repetition, priming and other relevant effects. The greater the consumption of total rehearsal or priming (analogous to S) time, the better the memory! In sum,

---

[2] Indirect and relaxed, because the strict TTH must be examined within a constant total time. The property herein discussed is inferred from TTHs: The greater the total time, the greater the learning/performance.

the frequency, repetition, rehearsal, priming and other relevant effects are all inseparably confounded by total time effects.

The Presentation Duration Effects and the Total Time Effects

The S (study) time, or presentation duration effect, has been similarly well established. For instance, suppose that each S trial was presented at a 1 sec rate in Presentation Program 9.3, for a total of three S cycles in one condition, as compared to a 3 sec exposure rate in Program 9.4. Note that the horizontal spacing of the S cycles corresponds to the groups' exposure rates for each item (1 vs. 3 sec). The independent variable here is the presentation duration rate for each item in List Y.

$$
\begin{array}{lll}
\text{1 sec condition:} & \underline{\text{SSS}}\ \text{T} & (9.3) \\
\text{3 sec condition:} & \underline{\text{S}\quad \text{S}\quad \text{S}}\ \ \text{T} & (9.4)
\end{array}
$$

The general findings indicate that learners in the condition with the 3 sec exposure rate outperform those given a 1 sec exposure rate, the positive duration effect. Indeed, this demonstrates that the longer the S duration, the better the learning!

However, this duration effect can also be accounted for by TSTH (total study-time hypothesis), since the total S time expended for n-items in List Y is 1 x $n = n$ sec S time (Prog. 9.3). Compare that with the same n S items presented at a 3 sec rate, consuming 3 x $n = 3n$ sec (Prog. 9.4). The superior performance of the 3-sec presentation as opposed to the 1-sec presentation might, therefore, be attributed to longer total S time in addition to the exposure duration effect: The longer the total time, the better the performance.

Distributed (Spaced) Practice or Spacing Effects and the Total Time Effects

The distributed practice effect may be demonstrated by comparing Presentation Programs 9.5 and 9.6, which depict, respectively, massed and spaced practice, the latter alone containing r (rest) between S cycles:

$$
\begin{array}{lll}
\text{Massed Practice:} & S_1\ S_2\ S_3, \ldots, S_n\ T & (9.5) \\
\text{Spaced Practice:} & S_1\ r_1\ S_2\ r_2\ S_3\ r_3, \ldots, r_{n-1}\ S_n\ T & (9.6)
\end{array}
$$

The independent variable here is the presence or absence of an r (rest) period between S cycles.

From clear comparisons of Programs 9.5 and 9.6, spaced practice requires a much longer total time than massed practice does. More precisely, considering that nS cycles are given successively with no r (rest) periods in massed practice (Prog. 9.5), the time required was nd sec where d sec are expended for each S cycle, n in all cycles. In contrast, under spaced practice (Prog. 9.6), we need $(n - 1)r$ sec additional time because of the $n-1$ rest periods afforded between adjacent S trials, r seconds each, thus the total sec in real time is $nd + (n - 1)r$. Therefore, the superiority of spaced practice may be attributed to TTH at an indirect and relaxed level: the greater the total time (spaced Prog. 9.6), the better the performance (compared to massed Prog. 9.5).

However, the above rationale is incorrect, and TTH is misapplied, because "time" in TTH is defined as S time only, not including time spent on unspecified activities that occur during an r (rest) period. Refer to Programs 9.5 and 9.6 again: Both massed and spaced practice conditions have exactly the same amount of total S time, nd sec (r periods being irrelevant). Consequently, TTH must predict equal performances for both. This prediction contradicts the prevailing data (e.g., Hintzman, 1974; Izawa, 1968, 1970a, 1971a, 1988, 1992a, 1992b).

If TTH were to accommodate the empirical superiority of spaced practice, it would have to be modified to include time other than just S time, for example, the r period (Izawa, 1993a). Once we broaden the original definition of S time, a host of activities that may occur between S trials (including test, T, trials) must also be considered. To differentiate between the original TTH and a variety of modified versions, let us henceforth change TTH to TSTH (total study time hypothesis), and let us use the designation TT(+r)H when including r (rest) time.

Contamination by time effects has been widespread. Portions of Izawa's 30-year-long research on study-test-rest (S-T-r) presentation programs are no exception. For example, many comparisons were made among different Integers j and k in conditions derived from Presentation Program 9.7:

$$S_1S_2 \ldots S_j\, T_1T_2 \ldots T_k \qquad (9.7)$$

including Condition S vs. ST, SS vs. SST, SSS vs. SSST, S vs. $ST_1T_2...T_k$ (e.g., Izawa, 1968, 1969, 1970b, 1970c, 1971b, 1988; Izawa & Patterson, 1989). Here, the superiority of Condition ST over Condition S, for instance, may be partially attributable to the greater total time in the former despite the presence of other pertinent factors.

These few examples are in effect simple transformations of a version of TTH at an indirect and relaxed level. If correct, these and relevant phenomena argue for careful reconsideration of the original TTH (now referred to as TSTH).

However, note that the theories of major human learning phenomena outlined above, including the frequency-, repetition-, familiarity-, rehearsal-, priming-, presentation duration-/rate- and distributed-practice-effects, as well as some of the S-T-r program effects that seem to support TTH, are not only indirect, but are also only detectable at a global level. In sum, for rigorous inquiries, these theories are less precise than we desire. What we need, therefore, is more direct testing of this hypothesis.

Total Time Hypothesis (TTH): A New Approach and Further Examination and Modification

One way to systematically examine TSTH (total study time hypothesis) is to strictly control all temporal variables, independent of the frequency and duration of S (study) presentations. Here, S duration and frequency become salient experimental variables. It is crucial to isolate these effects from the influence of total S time. This can be accomplished by holding the total S time strictly constant and varying only the frequency and duration of S, with all other temporal intervals (r and T) held constant in each of the presentation programs (Izawa, 1993a).

The effects of r (rest) in the S-T-r presentation program hypothesis have already been investigated extensively at both empirical and theoretical levels, both with respect to the item and the list (e.g., Izawa, 1970a, 1971a) in a large family of S-T-r presentation programs derived from Program 9.8 (e.g., Izawa, 1968, 1970a, 1971b, 1976, 1988, 1992; Izawa & Hayden, 1993 for reviews). These programs provided the bulk of compelling evidence that r effects enhance acquisition and retention. Thus, Izawa (e.g., 1993a, 1993b, in press) concentrated on varying the program effects of the other principal variables, S and T. Throughout these systematic investigations, the learning materials were held constant by using the same CVC-CVC paired-associates, which were based on extant norms (*cf.* Izawa, 1993a).

Considering the constant total S time among the seven conditions in two experiments run simultaneously by Izawa (1993a), the TSTH and all other variants of Bugelski's TTH predicted identical performances among the conditions, but that identity turned out to be quite limited in scope. The data were far more in line with Izawa's S-T-r presentation program hypothesis, which predicted differential results as a function of how S, T, and r events were programmed.

Within these two experiments, the learner's use of time was not limited to the S and r intervals discussed so far; it also included time for testing (T). As often noted by Izawa already (e.g., Izawa, 1992, 1993a, 1993b; Carrier & Pashler, 1992; Rose, 1992), T trials control both acquisition and retention in major ways. For a summary see, for example, Izawa (1992a, in press) in which the general repetitive presentation pattern is applied as in Presentation Program 9.8:

$$S_1 S_2 ... S_i \, r_1 r_2 ... r_j \, T_1 T_2 ... T_k \, r_1 r_2 ... r_m \, T_1 T_2 ... T_n, \; \cdots \quad (9.8)$$

where subscripts indicate i-, j-, k-, m-, and n-th cycle ($i \geq 1$; j, k, m, $n \geq 0$), respectively. For example, we could fill the time with successive Ts (tests) following a S (study) trial (by letting $i = 1$, $k = 7$, and j, m, $n = 0$, respectively) as in Presentation Program 9.9:

$$STTTTTTT \qquad (9.9)$$

which became Condition 1 (Izawa, 1992a); eight other conditions were also generated by varying the number of cycles j, k, m, n of T and r (=N, neutral) trials per repetition unit of S-T-r programs. They were Conditions STrTrTrT, STrrTrrT, STrrrrrT, STrrrrrr, STTTrrrr, SrrTTTrr, and SrrrrTTT.

The efficiency of learning was controlled by the pattern of real time programming following each S, and the conditions differed significantly despite both total S and real times being held strictly constant among the nine conditions. Izawa's findings (1992a, 1992b) uncovered the forgetting-prevention effects of positive spaced-T, even when Ts were interspersed with rests (Conditions STrTrTrT, STrrTrrT, and STrrrrrT).

Given the highly significant positive effects of unreinforced Ts, Izawa (1993b) then varied the frequency and duration of Ts while holding the total S, r, as well as T times constant among another set of seven conditions in two experiments conducted simultaneously. Within these conditions, the family of all TTHs (original/modified) predicted identical performances, but the data again contradicted this prediction, and lent stronger support for the S-T-r presentation program hypothesis.

Next, Izawa (in press) co-varied the frequency and duration of S and T presentations, while still holding the total S, T, and r times constant, respectively, among the 10 conditions in three experiments. Again, the entire TTH family expected identical performances from all 10 conditions in the three experiments. But, once again, highly significant differences were found in both STM and LTM. These complex yet orderly data could be accounted for by the S-T-r presentation program hypothesis; it expected different results from different S, T, and r programs.

However, a small subset of experimental conditions were manipulated to maximally favor TTHs; this subset was the item-repetition program in Izawa's past experiments (1993a, 1993b, in press). When analyses were limited to the four conditions under this particular program (item-repetition program), TTHs were supportable. In the overall analyses, however, TTHs were hardly supported in any of the above three investigations.

One main goal in the current three experiments, which were newly designed and executed specifically for this chapter, was to pursue the special phenomenon within the item-repetition program of Izawa (in press). Throughout 10 experiments in a series of four investigations (Izawa 1993a, 1993b, in press and current chapter, with 2, 2, 3, and 3 experiments, respectively), there are

S and T Presentation Programs Condition (Name, Rate)	Study (S) and Test (T) Phases $S_{(1)}$	$T_{(1)}$	. . .	$S_{(10)}$	$T_{(10)}$
Experiment 1, S+T List-Repetition Program					
1 (ST, 6 sec)	S_1	T_1^*	. . .	S_{10}	T_{10}^*
2 (SSTT, 3 sec)	S_1 S_2	T_1 T_2^*	. . .	S_{19} S_{20}	T_{19} T_{20}^*
3 (SSSTTT, 2 sec)	S_1 S_2 S_3	T_1 T_2 T_3^*	. . .	S_{28} S_{29} S_{30}	T_{28} T_{29} T_{30}^*
4 (SSSSSSTTTTTT, 1 sec)	S_1 S_2 S_3 S_4 S_5 S_6	T_1 T_2 T_3 T_4 T_5 T_6^*	. . .	S_{55} S_{56} S_{57} S_{58} S_{59} S_{60}	T_{55} T_{56} T_{57} T_{58} T_{59} T_{60}^*
Experiment 2, S+T Item-Repetition Program					
1 (S'T', 6 sec)	S'_1	$T'_1{}^*$	. . .	S'_{10}	$T'_{10}{}^*$
5 (S'S'T'T', 3 sec)	S'_1 S'_2	T'_1 $T'_2{}^*$	. . .	S'_{19} S'_{20}	T'_{19} $T'_{20}{}^*$
6 (S'S'S'T'T'T', 2 sec)	S'_1 S'_2 S'_3	T'_1 T'_2 $T'_3{}^*$	. . .	S'_{28} S'_{29} S'_{30}	T'_{28} T'_{29} $T'_{30}{}^*$
7 (S'S'S'S'S'S'T'T'T'T'T'T', 1 sec)	S'_1 S'_2 S'_3 S'_4 S'_5 S'_6	T'_1 T'_2 T'_3 T'_4 T'_5 $T'_6{}^*$	. . .	S'_{55} S'_{56} S'_{57} S'_{58} S'_{59} S'_{60}	T'_{55} T'_{56} T'_{57} T'_{58} T'_{59} $T'_{60}{}^*$
Experiment 3, S/T Alternation Program					
1 (ST, 6 sec)	S_1	T_1^*	. . .	S_{10}	T_{10}^*
8 (STST, 3 sec)	S_1 T_1	S_2 T_2^*	. . .	S_{19} T_{19}	S_{20} T_{20}^*
9 (STSTST, 2 sec)	S_1 T_1 S_2	T_2 S_3 T_3^*	. . .	S_{28} T_{28} S_{29}	T_{29} S_{30} T_{30}^*
10 (STSTSTSTSTST, 1 sec)	S_1 T_1 S_2 T_2 S_3 T_3	S_4 T_4 S_5 T_5 S_6 T_6^*	. . .	S_{55} T_{55} S_{56} T_{56} S_{57} T_{57}	S_{58} T_{58} S_{59} T_{59} S_{60} T_{60}^*

T*= Target T
S = Study trial presented by the S list-repetition program
T = Test trial presented by the T list-repetition program
S' = Study trial presented by the S item-repetition program
T' = Test trial presented by the T item-repetition program

FIG. 9.1. Izawa's (in press) Study-Test-rest (S-T-r) acquisition presentation programs for 10 conditions in three experiments. Total times of S, T, S+T, and r trials were held constant.

several common features, differing only in S-T-r presentation programs. These common features are:

1. The learning materials, a list of 12 CVC-CVC paired-associates (except for current Experiment 3, which used digits as the targets, B-terms of the pairs, and the same CVCs as the cues, A-terms). List-length $n = 12$.

2. Within each experiment, the total S, T, S+T and r times were, respectively, identical except for two conditions in current Experiments 2 and 3, where 50% longer total times were included.

3. Within each investigation, all conditions in all experiments were conducted simultaneously, in order to control the participant-variables; 1-2 common control condition(s) was(were) used.

4. For varied S, T, or both phases of Izawa (1993a, 1993b, & in press), or the current Conditions 1-4, 7-8, each S or T phase lasted 72 sec. With this restriction, S or T presentation frequencies and durations were inversely related; during one S (or T) phase of 72 sec, each S (or T) item was presented 1, 2, 3, or 6 times/cycles, respectively, at the 6, 3, 2, or 1 sec presentation rates.

5. In all conditions in all of the four investigations, S and T phases were administered alternately until the 10th set was completed, and this was followed by an interpolated task and two unannounced successive delayed T cycles. See Presentation Program 9.10 design:

$$S_{(1)}T_{(1)}S_{(2)}T_{(2)}S_{(3)}T_{(3)},...,S_{(10)}T_{(10)}$$

$$--- <\text{Int. task}> --- T_{d1}T_{d2}. \qquad (9.10)$$

Through presentation Program 9.10 and Figure 9.1, Izawa (in press) investigated 10 conditions, run simultaneously. Of special interest in the present experiments was a comparison between programs of S and T co-varied (S+T) list- and item-repetition at a fast (1 sec) presentation rate (Cond. 4 vs. 7). In the continuing current series of 3 experiments, a clear distinction among S (study) and T (test) *items*, *cycles*, and *phases* is essential.

An S (study) *item* is the presentation of both cue and target terms of a pair (A_j-B_j for Pair$_j$) for learning, or the presentation of the cue term alone as a T (test) *item* (A_j-?) where the participant is asked to supply the target, B_j. An S (or T) *cycle* involves one presentation of all S (or T) items in the list (A_j-B_j for an S, and for A_j-? for a T, $1 \leq j \leq n$, list length here $n = 12$), one S (or T) item at a time. An S (or T) *phase* is the largest presentation unit, and is defined as a 72 sec S (or T) period in Izawa (in press) and in the current Conditions 1, 2, 3, 4, 7, and 8 (Exps. 1, 2, & 3), and as a 108 sec period in Conditions 5, 6, 9, and 10 (Exps. 2 & 3). The *phase* is differentiated from the cycle by a parenthetical subscript. For example, S_1 indicates the first study *cycle*, whereas $T_{(2)}$, the

S(1) Phase			T(1) Phase		
S_1-Cycle	S_2-Cycle	S_3-Cycle	T_1-Cycle	T_2-Cycle	T_3-Cycle
$A_1 - B_1$	$A_2 - B_2$	$A_6 - B_6$	$A_8 - ?$	$A_n - ?$	$A_j - ?$
$A_2 - B_2$	$A_j - B_j$	$A_n - B_n$	$A_5 - ?$	$A_{12} - ?$	$A_1 - ?$
$A_3 - B_3$	$A_5 - B_5$	$A_j - B_j$	$A_n - ?$	$A_j - ?$	$A_{10} - ?$
.	.	.	.	.	.
.	.	.	.	.	.
$A_j - B_j$	$A_n - B_n$	$A_3 - B_3$	$A_9 - ?$	$A_7 - ?$	$A_n - ?$
.	.	.	.	.	.
.	.	.	.	.	.
$A_n - B_n$	$A_9 - B_9$	$A_{10} - B_{10}$	$A_j - ?$	$A_4 - ?$	$A_{11} - ?$

FIG. 9.2. Schema of list-repetition presentation for an n-item list cued-recall or paired-associate learning (PAL) for the first S ($S_{(1)}$) and T ($T_{(1)}$) phases, used in Condition 1 (SSSTTT) of Experiment 1, where the list-length $n = 12$ (single item presentation per cycle with multiple cycles per phase).

S'S'S'T'T'T' (Cond. 2, 2 sec rate)		S'S'S'S'S'S'T'T'T'T'T'T' (Cond. 4, 1 sec rate)	
S' Cycle	T' Cycle	S' Cycle	T' Cycle
$A_1 - B_1$	$A_j - ?$	$A_1 - B_1$ $A_1 - B_1$	$A_j - ?$ $A'_j - ?$
$A_1 - B_1$	$A_j - ?$	$A_1 - B_1$ $A_1 - B_1$	$A'_j - ?$ $A'_j - ?$
$A_1 - B_1$	$A_j - ?$	$A_1 - B_1$ $A_1 - B_1$	$A'_j - ?$ $A'_j - ?$
$A_2 - B_2$	$A_7 - ?$	$A_2 - B_2$ $A_2 - B_2$	$A_7 - ?$ $A_7 - ?$
$A_2 - B_2$	$A_7 - ?$	$A_2 - B_2$ $A_2 - B_2$	$A_7 - ?$ $A_7 - ?$
$A_2 - B_2$	$A_7 - ?$	$A_2 - B_2$ $A_2 - B_2$	$A_7 - ?$ $A_7 - ?$
.	.	.	.
.	.	.	.
.	.	.	.
$A_j - B_j$	$A_n - ?$	$A_j - B_j$ $A'_j - B'_j$	$A_n - ?$ $A_n - ?$
$A_j - B_j$	$A_n - ?$	$A'_j - B'_j$ $A'_j - B'_j$	$A_n - ?$ $A_n - ?$
$A_j - B_j$	$A_n - ?$	$A'_j - B'_j$ $A'_j - B'_j$	$A_n - ?$ $A_n - ?$
.	.	.	.
.	.	.	.
.	.	.	.
$A_n - B_n$	$A_4 - ?$	$A_n - B_n$ $A_n - B_n$	$A_4 - ?$ $A_4 - ?$
$A_n - B_n$	$A_4 - ?$	$A_n - B_n$ $A_n - B_n$	$A_4 - ?$ $A_4 - ?$
$A_n - B_n$	$A_4 - ?$	$A_n - B_n$ $A_n - B_n$	$A_4 - ?$ $A_4 - ?$

FIG. 9.3. Schema of item-repetition presentation for n-item list paired-associate learning (PAL) for the first S ($S_{(1)}$) and T ($T_{(1)}$) phases in Conditions 2 (S'S'S'T'T'T') and 4 (S'S'S'S'S'S'T'T'T'T'T'T') in Experiment 1. List-length $n = 12$ (multiple item presentations per cycle, one cycle per phase, primes indicate the item-repetition program).

second test *phase*. This distinction is important: One S (or T) phase may have more than one S (or T) cycle depending on the presentation rate.

For example, in Condition 1, Experiment 1, there were 3 S (or T) cycles per 1 S (or T) phase with the 2 sec presentation rate. See Fig. 9.2 for the S+T list-repetition program (a single item presentation per cycle, with multiple cycles per phase), a time-honored list-repetition program over a century. For other examples, see Fig. 9.1 (Izawa's in press design).

Izawa (in press) introduced a novel S+T item-repetition program, in which each S or T phase had only one S or T cycle, but each S or T item was successively repeated for a specified number of times to fill the 72 sec duration. In a 2 sec presentation condition, for example, each item was repeated 3 times successively, as seen in the first column of Fig. 9.3 (Exp. 1, Cond. 2), a total of 6 sec elapsed before proceeding to the next item of the list. For Condition 4, each item was repeated 6 times successively at 1 sec rate (multiple item-presentation per cycle, a single cycle per phase; right column, Fig. 9.3). The items presented under the S+T item-repetition program are identified by primes (S' & T').

The S+T item-repetition program was created for four reasons: (*a*) In order to favor TTH, each item was repeated multiple times (for a total of 6 sec) to equalize all item-repetition conditions in current Experiment 1 (& in Izawa's Exp. 2, in press). For example, using a memory drum, it would not matter whether each item was presented three times successively at a 2 sec rate or was presented 6 times in succession at a 1 sec rate (Conds. 2 vs. 4, Fig. 9.3) because the presentations are technically similar, and the total time is identical. (*b*) On the other hand, blinking advertising signs, for example, attract more attention than the ones which do not. What effects do these presentation methods produce upon learning and retention? (*c*) Notice also: When seeking to commit a new item to memory (e. g., foreign words, name, telephone number, ID), our natural strategy is to repeat it a few times to ourselves. (*d*) Adult learning of tens of thousands of paired-associates in 5 languages (*cf*. Izawa, 1989b) is maximized by the item-repetition program, rather than by the traditional list-repetition program that is pervasive in laboratories. The soundness of the item-repetition program in difficult learning situations is indeed supported by real-life events.

Experiments 1, 2, and 3

Findings of theoretical and empirical importance require replication, especially those which could help to rectify the nation's educational deficits (*cf*. Izawa & Hayden, 1993; Stevenson, Chen, & Lee, 1993). What was missing in the previous series of investigations was the effects of learning difficulties. Can the phenomena unveiled earlier with difficult learning materials (e.g., Izawa, in press) hold for intermediate to easy learning materials and situations? Efficient learning strategies may depend heavily on learning difficulty level. If so, our theoretical interests, that is, the effects of total time, S-T-r programs, presentation duration and frequency, and relevant effects must be examined across the spectrum of difficulty. This was done in Experiments 1, 2, and 3, conducted concurrently in this chapter.

Moreover, Izawa's (in press) 1-sec S+T item-repetition condition, S'S'S'S'S'S'T'T'T'T'T', requires serious consideration: A highly unstable zigzag response pattern was displayed over the 6 repetitive T's. There are three possible explanations: (1) participant variability, (2) a fast presentation rate, or (3) the difficulty of the learning task (12 CVC-CVC pairs with low to intermediate meaningfulness/association values, which might have been too difficult for participants fresh out of high school). Each combination thereof directly relates to learning difficulty.

To examine the effects of these critical factors, three new experiments with a total of 10 conditions were conducted simultaneously. (4) The fourth issue addressed the effect of expanding the total time factor (small vs. large), which is also relevant to learning difficulty.

Experiment 1: Participant Variable--Participants' Experiences in a Difficult Learning Situation

In Experiment 1, a list of 12 CVC-CVC pairs by Izawa (1993a, 1993b, in press) was used in all four conditions: with 2 and 1 sec presentation rates under both list- and item-repetition (differentiated by primes) programs. Conditions 1, 2, 3, and 4 were programmed as: SSSTTT, S'S'S'T'T'T', SSSSSSTTTTTT, and S'S'S'S'S'S'T'T'T'T'T'T', holding the 72 sec S (study) and T (test) phases constant, respectively, among all conditions (Prog. 9.10).

The naïve freshmen in Izawa's (in press, Figs. 3 & 4) 1 sec item-repetition Condition S'S'S'S'S'S'T'T'T'T'T' complained vehemently that the pace was too fast, and was forcing them to skip some Ts, often every other T. This pervasive post-experimental report corresponds to the freshmen's response pattern; extreme fluctuations from one T to the next over the repetitive 6 T's. Is this erratic zigzag response pattern general enough to be replicable? Or, does it reflect an idiosyncratic aversion attributable to the naïveté of the young and inexperienced? To examine this point in each of the current experiments, we sought out psychology majors (2.5-3.5 years older than Izawa's in press participants), highly experienced in verbal learning experiments.

More importantly, if this instability was idiosyncratic, how about other major findings by Izawa utilizing the same freshmen? Are they also idiosyncratic, or generalizable? To learn more, four of her conditions were replicated with *experienced* subjects in Experiment 1, see Fig. 9.4. In all current experiments, conditions with *odd* numbers were run under the list-repetition

FIG. 9.4.

S and T Presentation Programs Condition (Name, Rate)	Study (S) and Test (T) Phases				
	$S_{(1)}$	$T_{(1)}$	⋯	$S_{(10)}$	$T_{(10)}$
S+T List-Repetition Program					
1 (SSSTTT, 2 sec)	$S_1\ S_2\ S_3$	$T_1\ T_2\ T_3^*$	⋯		
3 (SSSSSSTTTTTT, 1.5 sec)	$S_1\ S_2\ S_3\ S_4\ S_5\ S_6$	$T_1\ T_2\ T_3\ T_4\ T_5\ T_6^*$	⋯	$S_{55}\ S_{56}\ S_{57}\ S_{58}\ S_{59}\ S_{60}$	$T_{55}\ T_{56}\ T_{57}\ T_{58}\ T_{59}\ T_{60}^*$
5 (SSSSSSTTTTTT, 1.5 sec)	$S_1\ S_2\ S_3\ S_4\ S_5\ S_6$	$T_1\ T_2\ T_3\ T_4\ T_5\ T_6^*$	⋯	$S_{55}\ S_{56}\ S_{57}\ S_{58}\ S_{59}\ S_{60}$	$T_{55}\ T_{56}\ T_{57}\ T_{58}\ T_{59}\ T_{60}^*$
7 (SSSSSSTTTTTT, 1 sec)	$S_1\ S_2\ S_3\ S_4\ S_5\ S_6$	$T_1\ T_2\ T_3\ T_4\ T_5\ T_6^*$	⋯	$S_{55}\ S_{56}\ S_{57}\ S_{58}\ S_{59}\ S_{60}$	$T_{55}\ T_{56}\ T_{57}\ T_{58}\ T_{59}\ T_{60}^*$
9 (SSSSSSTTTTTT, 1.5 sec)	$S_1\ S_2\ S_3\ S_4\ S_5\ S_6$	$T_1\ T_2\ T_3\ T_4\ T_5\ T_6^*$	⋯	$S_{55}\ S_{56}\ S_{57}\ S_{58}\ S_{59}\ S_{60}$	$T_{55}\ T_{56}\ T_{57}\ T_{58}\ T_{59}\ T_{60}^*$
S+T Item-Repetition Program					
2 (SSSTTT, 2 sec)	$S'_1\ S'_2\ S'_3$	$T'_1\ T'_2\ T'_3{}^*$	⋯		
4 (S'S'S'S'S'S'TTTTTTT, 1 sec)	$S'_1\ S'_2\ S'_3\ S'_4\ S'_5\ S'_6$	$T'_1\ T'_2\ T'_3\ T'_4\ T'_5\ T'_6{}^*$	⋯	$S'_{55}\ S'_{56}\ S'_{57}\ S'_{58}\ S'_{59}\ S'_{60}$	$T'_{55}\ T'_{56}\ T'_{57}\ T'_{58}\ T'_{59}\ T'_{60}{}^*$
6 (S'S'S'S'S'S'TTTTTTT, 1.5 sec)	$S'_1\ S'_2\ S'_3\ S'_4\ S'_5\ S'_6$	$T'_1\ T'_2\ T'_3\ T'_4\ T'_5\ T'_6{}^*$	⋯	$S'_{55}\ S'_{56}\ S'_{57}\ S'_{58}\ S'_{59}\ S'_{60}$	$T'_{55}\ T'_{56}\ T'_{57}\ T'_{58}\ T'_{59}\ T'_{60}{}^*$
8 (S'S'S'S'S'S'TTTTTTT, 1 sec)	$S'_1\ S'_2\ S'_3\ S'_4\ S'_5\ S'_6$	$T'_1\ T'_2\ T'_3\ T'_4\ T'_5\ T'_6{}^*$	⋯	$S'_{55}\ S'_{56}\ S'_{57}\ S'_{58}\ S'_{59}\ S'_{60}$	$T'_{55}\ T'_{56}\ T'_{57}\ T'_{58}\ T'_{59}\ T'_{60}{}^*$
10 (S'S'S'S'S'S'TTTTTTT, 1.5 sec)	$S'_1\ S'_2\ S'_3\ S'_4\ S'_5\ S'_6$	$T'_1\ T'_2\ T'_3\ T'_4\ T'_5\ T'_6{}^*$	⋯	$S'_{55}\ S'_{56}\ S'_{57}\ S'_{58}\ S'_{59}\ S'_{60}$	$T'_{55}\ T'_{56}\ T'_{57}\ T'_{58}\ T'_{59}\ T'_{60}{}^*$

T^* = Target T
S = Study trial presented by the S list-repetition program
T = Test trial presented by the T list-repetition program
S' = Study trial presented by the S item-repetition program
T' = Test trial presented by the T item-repetition program

Experiment 1 with Conditions 1, 2, 3, 4
Experiment 2 with Conditions 3, 4, 5, 6
Experiment 3 with Conditions 7, 8, 9, 10

FIG. 9.4. Ten simultaneous Study-Test-rest (S-T-r) presentation programs for Experiments 1, 2, and 3; Conditions 3 and 4 served as base-line for both Experiments 1 and 2.

program, and those with *even* numbers, under the item-repetition program.

Thus, Conditions 1 (SSSTTT) and 3 (SSSSSSTTTTTT) were run with the list-repetition program at 2 sec (Fig. 9.2) and 1 sec presentation rates, respectively, in which each item was presented once per cycle, with 3 and 6 S and T cycles per each S and T phase under Program 9.10. In contrast, each item in Conditions 2 (S'S'S'T'T'T') and 4 (S'S'S'S'S'S'T'T'T'T'T'T') was presented repetitively 3 and 6 times (Fig. 9.3) with one S or T cycle per S and T phase, while maintaining the same durations and frequencies as in Conditions 1 and 3, respectively (Fig. 9.4). Note that the total times of the S and T phases were identical for the first four conditions, and that their durations and S and T frequencies were inversely related.

Experiment 2: Exposure Duration Effects and the Differential Total Time Effect in an Intermediately Difficult Learning Situation

In Izawa's (in press) study, the zigzag response irregularity was limited to the 1 sec item-repetition condition S'S'S'S'S'S'T'T'T'T'T'T' which may have been too difficult for freshmen. One must ask if the increased efficacy of an item-repetition program still holds when compared to a list-repetition program where the ease of learning was enhanced by a 50% longer exposure duration (1.5 sec).

Another issue raised in the current investigation was the total time effects viewed from a different perspective than Experiment 1. Discussed at a global level, the arrangements planned in Experiment 2 were impossible with a constant total time constraint such as in Experiment 1 (and in Izawa, 1993a, 1993b, & in press). Here, duration effects were examined while holding the presentation frequency constant (*cf.* Prog. 9.3 vs. 9.4): short vs. long total times.

Consequently, in Experiment 2, the same standard 12 CVC-CVC pairs were learned at two presentation rates, with a constant frequency: Conditions 3 and 4 were run at a 1 sec rate, but Conditions 5 and 6 at a 1.5 sec rate. Conditions 3 and 5 used list-repetition SSSSSSTTTTTT, and Conditions 4 and 6 used item-repetition S'S'S'S'S'S'T'T'T'T'T'T' (Fig. 9.4). Conditions 3 and 4 applied to both Experiments 1 and 2, and served as the base line data for Conditions 5 and 6 in the latter, and for Conditions 1 and 2 in the former.

Experiment 3: Effects of Learning Material and Exposure Duration in an Extremely Easy Learning Situation

Another way to make learning easier, in addition to a longer total S, T, S+T, and r times, is via the learning material variable itself. Granted that either too easy or too difficult a learning situation may mask prominent learning and memory phenomena due to ceiling/floor effects (e.g., Izawa & Hayden, 1989), it is essential for us to examine total time, S-T-r program, and other major variable effects in extremely easy learning situations in addition to difficult (Exp. 1) and intermediately difficult (Exp. 2) learning situations.

For Experiment 3, therefore, an extremely easy list was derived from the standard list used in Experiments 1 and 2, as well as in Izawa (e.g., 1993a, 1993b, in press). The cue, A-terms of the Experiment 3 list consisted of the same CVCs from the standard list, while their target, B-terms were easy randomly-assigned numerals varying from 1 to 12. Via the 12 CVC-digit pair list, Conditions 7 and 9 were presented with the list-repetition program SSSSSSTTTTTT, while Conditions 8 and 10, with the item-repetition program S'S'S'S'S'S'T'T'T'T'T'T'. Conditions 7 and 8 learned at a 1 sec presentation rate, while Conditions 9 and 10, at a 1.5 sec rate (Fig. 9.4).

For Conditions 9 and 10 all variables including: learning materials, exposure duration, and participants (older and experienced), learning was extraordinarily easy, to facilitate in revealing limits, if any, for any determinants that control efficiency of learning and retention in STM and LTM.

General Method

Ten conditions of Experiments 1, 2, and 3 were conducted simultaneously, with 7 highly experienced participants per condition, 70 in total. They were paid volunteers from advanced undergraduate psychology courses.

Following the presentation programs specified in Presentation Program 9.10 and Fig. 9.4, each participant learned either a list of 12 CVC-CVC pairs (Exps. 1 & 2) or a list of 12 CVC-digit pairs (Exp. 3). Each S or T phase of Conditions 1, 2, 3, 4, 7, and 8 lasted 72 sec, while each phase in Conditions 5, 6, 9 and 10 lasted 108 sec. A Stowe Memory Drum presented items at a specified rate per condition (Fig. 9.4).

For Conditions 1-4 and 7-8, the total r (rest) intervals were held constant at 6 sec, 2 sec each after each S (or T) cycle for Condition 1, and 1 sec each for Conditions 3 and 7. However, 6 sec were given after each S or T phase for Conditions 2, 4, and 8. The total r times for Conditions 5, 6, 9, and 10 were 9 sec each per S and T phase, 1.5 sec after each S or T cycle in Conditions 5 and 9, and 9 sec after each S or T phase in Conditions 6 and 10.

In order to examine the long-term effects of the total time and S-T-r programs, two surprise delayed retention Ts (T_ds) were given at a 3 sec presentation rate for all 10 conditions after a 10 min interpolated (written-arithmetic) task, which was administered immediately following the main PAL task (Prog. 9.10).

Responses were made orally, and spelled out letter-by-letter, after the learner read the cue-term aloud. A practice PAL task preceded the main task for all participants, to familiarize them with the experimental task, as well as to check on group differences. No significant differences were found among the conditions within or between/among any combination of the three experiments. The current results, therefore, seem uninfluenced by pre-experimental group differences.

Theoretical Positions/Predictions to Be Investigated

The current design (Fig. 9.4) provided excellent opportunities for evaluating in-depth at least 5 theoretical facets, including 14 hypotheses (13 single-factored, 1 multi-factored) outlined in Table 9.1.

Total Time Hypotheses (TTHs), Original and Modified

At the end of the target tests (T*s, Fig. 9.4), all four conditions in Experiment 1 had the same total S, T, S+T, and r times, respectively. Because the "time" in the TTH originally referred exclusively to the S time (e.g., Bugelski, 1962), the original TTH (total time hypothesis) can be restated as TSTH (total study time hypothesis). Once we accept a modification of the original TTH to include r (rest) periods, to have TTH(+r), we can also formulate the total rest time hypothesis, TrTH. Similarly, we can generalize the total test time hypothesis (TTTH, Izawa, 1993b) and the total study-and-test time hypothesis (TS+TTH, Izawa, in press).

Because the design (Fig. 9.4) of Experiment 1 utilized identical total S, T, and S+T and r times, predictions made by the entire family of TTHs (TSTH, TTTH, TS+TTH, and TrTH; any combination thereof, or derivatives therefrom) call for identical performances: (a) among all conditions with 72 sec S and T phases: 4 conditions in Experiment 1 and Conditions 7-8 in Experiment 3, and (b) among all conditions with 108 sec S and T phases (Conds 5, 6, 9, & 10) in Experiments 2 and 3 (see Table 9.1), respectively.

The same prediction holds for the TTHs that include rest periods (TTH(+r), Izawa, 1992a), and the TTH which assumes virtual identity between S and T trials (*cf.* Whitten & Bjork, 1977). For more details of Hypotheses 2, 4, 5, and 6 in Table 9.1 (TTTH, TrTH, TTH(+r), TTH(S=T), respectively), see Izawa (1993a, 1993b, in press).

An inference from TTHs allows us to examine short vs. long total times situations as indirect tests of TTHs in Experiments 2 and 3. Here, conditions with longer S, T, S+T, and r total times are expected to have advantages than

TABLE 9.1.
Fourteen Hypotheses: Predictions, Determinants

Category	Hypothesis	Predictions/Determinants
Total Time	1. Total study time hypothesis (TSTH) (Original TTH)	A constant total time produces constant performances:
		Exp. 1: Cond. $1 = 2 = 3 = 4$
	2. Total test time hypothesis (TTTH)	Exp. 2: Cond. $3 = 4$, Cond. $5 = 6$
		[Conds. $3 = 4 <$ Conds. $5 = 6$]
	3. Total study and test time hypothesis (TS + TTH)	Exp. 3: Cond. $7 = 8$, Cond. $9 = 10$ [Conds. $7 = 8 <$ Conds. $9 = 10$]
	4. Total rest time hypothesis (TrTH)	
	5. Total time hypothesis inclusive of rest period (TTH(+r))	
	6. Total time hypothesis that assumes identity for study and test (TTH(S=T))	
Presentation Duration	7. Study (S) duration hypothesis (original duration hypothesis)	The longer duration, the better the performances:
		Exp. 1: Cond. $1 = 2 >$ Cond. $3 = 4$
	8. Test (T) duration hypothesis	Exp. 2: Cond $3 = 4$, Cond. $5 = 6$
		[Conds. $3 = 4 <$ Conds. $5 = 6$]
	9. Study and Test (S+T) duration hypothesis	Exp. 3: Cond. $7 = 8$, Cond. $9 = 10$ [Conds. $7 = 8 <$ Conds. $9 = 10$]
Presentation Frequency	10. Study (S) frequency hypothesis, (original frequency hypothesis), inclusive of familiarity, repetition, priming, rehearsal, and other relevant hypotheses	The greater frequency, the better the performances: Exp. 1: Conds. $1 = 2 <$ Conds. $3 = 4$ Exp. 2: Cond. $3 = 4$, Cond. $5 = 6$ [Cond. $3 = 4 = 5 = 6$] Exp. 3: Cond. $7 = 8$, Cond. $9 = 10$
	11. Test (T) frequency hypothesis	[Cond. $7 = 8 = 9 = 10$]
	12. Study and Test (S+T) frequency hypothesis	
Retrieval	13. Retrieval practice hypothesis	
Presentation Program	14. Study-Test-rest (S-T-r) presentation program hypothesis	S-T-r programs (e. g., Prog. 9.8), exhibited multiple factor interactions, including any or all determinants, e. g.: Repetition modes (list- vs. item-repetitions), and learning difficulty, presentation rates, learning materials, and participant attributes (see the text for details).
		Under constant total times for S, T, S+T, and r trials:
		(a) Performances may differ depending on S-T-r programs, and
		(b) Repetition mode performance may differ and interact with difficulty levels.
		(c) Under the list-repetition program in difficult learning situations, STM and LTM performances may vary due to LTM enhancement effects induced by fast successive Ts, e.g., Cond. 3. [Longer total times are advantaged over shorter ones.]

[ ] signifies entries of conditions with different total times.

shorter ones: Conditions 5 = 6 > Conditions 3 = 4, and Conditions 9 = 10 > Conditions 7 = 8. In a sense, however, this global level of TTHs may become indistinguishable from the duration hypotheses to be discussed next. Recall our discussion earlier, regarding Presentation Program 9.3 vs. 9.4 on page 168.

Presentation (Exposure) Duration Hypotheses, Original and Modified

Alternatives to TTHs include the presentation duration and frequency hypotheses (Izawa, 1993a, 1993b, in press; Izawa & Hayden, 1993). Traditionally both "duration" and "frequency" refer to those of the S (study) trials. Let us, then, call them the S duration and S frequency hypotheses, respectively.

In general, as seen in comparisons of Presentation Programs 9.3 and 9.4, (*a*) the longer the S duration, the better the performance in both STM and LTM. Thus, 2 sec exposures (Conds. 1 & 2) are expected to be more effective than the 1 sec (Conds. 3 & 4) exposures. Furthermore, (*b*) the S duration hypothesis predicts similar results from the conditions with the identical exposure duration, of which there were 5 sets in the current 10 conditions: Conditions 1 = 2, 3 = 4, 5 = 6, 7 = 8, and 9 = 10 (Table 9.1). Exactly the same predictions can be made from the T duration hypothesis (Izawa 1993b), or from the S+T duration hypothesis (Izawa, in press).

When the duration was incremented to 1.5 sec rate in Experiments 2 and 3, the duration hypotheses all expect better performances for the conditions with longer duration as compared with the shorter ones: Conditions 3 = 4 < Conditions 5 = 6, and Conditions 7 = 8 < Conditions 9 = 10, respectively.

Presentation Frequency Hypotheses, Original and Modified

Increases in familiarity, repetition, rehearsal, priming or practice increase frequency and thereby enhance acquisition (STM) and retention (LTM). Therefore, the S frequency hypothesis, along with both the T frequency (Izawa, 1993b) and S+T frequency (Izawa, in press) hypotheses predict that: (*a*) Conditions 1 and 2, which had the fewest S and T events (20 Ss, 20 Ts), would be worse than Conditions 3 and 4 (60 Ss, 60 Ts); and that (*b*) the conditions with identical presentation frequencies would lead to the same levels of encoding and retention in the same manner as with the duration hypotheses for 5 sets of two conditions each: Thus, Conditions 1 = 2, 3 = 4, 5 = 6, 7 = 8, and 9 = 10 in Experiments 1, 2, and 3. These predictions were made without contaminating effects of the total time differentials.

However, if we expand our discourse to the four conditions with greater total times in the current series of experiments, the following hold: The duration being irrelevant, the family of the frequency hypotheses expect all conditions with 6 Ss and 6 Ts per S and T phase, respectively, to obtain the same performance level: Conditions 1 = 2 < Conditions 3 = 4 = 5 = 6 in Experiments 1 and 2, and Conditions 7 = 8 = 9 = 10 in Experiment 3.

The Retrieval Practice Hypothesis

The superior performances observed among conditions with more Ts (tests) might be attributable to participants' improved retrieval skills (e.g., Gross & Bjork, 1991; Izawa, 1992a, 1993b; King, Zechmeister, & Shaughnessy, 1980; Longstreth, 1971). If correct, the present design also provides an excellent opportunity for testing the retrieval practice hypothesis. As was the case for the presentation frequency hypothesis, predictions from the retrieval practice hypothesis are the same as those made by the family of frequency-related hypotheses, shown in Table 9.1. Each hypothesis predicts that the more Ts, the better the performances.

Note that the above four families of 13 hypotheses do not differentiate between short-term acquisition and long-term retention processes, and therefore predict qualitatively similar data for both STM and LTM.

The Study-Test-rest[1] (S-T-r) Presentation Program Hypothesis

In direct contradiction to all versions of the TTHs, the S-T-r program hypothesis assumes that: (1) learning and retention are controlled by time management factors inherent in S, T, S+T, and r programming for a given set of learning materials and a defined pool of participants, and (2) these factors interact. Depending on S-T-r presentation programs, (3) within a defined Total Time X, it is possible to enhance learning efficiency and improve retention, (4) the optimal S-T-r program may vary depending on learning difficulty levels, and (5) participants' attributes. (6) STM and LTM performances may vary due to LTM enhancement effects induced by fast successive T-list-repetition program in difficult learning situations. (7) With a constant learning materials and subject characteristics, the relevant determinants include: (a) S-T-r programs (e.g., Program 9.8), (b) repetition modes (e.g., list vs. item), (c) density of S/T alternations (Izawa, 1992, in press), (d) the T effect (e.g., Izawa, 1966, 1967, 1992a, 1993b), (e) response search opportunities, and (f) S, T, and r durations, (g) S- and T-spacing effects (Izawa, 1971a, 1992).

Unlike the 13 single-factor hypotheses outlined above, which predict either monotonic or flat outcomes (Table 9.1), the S-T-r presentation program hypothesis, based on multiple interactive factors unveiled from Izawa's extensive empirical findings, is uniquely successful in accommodating the prevailing

---

[1] See footnote 1 on p. 166

curvilinear outcomes (a maximum point somewhere between the two extremes). See, for example, reviews by Izawa and Hayden, (1993) for duration and frequency factors, Izawa (1969) for the optimal test effect, Izawa (1985a, 1985b) and Izawa and Hayden (1989) for anticipation vs. study-test method differentials, and many studies cited above for S- and T-spaced practice effects. Notice also that clearly U-shaped outcomes might indicate the interaction of a greater numbers of independent variables, even if one factor generates a monotonic effect (an example given later in the chapter). The current design (Fig. 9.4) with 10 conditions simultaneously run in three experiments helped to determine the generalities and limitations of these 14 hypotheses at varied learning difficulty levels.

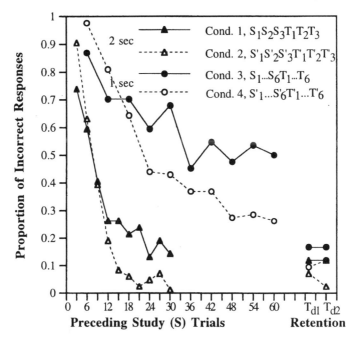

FIG. 9.5. Performances as proportions of incorrect responses to T_1 s and T'_1 s (first tests) of each T (test) phase. A function of preceding S (study) trials in all four conditions of Experiment 1. Total times of S, T, S+T and r were held respectively constant throughout. (Solid and open dots in this and subsequent figures show data from the list- and item-repetition presentation programs, respectively.)

Results and Discussion

Experiment 1: Participants' Experiences in a Relatively Difficult Learning Situation

Since the inception of learning theories such as Ebbinghaus' (1885) and Hull's (1943), the number of S (study) trials has been found to determine performance levels. Figure 9.5 shows performance levels of the four Experiment 1 conditions as a function of S trials in terms of proportions of incorrect responses to T_1/T'_1, the first T following each 6 sec S-experience per item. Recall that the family of total time hypotheses (TSTH, TTTH, TS+TTH, TrTH, TTH(+r), & TTH(S=T); Table 9.1) predicted identical performance levels among all four conditions.

   Contrary to that prediction of identity, the conditions' performances showed highly significant differences: Condition 2 (2 sec item-repetition) demonstrated the lowest error rate by far, followed by Conditions 1 (2 sec list-repetition), 4 (1 sec item-repetition), and 3 (1 sec list-repetition) in that order. The significance of the overall duration variable was a whopping $F(1, 24)= 53.15, p = 0.0001$. Although not great early in acquisition, differences between the list- and item-repetition programs did become significant toward the latter half: $F(1, 24) = 4.83, p = 0.038$. Duration x Program interactions, however, were nonsignificant, indicating a similar item-repetition program advantage for both durations.

   The significance found among both presentation duration and S-T-r program variables can, however, be accounted for by the S-T-r presentation program hypothesis as a matter of course, with absolutely no difficulty. It is because these four conditions differed in both their presentation modes (list- vs. item-repetitions) and in their exposure rates.

   Longer exposures (Conds. 1 & 2) led to significantly better performances (fewer errors) than shorter ones (Conds. 3 & 4), supporting the family of presentation duration hypotheses (S, T, & S+T, Table 9.1). Yet, significant differences between the two conditions with the same duration rate contradicted its prediction of equality. Greater difficulty was encountered by the family of frequency hypotheses, which predicted that greater S, T, and S+T frequencies would lower the proportion of incorrect responses (Table 9.1). To the contrary, performances were significantly worse under conditions with the greatest frequency (repetition, priming, familiarity).

   Figure 9.5 might be considered incomplete from the TTHs' perspective, because only the T_1s/T'_1s of the successive Ts/T's per T phase are shown as a function of S trials. Our technique here might have amplified performance differences among the conditions, while ignoring differences in time. Therefore, Fig. 9.6 shows performances of all Ts after a total of 6 sec of S trials per item.

   Even in Fig. 9.6, despite the seemingly similar performance levels between Conditions 2 (2 sec S'S'S'T'T'T') and 3 (1 sec SSSSSTTTTTT), the overall ANOVAs again decisively rejected the family of TTHs' (Table 9.1) performance identity prognostications among the conditions, no matter which or how many of the 6 successive Ts/T's were used. In the case of target Ts (Fig. 9.4) where identical total S, T, S+T, and r times were used among all four conditions, respectively, longer exposures were significantly superior to shorter ones: $F(1, 24) = 11.77, p < 0.01$. In addition, the novel item-repetition program was significantly superior to the traditional list-repetition program: $F(1, 24) = 16.74, p < 0.001$. Again, no Duration x Program interactions were obtained.

As for the presentation duration and frequency hypotheses, the overall outcome shown in Fig. 9.6 is similar to that in Fig. 9.5. However, the similar performances in Conditions 2 (2 sec item-repetition) and 3 (1 sec list-repetition) generated an additional difficulty for the duration hypotheses, which anticipated that Condition 2 would outperform Condition 3, because the former's S+T duration was twice as long.

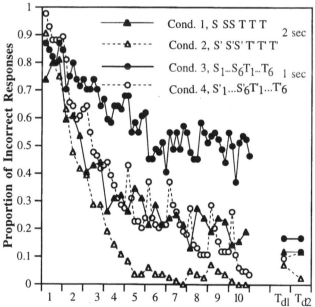

Preceding Blocks of 6 sec. (total) Study (S) Trials Retention

FIG. 9.6. Performances on all T/T' (test) trials in all four conditions in Experiment 1. The distance between each horizontal scale division represents a 6 sec T phase, with 3 T/T' entries in Conditions 1 and 2, whereas 6 entries in Conditions 3 and 4.

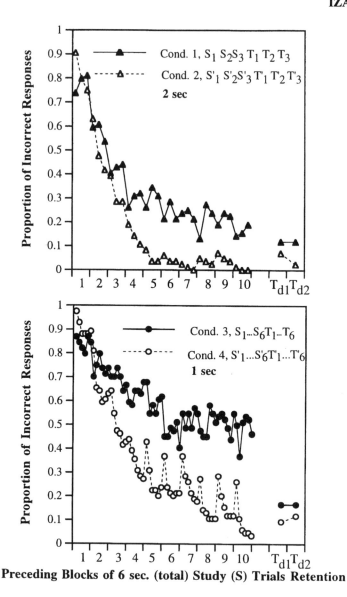

FIG. 9.7. Comparisons of list- and item-repetition presentations in Experiment 1, at 2 (upper panel) and 1 sec (lower panel) presentation rates. Total times of S, T, S+T, and r trials, as well as presentation durations and frequencies were constant for the two curves in each panel.

In contrast, the significant overall differences found among the four conditions, and similar levels of performance between Conditions 2 and 3, can be accommodated by the S-T-r presentation program hypothesis, which posits that the results depended on the programming of S, T, S+T, and r events, and which combined the effects of repetition methods (list- vs. item-repetitions) and exposure durations (multi-factors).

The overall outcomes, shown in Figs. 9.5 and 9.6, turned out to be universal. Performances of the current older and more experienced participants differed little qualitatively from Izawa's younger, inexperienced participants of 1993b and in-press studies.

More in-depth analyses of performances of the four conditions in relatively difficult learning situations (Exp. 1) are shown in Fig. 9.7. The upper and lower panels depict, respectively, the list-repetition (solid dots) vs. the item-repetition program (open dots) at 2 and 1 sec presentation rates. The two conditions in each panel had identical presentation durations, frequencies, and total S, T, S+T, and r times, and they differed only in their S-T-r presentation programs. Therefore, TTHs, frequency, and duration hypotheses all expected both curves to be identical or nearly identical. Only the S-T-r presentation hypothesis predicted that differential performances were likely to appear at this high level of learning difficulty.

Sharply contradicting the identity predictions from all 13 single-factor hypotheses, both panels of Fig. 9.7 show large differences in acquisition performances, despite much smaller differences among their delayed T performances. An overall ANOVA indicated that the item-repetition program was significantly superior to the traditional list-repetition programs at both presentation speeds: $F(1, 24) = 16.74, p < 0.001$.

Even more conservative, separate analyses for each presentation speed did not obscure the powerful effects of the S-T-r presentation programs: STM and LTM combined analyses for the 2 sec rate (top, Fig. 9.7) indicated that although limited very early in acquisition, the superiority of S'S'S'T'T'T' item-repetition program over the SSSTTT list-repetition program increased steadily and soon became statistically significant, for example, in the second half of acquisition: $F(1, 12) = 7.51, p < 0.02$. Results from the 1 sec rate were even more pronounced (bottom, Fig. 9.7): the item-repetitions S'S'S'S'S'S'T'T'T'T'T'T' proved far superior to the list-repetitions SSSSSSTTTTTT in all acquisition stages: $F(1, 12) = 10.66, p < 0.001$.

In sum, the significant results shown in both panels of Fig. 9.7 clearly support the S-T-r presentation program hypothesis and decisively contradict the expectations from each of the other 13 hypotheses in Table 9.1. These findings from older, practiced participants closely replicate Izawa's (in press, Exps. 1 & 2) with younger, inexperienced ones. However, overall performance levels were substantially better among the current pool of psychology majors than they were among Izawa's (in press) freshmen. An overall 3-way ANOVA between our

Experiment 1 vs. Izawa' (in press) relevant four conditions (3, 4, 6, & 7) confirmed the above, especially during the second half of acquisition. The experienced participants out-performed the naïve participants: $F(1, 80) = 232.824, p < 0.0001$. The same analyses also verified that both experiments' two other main factors were highly significant; the longer duration (2 sec over 1 sec) led to superior performances: $F(1, 80) = 160.019, p < 0.0001$, and the item-repetition program excelled the list-repetition program: $F(1, 80) = 66.092, p < 0.001$.

Most interestingly, the same ANOVA indicated that Duration x Program interactions were also highly significant: $F(1, 80) = 31.020, p < 0.0001$, suggesting that performance differences generated by different S-T-r programs interact differentially with presentation speeds depending on participants' sophistication, and therefore learning difficulty level. In Experiment 1, the same CVC-CVC list was hard for inexperienced freshmen (Izawa, in press), but significantly less difficult for the experienced psychology majors.

A new and intriguing phenomena emerged from the very fast-paced item-repetition program of Experiment 1 when experienced participants were used. To illustrate, see the lower curve of the bottom panel, Fig. 9.7. The wide and erratic fluctuations from one T to the next over the 6 successive T's among naïve learners in the 1 sec $S'S'S'S'S'S'T'_1T'_2T'_3T'_4T'_5T'_6$ item-repetitions (Izawa, in press, Fig. 4) are absent from Experiment 1. Instead, very orderly and systematic improvement resulted from the first T'_1 to the last T'_6 over a block of 6 repetitive T's! Experienced participants' overall improvements from T'_1 to T'_6 per T phase were dramatically significant: $t(6) = 6.435, p < 0.001$.

Indeed, participants' strategies for coping with rapid T's varied markedly depending on their prior experiences in verbal learning. Whereas the naïve lacked a consistent strategy, the experienced did not: The older participants might have regarded T'_1 as a warning signal, and might have been able to utilize the remaining 5 T's to retrieve items requiring more searches or a longer reaction time toward the end of the T block. Notice, though, that the older participants' orderly progress from T'_1 to T'_6 might have been overly exaggerated, due to substantial losses from T'_6 (last T' of the T' block) to the next T'_1 (first T' of the next T' block). However, by T'_2 these losses were for the most part made up to the level of the previous block, with participants showing slightly further improvement toward the end of the T' block. Therefore, we ought to be careful! The major contributors to the staggering improvements from T'_1 to T'_6 might have been attributable to T'_1's significant drop in performance: $t(6) = 3.16, p < 0.02$, from one T'_6 to the next T'_1, despite that one S' phase of 72 sec (6 S's/item) intervened. The improvements from T'_2 to T'_6 were small and nonsignificant.

No such phenomena obtained in Condition 3, whose participants had the same 1 sec presentation rate as those in Condition 4, although repetitions were in the list form. No significant differences were found among the 6 successive T cycles under the list-repetition program, which was consistently replicated since Izawa (1966).

Retention Phenomena, Including the LTM Enhancement Effect

Large differences in STM acquisition Ts in Experiment 1 were the major contributors to the overall significance among the four conditions and between the two presentation programs. Differences in the delayed LTM Ts were much smaller, although the rank order in absolute values was the same as that for STM acquisition Ts. Separate overall analyses of LTM (delayed Ts) among all four conditions revealed neither significant differences among the conditions nor significant losses/gains occurring over the 10 min interpolated task (except Cond. 3, to be discussed shortly). Nor were significant differences found between the list- and item-repetition programs on delayed Ts. Consideration of LTM performances alone might appear to strengthen TTHs. The same situation with LTM retention curves in Fig. 9.7 seems to favor both duration and frequency hypotheses approaches, despite lack of support from the STM acquisition data (Figs. 9.5 & 9.6). However, none of these hypotheses differentiate between STM and LTM. They are therefore unable to account for the staggering differences among the four conditions as well as differences between list- and item-repetition programs in STM acquisition performances.

More importantly, notice that the number of duration variations in the current investigation was limited to 2: 1 vs. 2 sec in Experiment 1, and 1 vs. 1.5 sec in Experiments 2 and 3, which may not have been large enough to detect more subtle LTM differentials. With larger variations such as 4, ranging from 1 to 6 sec, Izawa (in press, e.g., Fig. 1) did find significant differences in LTM among the 10 conditions albeit smaller in absolute magnitude than in STM, with the same learning materials and S-T-r programs.

Another phenomenon of importance is the remarkably significant LTM performance enhancement of Condition 3, SSSSSSTTTTTT over the 10 min interpolated task between the last acquisition T, T_a and the first delayed T, T_{d1}: $t(6) = 2.95$, $p < 0.05$. We therefore witnessed, for the third time, the reliable enhancement of LTM effects in the T list-repetition program (Izawa, 1993b, in press) in PAL with linguistic materials. The same effects were obtained in motor skill learning by Hagman (1983) and by Izawa and Patterson (1989). LTM performance levels were stable over the two retention Ts in this and all other 9 conditions in current experiments.

However, the LTM enhancement effects found here and elsewhere require further consideration. Condition 4, $S'S'S'S'S'S'T_1T'_2T'_3T'_4T'_5T'_6$ generated enormous improvements from T'_1 to T'_6 over 6 repetitive T's for the same item per T' phase at 1 sec rate. In contrast, all Ts in Condition 3, SSSSSSTTTTTT also had 1 sec each, but the T items always differed from each other within the list. It may follow, then, that if Condition SSSSSSTTTTTT had involved a longer response time, the differences between the two presentation programs during acquisition might have been smaller. However, the fact that longer Ts (2 sec) in Conditions 1 and 2 resulted in significance defeats this argument. Similarly, although the nonsignificance between the two conditions' LTM performances may reflect such an effect, that inference assumes some degree of similarity between STM and LTM processes. This, however, may not always be true. A case in point: the LTM enhancement effect found in the 1 sec list-repetition program.

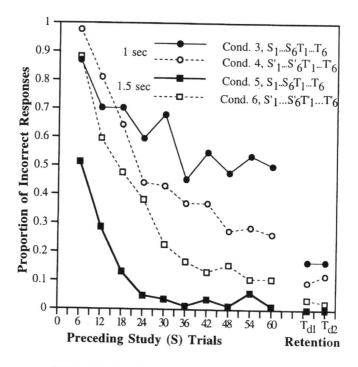

FIG. 9.8. Performances as proportions of incorrect responses on T_1s and T'_1s (first tests) on every T (test) phase as a function of preceding S (study) trials; all four conditions, Experiment 2.

Experiment 2: Effects of the Study-Test-rest (S-T-r) Program, the Exposure Duration, and the Total Time in an Intermediately Difficult Learning Situation

Izawa (in press) administered a difficult 12 CVC-CVC pair list to naïve freshmen under the $SSSSST_1T_2T_3T_4T_5T_6$ and $S'S'S'S'S'S'T'_1T'_2T'_3T'_4T'_5T'_6$, (list- & item-repetition) programs among others, and discovered interesting memory phenomena. The same learning materials and S-T-r programs were included in the current Experiment 1, but the participants here were older and experienced. Consequently, they found their PAL tasks less difficult. Yet, the results replicated the memory phenomena found in Izawa (in press), revealing the intriguing new phenomena above. In order to investigate learning-difficulty-dependent aspects of the S-T-r presentation programs more closely, Experiment 2 provided an overall intermediate level of difficulty with 50% longer exposures and total S, T, S+T, and r times for Conditions 5 and 6. In order to assess differences between the 1 sec and 1.5 sec rates (difficult vs. medium difficulty), Conditions 3 and 4 served as the base-line groups for both Experiments 1 (Conds. 1 & 2) and 2 (Conds. 5 & 6); see Fig. 9.4.

Figure 9.8 presents the major results for all T_1s/T'_1s in all four conditions of Experiment 2, which was overall substantially easier (yielded better performances) than the harder Experiment 1. The 50% longer S and T phases and longer presentation rates made the same CVC-CVC learning materials considerably easier to learn. Note that in Condition 5, nearly perfect learning was achieved one-quarter of the way in acquisition, while learners in the other conditions had to struggle to achieve far less.

With intermediately difficult learning, we again obtained large, significant differences among the conditions (Fig. 9.8). As for the duration main factor, Conditions 5 and 6 allowed 50% longer total times and showed significantly superior performances compared to the shorter Conditions 3 and 4: $F(1, 24) = 9.451$, $p = 0.005$. Another main factor (re the two S-T-r programs) differed significantly here once again: $F(1, 24) = 4.23$, $p = 0.05$. Thus far, the results closely agree with major findings by Izawa (1993a, 1993b, & in press), as well as with the results from Experiment 1.

However, given an overall intermediately difficult learning situation, as in Experiment 2, the results unearthed a new and highly intriguing phenomenon: The effects of S-T-r programs appear to be learning-difficulty-dependent! Earlier, when learning was very difficult (because of either too fast presentations, or too naïve subjects, or both), the item-repetition program was shown to be superior to the list-repetition program, where the total times were held strictly constant (e.g., Exp. 1; Izawa, 1993a, 1993b, in press). Differing drastically, in Experiment 2, where learning was easier because total time and exposures were 50% longer, the relative advantage of the item-repetition program over the list-repetition program was reversed! The list-repetition program showed significant advantage at the easy 1.5 sec rate (Cond. 5 over 6). This fact suggests significant Program x Duration interactions. This new finding was confirmed by ANOVAs: $F(1, 24) = 7.019$, $p = 0.01$!

Figure 9.9 supports the findings via all Ts for all four conditions in Experiment 2. Here again, interactions were highly significant: $F(1, 24) = 14.119$, $p < 0.001$, as were the duration effects: $F(1, 24) = 30.012$, $p < 0.0001$. However, Conditions 5 and 6, (50% longer duration and total S+T and r times) showed near perfect learning (floor effects for incorrect responses), but the overall effects of the programs were not reliable. The latter fact is important: When learning was intermediately difficult between two extremes (very difficult where item-repetition is favored and very easy where the list-repetition is advantaged), S-T-r program effects may have been small or nonsignificant.

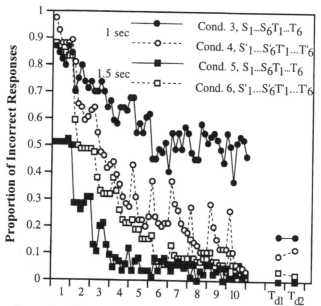

FIG. 9.9. Performances, all T/T' (test) trials, all four conditions, Experiment 2. The distance between each horizontal scale division represents a 6 sec T phase, with 6 T/T' entries per T phase in each condition.

Differences among the conditions' LTM performances (on delayed Ts) were smaller due to small experimental variations. Yet, the two longer-duration conditions showed a significant advantage over the two shorter ones in LTM (notwithstanding the powerful floor effects): $F(1, 24) = 6.400$, $p < 0.05$. All other effects were swamped by floor effects and were negligible.

For more in-depth analyses of the intermediately difficult learning situation in Experiment 2, see Fig. 9.10, which shows the 1 sec conditions at the top and the 1.5 sec conditions at the bottom. Note that, within each panel, both the list-repetition (solid dots) and the item-repetition program (open dots) had respectively identical total S, T, S+T, and r times, as well as identical presentation frequency and duration. The two conditions differed only in their S-T-r presentation programs. Therefore, all TTHs, duration, and frequency hypotheses, as well as their derivatives, predicted equivalent performances per panel, but large differences between the difficult and intermediate learning difficulty levels were possible in the S-T-r presentation program hypothesis.

Both panels of Fig. 9.10 revealed considerable differences between the two S-T-r programs, giving support to the S-T-r presentation program hypothesis, but contradicting the predictions of all other theories. In comparing Conditions 5 and 6 (longer durations and total times, 1.5 sec rate) with Conditions 3 and 4 (shorter durations, 1 sec rate), we observed the following: (a) The item-repetition program far surpassed the list-repetition program at the difficult 1 sec exposure rate, even a conservative analysis revealed significance: $F(1, 12) = 7.51$, $p < 0.001$. However, the opposite turned out to be true when learning was made easier via a longer (1.5 sec) rate (with concurrent increases in the total S, T, S+T, and r times; not so in Exp. 1 or in Izawa's 7 exps., 1993a, 1993b, in press). In significantly easier learning situations, the 1.5 sec conditions manifested floor effects (a lack of errors) halfway through acquisition. Consequently, in spite of some program differences early in acquisition: $F(1, 12) = 4.84$, $p < 0.05$, overall program differences were small and nonsignificant, in the manner expected from interactions of S-T-r program effects and learning difficulty level; a characteristic of intermediately difficult situation.

(b) As for the 6 repetitive T's per T phase within the item-repetition program, increments from T'_1 to T'_6 still appear in the lower panel of Fig. 9.10, where learning was made easier through a 1.5 sec presentation rate, as compared to the harder 1 sec rate shown in the upper panel, but here the trends were much smaller. When the overall increments from T'_1 to T'_6 were considered alone (disregarding all other T's), they reached significance at $p = 0.05$, $t(6) = 3.05$. But, when all T's within each T phase were considered together, overall differences among the 6 T's were not significant.

(c) Conspicuously absent in the item-repetition program (lower panel of Fig. 9.10, 1.5 sec rate) were significant performance losses from the end of one T phase to the beginning of the next (prevalent in the upper panel, 1 sec item-repetitions). Granting small deviations, on the average there was a trend for

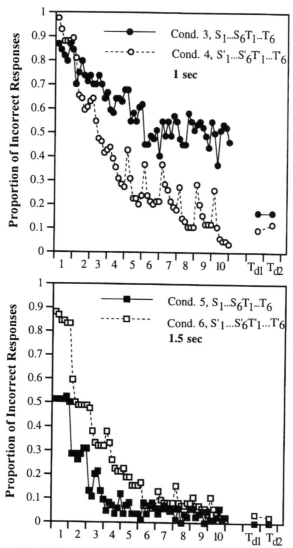

FIG. 9.10. Comparisons of the list- and
item-repetition presentations in Experiment 2, at
1 and 1.5 sec presentation rates, respectively, in
upper and lower panels. Total times of S, T, S+T,
and r trials, as well as presentation duration and
frequencies were constant for all curves in each
panel.

improvement from one T phase to the next in the item-repetition program (Cond. 6). Apparently, the significantly enhanced error rate from the end of one block of successive T's to the beginning of the next was limited to the difficult 1 sec condition among older, more experienced participants. These lapses, if any, were not large enough to be reliable in the easy 1.5 sec rate (lower panel, Fig. 9.10).

Experiment 3: Learning Materials, Presentation Rates, Differential Total Times and the S-T-r Presentation Programs in an Extremely Easy Learning Situation

Learning difficulty levels can be changed through presentation rates and total S and T times, as was done in Experiment 2. More practically, however, learning

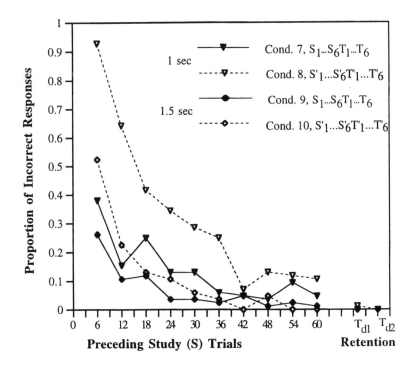

FIG. 9.11. Performances as proportions of incorrect responses to T_1s and T'_1s (first tests) for every T (test) phase in all four conditions in Experiment 3.

difficulty levels can also be altered through learning materials, especially through the target items used in paired-associate learning (PAL). Indeed, the irregular response pattern in Izawa's (in press) 1 sec item-repetition program may have been partly attributable to very difficult response learning. In Experiment 3, therefore, both factors were introduced concurrently via: (1) A 12 CVC-digit pair list, using the cues from the standard list of Experiments 1-2, but employing the digits 1-12 (no new learning required) as target terms. (2) The use of a 50% longer S+T item presentation rate (1.5 sec) in Conditions 9 and 10. In addition, because Experiment 3 used highly experienced participants, learning was extremely easy. Although very easy learning is likely to mask subtle memory phenomena due to floor/ceiling effects (*cf.* Izawa, 1980, 1989a, 1989b, Izawa & Hayden, 1989), such situations may nevertheless help reveal boundaries for the S-T-r program presentation effects and the total time, frequency, duration, and related effects.

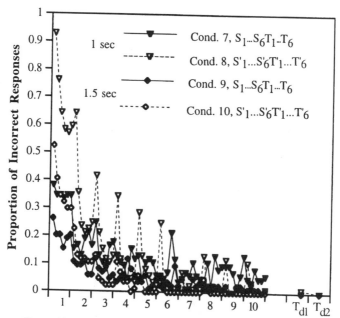

FIG. 9.12. Performances on all T/T' (test) trials, all four conditions in Experiment 3. The distance between each horizontal scale division represents a 6 sec T phase, with 6 T/T' entries per T phase in every condition.

Figure 9.11 shows all T_1/T'_1 performances in Experiment 3. When learning was made very easy, as in Experiment 3, the results were quite different from those in Experiment 1 (and in Izawa's 1993a, 1993b, in press). The new phenomenon associated with easy learning in Conditions 5 and 6 in Experiment 2 emerged again but were more prominent in an extraordinarily easy learning situation: Even here, prior to the onset of floor effects during the first half of acquisition, the powerful effects of the S-T-r presentation program favored list-repetition (Conds. 7 & 9) over item-repetition (Conds. 8 & 10) highly significantly: $F(1, 24) = 20.276, p = 0.0001$.

The duration/total time factor was also highly significant: $F(1, 24) = 22.613, p = 0.0001$, favoring a longer duration/total time (Conds. 9 & 10) as opposed to shorter ones (Conds. 7 & 8). Also significant were Program x Duration interactions: $F(1, 24) = 8.342. p < 0.008$, suggesting that the extent of the list-repetition's advantage was greater within the 1 sec than in the 1.5 sec rate.

Figure 9.12 shows performances for all Ts in the four conditions of Experiment 3. Clearly, learning here was extraordinarily easy, and, in general, floor effects set in one-third of the way through in acquisition, independent of program type and duration. However, only the duration factor demonstrated significant influence, but then only during the first half of acquisition: $F(1, 24) = 13.142, p = 0.0014$.

When learning was made extremely easy, as in Experiment 3, subtle memory phenomena were hard to detect due to strong floor effects; and the detection of overall differences between the list- vs. item-repetition programs was similarly hard. Fig. 9.13 shows that overall differences between the programs were minor, and that tangible differences were limited to performances immediately following the first S phase, $S_{(1)}$, where learning was still challenging. In a conservative analysis, all Ts examined in the $T_{(1)}$ phase under the 1 sec rate, Condition SSSSSSTTTTTT outperformed Condition S'S'S'S'S'S'T'T'T'T'T'T' significantly: $t(6) = 10.49, p < 0.001$, and this was also true for the 1.5 sec conditions (list- over item-repetitions): $t(6) = 5.413, p < 0.01$. However, the list-repetition program's margin of superiority over the item-repetition program declined when learning was made easier still by lengthening exposures and total times.

A novel phenomenon which was previously detected among older participants responding to 6 repetitive T's at a 1 sec rate in Condition 4, S'S'S'S'S'S'T'$_1$T'$_2$T'$_3$T'$_4$T'$_5$T'$_6$ (Exps. 1-2) using difficult CVC-CVCs, was again detected in Experiment 3's 1 sec Condition 8, which used very easy CVC-digits. Here, spectacular performance losses occurred from T'$_6$ of a T' block/phase to the next T'$_1$, but there were steady improvements from T'$_1$ to T'$_6$ of the same T' phase/block. Apparently, this response pattern persisted among older more experienced participants, independent of learning difficulty. See Figure 9.13. The total S, T, S+T, and r times, presentation frequencies and durations of both programs were identical within the top (1 sec) and bottom (1.5 sec) panels under the list- and item-repetition programs.

In Experiment 3, large, progressive improvements were found from T'_1 to T'_6 under the $S'S'S'S'S'S'T'_1T'_2T'_3T'_4T'_5T'_6$ item-repetition program. These improvements were highly significant: $t(6) = 8.03$, $p < 0.001$. Such dramatic improvements were primarily due to another peculiar phenomenon; participants' significant STM losses from one T'_6 to the next T'_1: $t(6) = 4.95$, $p < 0.01$. It appears that the 1 sec T' time was indeed too short. Upon noticing the pattern of 6 successive T's under the item-repetition program, participants might have regarded T'_1 as a signal, and became more attentive only after T'_2.

However, the short T time may not tell the entire story. No such response pattern was observed on T_1 of any T phase in the other 1 sec rate condition, list-repetition $SSSSST_1T_2T_3T_4T_5T_6$, and T_1 performance level was as good as all the others within a given T phase. Furthermore, the T_1s of the list-repetition program were significantly better than T'_1s of the item-repetition program in most T phases in Experiment 3 (Fig. 9.13, upper panel). In addition, very stable performances over successive Ts in the list-repetition program have been replicated countless times over the past 3 decades (since Izawa, 1966).

What lies behind these differences? Perhaps, the experienced participants' cleverer strategies for coping with the rapid 1 sec item-repetition condition? If correct, this might explain: (a) the significant loss from the end of one T' phase to the beginning of the next, despite an intervening S' phase, and (b) the spectacular improvements from T'_1 to T'_6 within each T' block/phase.

However, when duration and total time were increased by 50% to 1.5 sec (making learning easier), both (a) and (b) phenomena disappeared, as seen in the bottom panel of Fig. 9.13. Despite the superiority of the former on the first T phase, $T_{(1)}$: $t(6) = 5.41$, $p < 0.01$ and the large improvements evident between T'_1 to T'_6: $t(6) = 5.20$, $p < 0.01$, overall, the list-repetition program did not differ significantly from the item-repetition program here.

In Fig. 9.13, note the differences between the upper (1 sec rate) and lower (1.5 sec rate) panels: Shorter exposures, when compared to longer exposures, produced significantly inferior performances: $F(1, 24) = 9.93$, $p < 0.01$ for both programs. The same level of significance was observed when analyses were limited to the first half of the acquisition period: $F(1, 24) = 12.83$, $p < 0.01$. This is not surprising: The greater the total time and the slower the presentation speed, with presentation frequency held constant, the better the performance (Program 9.3 vs. 9.4). Notice also that the absolute magnitude of differences between programs became even smaller with extremely easy learning, as seen in the lower panel.

From Fig. 9.13, it is clear that there were no significant LTM differences either among the four conditions or between the two presentation programs. This gives support to the families of TTHs, presentation duration and

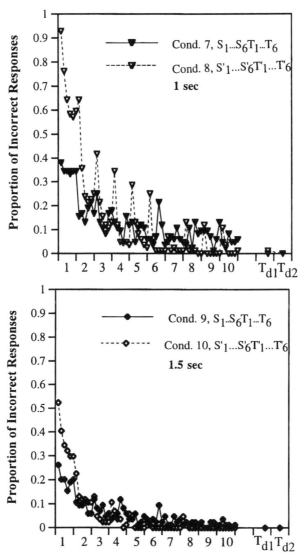

Preceding Blocks of 6 sec. (total) Study (S) Trials Retention

FIG. 9.13.   Comparisons of the list- and item-repetition presentations in Experiment 3, at 1 and 1.5 sec presentation rates. Total times of S, T, S+T, and r trials, as well as presentation durations and frequencies were held constant for all curves in each panel.

frequency hypotheses, as well as to the S-T-r presentation program hypotheses. However, considering the inherent limitations of extremely easy learning materials (the strong floor effects), caution is required in interpreting the results of Experiment 3: The degree to which we can generalize is limited.

Comparisons of Experiments 2 and 3: Learning Material Differences

Finally, the phenomena discussed above were supported by 2 (durations) X 2 (programs) X 2 (materials) ANOVA results of all Ts from Experiments 2 and 3. Experiment 3 with its easy CVC-digits yielded significantly fewer incorrect responses than Experiment 2 with its harder CVC-CVCs: $F(1, 48) = 65.500$, $p = 0.0001$. The duration main factor was also highly significant: $F(1, 48) = 42.279$, $p = 0.0001$. In addition, Duration x Program, Duration x Experiment, and Duration x Program x Experiment interactions were all significant: $F(1, 48)$s being 11.117, 11.972, and 12.659, each $p < 0.002$.

Despite the powerful floor effects (which masks subtle factors) in the extremely easy Experiment 3, and because far larger effects obtained in the intermediately difficult Experiment 2, the jointly considered S-T-r programs resulted in large and significant effects during the second half of acquisition: $F(1, 48) = 19.746$, $p = 0.001$. The differences in S-T-r presentation program effects between Experiments 2 and 3 suggested strong Experiment x Program interactions. This, furthermore, was supported by: $F(1, 48) = 9.012$, $p = 0.004$. Whereas the item-repetition program held a greater advantage supported by statistical results in both STM acquisition and LTM retention when learning was difficult, the reverse was true when learning was easy. This is a very interesting discovery!

An Examination of the Identity Assumption of Study and Test in TTH (S=T)

Many studies have distinguished between S and T trials (e.g., Izawa, 1969, 1992a, 1993b), while others have assumed them to be virtually identical (e.g., Whitten & Bjork, 1977). Given no dispute on the fact that new encoding occurs on S trials, the core issue boils down to this question: Can new encoding occur on T trials? New encoding, or gaining new information, differs sharply from hypermnesia, the recovery of old information that was once lost. New learning can be manifested by a T performance superior to the best previous performance among all acquisition Ts.

Because the 10 current conditions in the three experiments had 3 or 6 successive T trials following each S phase, they provided excellent opportunities

TABLE 9.2

Encoding Probabilities on Study (S) Trials: Estimated from Conditional Probabilities of Correct Responses Made for the First Time Given Incorrect Responses on All Previous Trials in All 10 Conditions (Experiments 1, 2, and 3)

Condition		$S_{(1)}$	$S_{(2)}$	$S_{(3)}$	$S_{(4)}$	$S_{(5)}$	$S_{(6)}$	$S_{(7)}$	$S_{(8)}$	$S_{(9)}$	$S_{(10)}$	$M_{(S)}$
S+T List-Repetition Condition												
1, SSSTTT		.262	.246	.310	.250	.176	.214	.200	.333	---	---	.256
2 sec, CVC- CVC	N	84	61	42	24	17	14	10	6	---	---	
3, SSSSSSTTTTTT		.131	.180	.114	.083	.077	.200	.000	.071	.167	.000	.122
1 sec, CVC- CVC	N	84	61	44	36	26	20	15	14	12	7	
5, SSSSSSTTTTTT		.488	.421	.625	---	---	---	---	---	---	---	.485
1.5 sec, CVC - CVC	N	84	38	16	---	---	---	---	---	---	---	
7, SSSSSSTTTTTT		.619	.500	---	---	---	---	---	---	---	---	.602
1 sec, CVC- #	N	84	14	---	---	---	---	---	---	---	---	
9, SSSSSSTTTTTT		.738	.571	---	---	---	---	---	---	---	---	.725
1.5 sec, CVC- #	N	84	7	---	---	---	---	---	---	---	---	
S+T Item-Repetition Condition												
2, S'S'S'TTT'		.095	.270	.212	.526	.571	---	---	---	---	---	.223
2 sec, CVC-CVC	N	84	63	33	19	7	---	---	---	---	---	
4, S'S'S'S'S'S'TTTTTT'		.024	.123	.167	.115	.167	.000	.000	.333	---	---	.098
1 sec, CVC-CVC	N	84	73	48	26	18	12	8	6	---	---	
6, S'S'S'S'S'S'TTTTTT'		.119	.286	.220	.080	.188	.364	.400	---	---	---	.199
1.5 sec, CVC-CVC	N	84	70	41	25	16	11	5	---	---	---	
8, S'S'S'S'S'S'TTTTTT'		.071	.174	.133	.143	---	---	---	---	---	---	.112
1 sec, CVC- #	N	84	46	15	7	---	---	---	---	---	---	
10, S'S'S'S'S'S'TTTTTT'		.476	.560	.667	---	---	---	---	---	---	---	.504
1.5 sec, CVC- #	N	84	25	6	---	---	---	---	---	---	---	

N = Number of cases
$M_{(S)}$ = Mean

TABLE 9.3

Response Recoveries over Successive Tests (Ts) Estimated from Responses Made for the First Time Given Incorrect on All Previous Trials Evaluated on the Second or Later Tests on Successive Tests Within Each Test Phase in All S+T List-Repetition Conditions in Experiments 1 and 2

Condition		Preceding Study (S) Phase										
		$S_{(1)}$	$S_{(2)}$	$S_{(3)}$	$S_{(4)}$	$S_{(5)}$	$S_{(6)}$	$S_{(7)}$	$S_{(8)}$	$S_{(9)}$	$S_{(10)}$	$M_{(T)}$
1, $SSST_1T_2T_3$	T_2	.016	.043	.103	.000	.000	.091	.250	---	---	---	.048
2 sec, CVC-CVC	N	62	46	29	18	14	11	8	---	---	---	
	T_3	.000	.045	.077	.056	.000	.000	.000	---	---	---	.028
	N	61	44	26	18	14	10	6	---	---	---	
3, $SSSSSST_1T_2T_3T_4T_5T_6$	T_2	.068	.040	.000	.061	.042	.063	.067	.000	.100	.000	.046
1 sec, CVC-CVC	N	73	50	39	33	24	16	15	13	10	7	
	T_3	.059	.000	.026	.032	.043	.000	.000	.077	.000	.000	.030
	N	68	48	39	31	23	15	14	13	9	7	
	T_4	.047	.042	.000	.033	.091	.000	.000	.000	.111	.143	.039
	N	64	48	38	30	22	15	14	12	9	7	
	T_5	.000	.022	.026	.069	.000	.000	.000	.000	.125	.000	.020
	N	61	46	38	29	20	15	14	12	8	6	
	T_6	.000	.022	.027	.037	.000	.000	.000	.000	.000	.000	.012
	N	61	45	37	27	20	15	14	12	7	6	
5, $SSSSSST_1T_2T_3T_4T_5T_6$	T_2	.047	.091	.500	---	---	---	---	---	---	---	.099
1.5 sec, CVC-CVC	N	43	22	6	---	---	---	---	---	---	---	
	T_3	.073	.100	---	---	---	---	---	---	---	---	.082
	N	41	20	---	---	---	---	---	---	---	---	
	T_4	.000	.056	---	---	---	---	---	---	---	---	.018
	N	38	18	---	---	---	---	---	---	---	---	
	T_5	.000	.000	---	---	---	---	---	---	---	---	.000
	N	38	17	---	---	---	---	---	---	---	---	
	T_6	.000	.059	---	---	---	---	---	---	---	---	.018
	N	38	17	---	---	---	---	---	---	---	---	

N = Number of cases
$M_{(T)}$ = Mean

TABLE 9.4
Response Recoveries over Successive Tests (Ts) Estimated from Responses
Made for the First Time Given Incorrect on All Previous Trials, Evaluated on
the Second or Later Tests on Successive Tests Within Each Test Phase
in All S+T Item-Repetition Conditions in Experiments 1 and 2

Condition		$S_{(1)}$	$S_{(2)}$	$S_{(3)}$	$S_{(4)}$	$S_{(5)}$	$S_{(6)}$	$S_{(7)}$	$S_{(8)}$	$S_{(9)}$	$S_{(10)}$	$M_{(T)}$
						Preceding Study (S) Phase						
2, $S'S'ST_1T_2T_3$	T'_2	.118	.152	.231	.111	---	---	---	---	---	---	.146
2 sec, CVC-CVC	N	76	46	26	9	---	---	---	---	---	---	
	T'_3	.060	.154	.050	.125	---	---	---	---	---	---	.090
	N	67	39	20	8	---	---	---	---	---	---	
4, $S'S'S'S'S'ST_1T_2T_3T_4T_5T_6$	T'_2	.049	.156	.100	.087	.067	.333	.000	---	---	---	.102
1 sec, CVC-CVC	N	82	64	40	23	15	12	8	---	---	---	
	T'_3	.051	.037	.139	.048	.071	.000	.000	---	---	---	.059
	N	78	54	36	21	14	8	8	---	---	---	
	T'_4	.000	.077	.065	.050	.000	.000	.125	---	---	---	.039
	N	74	52	31	20	13	8	8	---	---	---	
	T'_5	.014	.000	.103	.053	.077	.000	.000	---	---	---	.030
	N	74	48	29	19	13	8	7	---	---	---	
	T'_6	.000	.000	.000	.000	.000	.000	.143	---	---	---	.005
	N	73	48	26	18	12	8	7	---	---	---	
6, $S'S'S'S'S'ST_1T_2T_3T_4T_5T_6$	T'_2	.014	.160	.125	.043	.000	.286	---	---	---	---	.081
1.5 sec, CVC-CVC	N	74	50	32	23	13	7	---	---	---	---	
	T'_3	.027	.024	.107	.136	.077	.000	---	---	---	---	.054
	N	73	42	28	22	13	5	---	---	---	---	
	T'_4	.000	.000	.000	.105	.083	.000	---	---	---	---	.017
	N	71	41	25	19	12	5	---	---	---	---	
	T'_5	.014	.000	.000	.059	.000	.000	---	---	---	---	.012
	N	71	41	25	17	11	5	---	---	---	---	
	T'_6	.000	.000	.000	.000	.000	.000	---	---	---	---	.000
	N	70	41	25	16	11	5	---	---	---	---	

N = Number of cases
$M_{(T)}$ = Mean

to investigate new encoding possibilities for unreinforced Ts. The encoding probabilities of S (study) trials can be estimated using the conditional probability of a correct response for the first time, given incorrect responses on all previous trials. Table 9.2 displays these probabilities for the list- and item-repetition programs, in the top and bottom sections, respectively. The extreme right column gives the weighted mean for each condition. In accord with our analyses in Figs. 9.5 to 9.7, using the same CVC-CVCs with a constant total time in Experiment 1, the less frequent but longer duration conditions were superior (larger encoding probabilities) to the shorter and more frequent ones under both list- and item-repetition programs; Conditions 1 and 2 > Conditions 3 and 4.

Furthermore, in Experiment 2 (Figs. 9.8 to 9.10), these trends continued when the total S, T, S+T, and r times were increased by 50% for both repetition programs (same CVC-CVCs): The encoding probabilities of Conditions 5 and 6 (1.5 sec rate) were more than twice as large as those of Conditions 3 and 4 (1 sec rate). The same held true in Experiment 3 (easier CVC-digits, Figs. 9.11 - 9.13), where the 1.5 sec conditions (Conds. 9 &10) produced distinctly larger encoding probabilities than the 1 sec conditions (Conds. 7 & 8).

S encoding probability differentials between list- and item-repetition programs did not differ greatly when learning was fairly difficult as in Experiment 1 (Conds. 1-4). It is significant, however, that if learning was made easier (via longer duration, easier materials, or both, Exps. 2-3, Conds. 5-10), the S encoding probabilities were distinctly larger among the list-repetition program than among the item-repetition program, as per our earlier analyses in this chapter, i. e., internally consistent.

The same conditional probabilities were computed for successive T trials (on T_2-T_6/T'_2-T'_6) in Experiments 1 and 2. See Tables 9.3 and 9.4 for the list- and item-repetition results, respectively. Notice the conspicuous difference in magnitude between Table 9.2 (S encoding) and Tables 9.3 and 9.4 (T response recovery). In general, granting a small deviation (Cond. 4), S encoding greatly exceeded T encoding, if any. Considering this fact, together with our earlier inquiries (e.g., Izawa, 1993d), the statistics in Tables 9.3 and 9.4 generally seem to represent participants' response recovery, rather than their new learning from prior Ts. In support of this interpretation, the statistics were found to diminish in general from T_2/T'_2 to T_k/T'_k ($2 < k \leq 6$): What could be recovered from these Ts/T's (continuously decreasing from T_k/T'_k to T_{k+1}/T'_{k+1}) in each condition was recovered. But in the absence of new encoding within each T/T' phase, the statistics (Tables 9.3 & 9.4) did not improve from T_2/T'_2 to T_k/T'_k, or even maintain the same levels as T_2/T'_2. If new learning were to occur on Ts/T's per se, it would be difficult to see why such new learning diminishes dramatically from T_2/T'_2 to T_6/T'_6.

The same T/T' response recovery statistics for the four conditions in Experiment 3 (very easy CVC-digits) are unstable because of the very small number of cases applicable, $N \geq 5$, due to the extremely early onset of the floor effect. Despite minor deviations from this limitation, the general trends observed in Experiments 1 and 2 held more often than not in Experiment 3. The $M_{(T)}$s, mean conditional probabilities of first correct responses, given incorrect responses on all previous trials on T_2/T'_2, T_3/T'_3, T_4/T'_4, T_5/T'_5, and (with N $\leq$ 5) were: .308, .185, .006, .004, .004 in Condition 7 (1 sec); .025, .000, .020, .016, .000 in Condition 9 (1.5 sec) under the list-repetitions; .244, .186, .113, .028, .014 in Condition 8 (1 sec); and .236, .143, .056, .088, .000 in Condition 10 (1.5 sec) under the item-repetitions.

Unlike the systematic downward trend for successive Ts/T's (response recovery, e.g., Tables 9.3 & 9.4), no such trend was observed for successive S phases (especially early ones with sufficient cases, Table 9.2). To the contrary, some trends seemed to veer up under the item-repetition program, again underlining the fundamental differences between S/S' and T/T' trials. The present findings consistently replicate those of different S-T-r presentation programs (e.g., Izawa, 1966, 1992a, 1993b, in press). They convincingly suggest that the basic premise of the total time hypothesis that assumes identity of S and T trials, TTH(S=T), is not on sound footing. In addition, all TTHs, original or modified, have encountered many difficulties while being examined in the current series of experiments.

Interactions of List-/Item-Repetition Presentation Programs and Learning Difficulty Levels

Most intriguingly, we discovered that the efficiency of S-T-r programs is learning-difficulty-dependent. Specifically, the item-repetition program held a distinct advantage over the list-repetition program when learning was difficult, a finding which might be attributable to participants' experience, maturity as well as the learning materials, presentation rates, total S, T, S+T, r times, or any combination thereof. When learning was made easier, however, the reverse occurred: Here, the list-repetition program showed superiority (except in learning situations that were too easy). The interactions occurred even when the two programs' respective total S, T, S+T, and r times, presentation durations, and frequencies were held constant (Figs. 9.7, 9.10, & 9.13). The phenomenon was also replicated by Izawa (1993a, Fig. 3.8; 1993b, Fig. 4.5; in press, Fig. 4). In sum, our findings clearly contradict all single-factor predictions made by the first 13 hypotheses in Table 9.1 as well as their derivatives.

Conjectures

A viable candidate to account for the clear interactions demonstrated here is the S-T-r program hypothesis. That is, if one can assume that the two programs, list- vs. item-repetitions, might produce opposite effects as a function of learning difficulty, (hypothetically schematized in Fig. 9.14 and expressed in terms of probable errors inferred from empirical data), we can account for the seemingly complex results via the effects of list- and item-repetition programs, respectively.

If one posits that the advantages of item-repetition dominate when learning is difficult, and those of the list-repetition are in control when learning is easy (see thick line), somewhere between hard and easy learning, there must be points where the two programs do not differ significantly: That seems supported by Izawa (1993a, Fig. 3.8), and the significant superiority of the item-presentation program when learning was difficult at the 1 sec presentation rate. However, there were no visible differences at all at the intermediate 2 sec rate, whereas at the easy 3 sec rate, the superiority of the list-repetition was apparent.

These findings have distinct educational implications.   Indeed, the benefits of item- vs. list-repetition may be tailored to fit specific educational situations.   In difficult learning situations because of either hard materials (such as foreign words, chemical formulae, and telephone or ID numbers) or learner attributes (such as young/naïve or intellectually disadvantaged), the item-repetition program has an edge.   However, for easy learning situations, the list-repetition program is advantageous, and for intermediately difficult situations either will do.

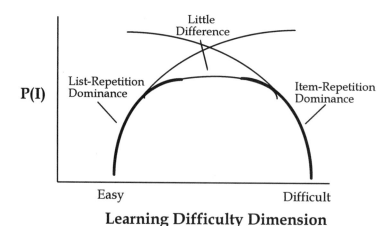

Learning Difficulty Dimension

FIG. 9.14.   A potential theoretical explanation for the empirical dominance of list- or item-repetitions interacting with learning difficulty levels.

Summary

In pursuit of optimal acquisition, psychology majors, well experienced in verbal learning experiments, participated in three simultaneous experiments containing 10 conditions. Systematically varied were S-T-r (Study-Test-rest) presentation programs (list- vs. item-repetitions), presentation durations (1 vs. 2 or 1.5 sec), frequencies (3 or 6 time per S or T phase), total S, T, S+T, and r times (72 or 108 sec per S or T phase; 6 or 9 sec for r per phase), and learning difficulty levels (difficult, medium, and very easy). Examined were 13 single-factor hypotheses from the three families of TTHs (total time hypotheses), presentation duration and frequency hypotheses and one multi-factor S-T-r presentation program hypothesis were examined.

When total times, durations, and frequencies were held constant in difficult learning situation in Experiment 1 (CVC-CVCs), significant differences resulted among the conditions, despite identical predictions from the 13 single factor hypotheses. The same held for Experiment 2 (intermediate CVC-CVCs with longer total times) and for the very early challenging part of Experiment 3, but thereafter its CVC-digits were very easy to master. Thus, the 13 single-factor hypotheses were challenged but the multi-factor S-T-r presentation program hypothesis received strong support.

We also discovered that S-T-r presentation program effects interacted with learning difficulty levels: The item-repetition program was significantly superior to the list-repetition program in difficult learning situations (Exp. 1), whereas the list-repetition program showed distinct strengths in easier learning situations (Exp. 2, Cond. 5 over 6; very early in Exp. 3). Over 6 successive T's in the 1 sec item-repetition programs $S'S'S'S'S'S'T'_1T'_2T'_3T'_4T'_5T'_6$ with both difficult CVC-CVCs and easy CVC-digit materials, the older and experienced participants, in contrast to young naïve freshmen (Izawa, in press), showed significant regression on T'_1 from the previous T'_6, but progressively and significantly improved performances T'_1 to T'_6 per T phase. The LTM enhancement effect is now well established, having been replicated here for the third time in a 1 sec Condition, SSSSSSTTTTT, in a difficult learning situation: Here LTM remains significantly superior to STM!

In conclusion, acquisition efficiency appears to be controlled by S-T-r (Study-Test-rest) presentation programs in conjunction with learning difficulty levels. Other influences include the powerful effects of T and r (e.g., Izawa, 1966, 1967, 1971a, 1971b, 1992a, in press), S/T interactions (e.g., Izawa, 1988, 1992a, in press), and S and T spacing (e.g., Izawa, 1989, 1992, in press) among others enumerated in this chapter. Total time alone is not an adequate explanation for acquisition efficiency! In that sense, our persistent efforts to find optimal learning and retention for acquisition efficiency parameters were rewarded.

Acknowledgments

This research was supported in parts by grants from NIMH (MH 12970-01 and - 02), and from the Flowerree Foundation (FF 6-25278). The author gratefully acknowledges the contributions of Elaine Blesi who ran all 70 experimental participants. Completion of this chapter owes much to the competent processing, proofing, tabulating, illustrating, reference-checking, and statistical treatments provided by Julie Bourbon, Maria Toledo, Eun-sil Lee, Althea Izawa-Hayden, Lieuko Nguyen, and Erica Sherer. Their devotion and professionalism have made it possible to complete this chapter in a timely manner.

References

Bugelski, B. R. (1962). Presentation time, total time, and mediation in paired-associate learning. *Journal of Experimental Psychology, 63*, 409-412.

Carrier, M., & Pashler, H. (1992). The influence of retrieval on retention. *Memory & Cognition, 20(6)*, 633-642.

Cooper, E. H., & Pantle, A. J. (1967). the total-time hypothesis in verbal learning. *Psychological Bulletin, 68*, 221-234.

Ebbinghaus, H. (1885). *Ueber das Gedaechtnis: Untersuchungen zur experimentellen Psychologie* [On Memory: Investigations in experimental psychology]. Leipzig, Germany: Duncker & Humbolt.

Estes, W. K. (1991). Cognitive architectures from the standpoint of an experimental psychologist. *Annual Review of Psychology, 42*, 1-28.

Eysenck, M. W. (1990). *The Blackwell dictionary of cognitive psychology.* Colchester, VT: Blackwell.

Gross, T. M., & Bjork, R. A. (1991, November) *Developing episodic distinctiveness via retrieval practice: Insulation from associate interference.* Paper presented at the 32nd Annual Meeting of the Psychonomic Society, San Francisco.

Hagman, J. D. (1983). Presentation- and test-trial effects on acquisition and retention of distance and location. *Journal of Experimental Psychology: Learning, Memory, and Cognition, 9*, 334-345.

Hintzman, D. L. (1970). Effects of repetition and duration of therapy. *Journal of Experimental Psychology, 83*, 435-444.

Hintzman, D. L. (1974). Theoretical implications of the spacing effect. In R. L. Solso (Ed.), *Theories in cognitive psychology: The Loyola Symposium* (pp. 77-99). Potomac, MD: Lawrence Erlbaum Associates.

Hoffman, R. R., & Deffenbacher, K. A. (1992). A brief history of applied cognitive psychology. *Applied Cognitive Psychology, 6*, 1-48.

Hull, C. L. (1943). *Principles of behavior.* New York: Appleton-Century-Crofts.

Izawa, C. (1966). Reinforcement-test sequences in paired-associate learning. *Psychological Reports, Monograph Supplement, 3-V18,* 879-919.

Izawa, C. (1967). Function of test trials in paired-associate learning. *Journal of Experimental Psychology, 75,* 194-209.

Izawa, C. (1968). Effects of reinforcement, neutral and test trials upon paired-associate acquisition and retention. *Psychological Reports, 23,* 947-959.

Izawa, C. (1969). Comparison of reinforcement and test trials in paired-associate learning. *Journal of Experimental Psychology, 81,* 600-603.

Izawa, C. (1970a). List versus items in distributed practice in paired-associate learning. *Proceedings, 78th Annual Convention,* APA, 87-88.

Izawa, C. (1970b) Optimal potentiating effects and forgetting-prevention effects of tests in paired-associate learning. *Journal of Experimental Psychology, 83,* 340-344.

Izawa, C. (1970c). Reinforcement-test-blank acquisition programming under the unmixed list design in paired-associate learning. *Psychonomic Science, 19,* 75-77.

Izawa, C. (1971a). Massed and spaced practice in paired-associate learning: List versus item distributions. *Journal of Experimental Psychology, 89,* 10-21.

Izawa, C. (1971b). The test trial potentiating model. *Journal of Mathematical Psychology, 8,* 200-224.

Izawa, C. (1976). Vocalized and silent tests in paired-associate learning. *American Journal of Psychology, 89,* 681-693.

Izawa, C. (1980). Empirical examinations of the retention interval hypothesis: Comparisons of learning methods when learning is difficult. *Journal of General Psychology, 103,* 117-129.

Izawa, C. (1985a). A test of the differences between anticipation and study-test methods of paired-associate learning. *Journal of Experimental Psychology: Learning, Memory, and Cognition, 11,* 165-184.

Izawa, C. (1985b). The identity model and factors controlling the superiority of the study-test method over the anticipation method. *Journal of General Psychology, 112,* 65-78.

Izawa, C. (1988). A search for the control factors of the repetition effect. *Japanese Psychological Review, 31,* 367-403.

Izawa, C. (1989a). A test of the identity model: Encoding processes differ little between anticipation and study-test methods. In C. Izawa (Ed.), *Current issues in cognitive processes: Tulane Flowerree symposium on cognition* (pp. 210-245). Hillsdale, NJ: Lawrence Erlbaum Associates.

Izawa, C. (1989b). Similarities and differences between anticipation and study-test item information presentation methods. In C. Izawa (Ed.), *Current issues in cognitive processes: The Tulane Flowerree symposium on cognition* (pp. 201-209). Hillsdale, NJ: Lawrence Erlbaum Associates.

Izawa, C. (1992a). Test trials contributions to optimization of learning processes: Study/test trials interactions. In A. Healy, S. W. Kosslyn, & R. M. Shiffrin (Eds.), *From learning processes to cognitive processes: Essays in honor of William K. Estes, Vol 2*, (pp. 1-35). Hillsdale, NJ: Lawrence Erlbaum Associates.

Izawa, C. (1992b, August). *The study-test-rest (S-T-r) program hypothesis.* Presented at the Patrick Suppes Retirement Seminar, 1992 Mathematical Psychology Meeting, Stanford, CA.

Izawa, C. (1993a). Efficient learning: The total time, exposure duration, frequency, and programming of the study phase. In C. Izawa (Ed.), *Cognitive psychology applied* (pp. 43-78). Hillsdale, NJ: Lawrence Erlbaum Associates.

Izawa, C. (1993b). Power behind the scenes: Hidden effects of test trials unveiled. In C. Izawa (Ed.), *Cognitive psychology applied* (pp. 79-110). Hillsdale, NJ: Lawrence Erlbaum Associates.

Izawa, C. (in press). Total time and efficient time management: In search of optimal learning and retention via Study-Test-rest presentation programs. *Journal of American Psychology.*

Izawa, C., & Hayden, R. G. (1989). Comparisons of visual and auditory information processing under the two different item presentation procedures. In C. Izawa (Ed.), *Current issues in cognitive processes: The Tulane Flowerree symposium on cognition* (pp. 246-278). Hillsdale, NJ: Lawrence Erlbaum Associates.

Izawa, C., & Hayden, R. G. (1993). Race against time: Toward the principle of optimization in learning and retention. In C. Izawa (Ed.), *Cognitive psychology applied* (pp. 15-41). Hillsdale, NJ: Lawrence Erlbaum Associates.

Izawa, C., & Patterson, D. J. (1989). Effects of the item presentation methods and test trials on Euclidean distances and location learning via the tactile sense. In C. Izawa (Ed.), *Current issues in cognitive processes: The Tulane Flowerree Symposium on cognition* (pp. 279-312). Hillsdale, NJ: Lawrence Erlbaum Associates.

King, J. F., Zechmeister, E. B., & Shaughnessy, J. J. (1980). Judgments of knowing: The influence of retrieval practice. *American Journal of Psychology, 93*, 329-343.

Longstreth, L. E. (1971). Relationship between response learning and recall of feedback in tests of the law of effect. *Journal of Experimental Psychology, 90*, 149-151.

Murdock, B. B., Jr. (1960).   The immediate retention of unrelated words. *Journal of Experimental Psychology, 60*, 222-234.

Newman, S. E. (1964).   Effects of pairing-time and test-time on performance during and after paired-associate training.   *American Journal of Psychology, 77*, 634-637.

Postman, L., & Goggin, J. (1966).   Whole versus part learning of paired-associate lists. *Journal of Experimental Psychology, 71*, 867-877.

Rose, R. J. (1992).   Degree of learning, interpolated tests, and rate of forgetting. *Memory & Cognition, 20(6)*, 621-632.

Slamecka, N. (1969).   A temporal interpretation of some recall phenomena. *Psychological Review, 76*, 492-503.

Stevenson, H. W., Chen, C., & Lee, S. (1993).   Mathematics achievements of Chinese, Japanese, and American children: Ten years later. *Science, 259*, 53-58.

Underwood, B. J. (1970).   A breakdown of the total time law in free-recall learning. *Journal of Verbal Learning and Verbal Behavior, 9*, 573-580.

Whitten, W. B., II., & Bjork, R. A. (1977).   Learning from tests: Effects of spacing. *Journal of Verbal Learning and Verbal Behavior, 16*, 465-478.

Chapter 10

Recalling to Recognize and Recognizing Recall

Steven E. Clark
University of California, Riverside, USA

The influence of the Atkinson-Shiffrin (1968) model is far-reaching to the point that one current memory textbook refers to it as the "modal model" (Schwartz & Reisberg, 1991). The Atkinson-Shiffrin chapter focussed on cued and free recall, proposing a serial search as the control process underlying retrieval in these tasks. However, in a last section on "Further considerations..." they previewed what has become one of the most central controversies regarding models of recognition memory.

> *Search processes seem at first glance to offer an easy means for the analysis of differences between recognition and recall. One could assume, for example, that ... the search component ... is not part of the recognition process; that is, one might assume that in recognition the relevant information in LTS is always found and retrieval depends solely on matching the stored information against the item presented for test.* (p. 186)

In the next sentence they suggest that the no-search hypothesis will be contradicted by data from experiments varying list length. Implicitly, they assumed the match function to be invariant across list length. In fact, it had already been shown that recognition performance decreases as list length increases (Strong, 1912). The question, of course, is whether the list-length results (which have since been replicated by Gronlund & Elam, 1994; Ratcliff, Clark, & Shiffrin, 1990) contradicted the no-search hypothesis in general, or just one version of it.

The no-search model for recognition has since come to be called by various names including strength model, familiarity model, and matching model. The question is whether recognition operates on the basis of strength, familiarity, or matching *only*, or whether a search, or some other *recall-like* component also operates in making recognition memory decisions. The question is also framed as one between single-process versus two-process models.

The commemorative nature of this book suggests an historical organization, beginning with two-process models of recognition proposed by Atkinson and Juola (1974), Humphreys (1978) and Mandler (1980). The 1980s saw the development of a new and improved variety of single-process models called *global memory* or *global matching* models (see Clark & Gronlund, 1996, for a review). Interest in two-process models was resurrected in 1991 with the publication of Jacoby's dual-process model, and by several other empirical results which seemed problematic for global matching models. The historical organization also reflects the interplay of theory and data which has guided research in this area.

Matching and Dual-Process Models

The defining feature of matching models is that retrieval is direct rather than indirect (Gillund & Shiffrin, 1984). By direct retrieval we mean that the relevant information for recognition is accessed directly; it does not need to be "found." This has the advantage of allowing fast reaction times. The basic model was simple; the match of the test item T returns an index of familiarity F(T). If F(T) is above a decision criterion C, the test item is called "old", and is called "new" otherwise. Two kinds of matching models have been proposed, referred to as local and global matching models. In local matching models, recognition is based on the test item's match to its locally-stored representation (for example a node in an associative network, Anderson, 1972). Two problems with local match models became quickly evident: they could not produce list-length effects or context effects. These two problems led to the development of two-process theories proposed by Atkinson and Juola (1974), Humphreys (1978), and Mandler (1980).

List Length Effect: Atkinson-Juola Model. Atkinson and Juola modified the simple local matching model by assuming there would be cases in which decisions could not be made on the basis of familiarity alone, requiring that the subject search through episodic memory. The modified two-process model assumed two decision criteria. If the familiarity is above a high criterion C_H the subject could quickly call the item "old," and if the familiarity is below a low criterion C_L, the subject could quickly call the item "new." Test items whose familiarity falls between C_H and C_L would require recall of the relevant information via a search of episodic memory. These assumptions provided excellent fits to response time data. Increases in response time with list length were due to longer search times, and yet very fast yes and no responses could be explained by very high or very low familiarity.

Context Effects: Humphreys and Mandler Models. Several studies have shown that recognition of words from a studied list is better when the words are tested with their original verbal study context than when tested in a different context (Tulving & Thomson, 1971). Schematically, for study of word pairs AB, CD, EF, etc., recognition of B is better when tested as AB than when tested as _B (context removed) or as CB (context changed). A related finding is the ability to distinguish between intact (AB) and rearranged (AD) pairs in associative recognition. A simple local-matching model, without modification, could not account for these results. One familiarity-based explanation, that context influenced the encoding of items at study and test was shown to have problems with some data (Humphreys, 1976; Underwood & Humphreys, 1979). Humphreys (1978) and Mandler (1980) proposed recall-based accounts which varied in some respects, but which both assumed that at the time of test, the context item provides a second cue to recognize the test item. Thus, even if word B cannot be recognized alone, the context word A may be used as a cue to recall the original A-B study pairing.

Familiarity-only models were shown to be inadequate to handle list-length and context-effect results, and recall-based explanations seemed to be just the right kind of "fix". But what do we mean when we say that recall processes operate in recognition memory? One way to answer that question is to consider the most prominent dual-process model (so prominent that it is often referred to as *the* dual-process model).

The Mandler-Jacoby Dual-Process Model

Mandler (1980) and later Jacoby (1991) formulated dual-process models which assumed that recognition decisions are based on the independent contributions of familiarity and recall processes. For both models, the probability of calling a test item B old is given as

$$p(\text{Rgn B}) = F_b + (1 - F_b)R_b \tag{10.1}$$

where F_b and R_b denote the familiarity and recall components. The test item is recognized if it is familiar or if it is recalled. At this level Jacoby's and Mandler's approaches are identical. What differentiates the two is how they estimate the recall and familiarity components. Inherent in the estimation procedures are important assumptions about the nature of the recall processes operating in recognition.

Mandler's Estimation Procedure

In Mandler's procedures, participants study word pairs AB, CD, etc., and the F and R components are estimated from three kinds of data: recognition of items tested with study context (AB), items tested without study context (_B), and cued recall (of A given B as a cue A|B, and B given A, B|A). According to the model, the advantage for recognition of items in context is due to the very same recall processes that underlie cued recall, so the level of cued recall performance and the amount of context-based facilitation in recognition are related. The probabilities for recognition of B alone, and for B within the AB pair are

$$p(\text{Rgn B}) = F_b + R_{ab|b} - F_b R_{ab|b} \tag{10.2}$$

and

$$p(\text{Rgn AB}) = F_b F_a + R_{ab} - F_a F_b R_{ab} \tag{10.3}$$

where it is assumed that $F_a = F_b$, and R_{ab} is given by the recall probabilities,

$$R_{ab} = p(A|B) + p(B|A) - p(A|B)p(B|A) \tag{10.4}$$

Familiarity is also derived from data, where

$$F_b = p(\text{Rgn B}) - R_{ab|b} / (1 - R_{ab|b}) \tag{10.5}$$

The F_a term is derived in the same manner from $p(\text{Rgn A})$ and $R_{ab|a}$.

Jacoby's Estimation Procedure

Jacoby's (1991) experimental procedure has been called the *process dissociation* or the *inclusion/exclusion* procedure. Two groups of items are studied, A and B, both of which are to be distinguished from new items X. In the inclusion condition the participant is instructed to respond old to both A and B items, whereas in the exclusion condition, the subject is to respond old to A and new to B.

In the inclusion condition, the participant may recognize a B item as old by recalling the item, but even if that fails, may still recognize the item based on familiarity. The probability of recognizing B in the inclusion condition is given by Eq. 10.1, which may be rewritten as

$$P(\text{Old}|B, \text{Include}) = R_b + (1-R_b) F_b \tag{10.6}$$

In the exclusion condition, B is erroneously called old if the participant fails to recall it, but responds on the basis of familiarity. Again, in the two-process model,

$$P(\text{Old}|B, \text{Exclude}) = (1-R_b) F_b \tag{10.7}$$

Equations for the Include and Exclude condition differ only in the R term in the Include condition. Thus, the recollective component R can be estimated from the difference in P(Old) for the include and exclude conditions, or

$$R = P(\text{Old}|B, \text{Include}) - P(\text{Old}|B, \text{Exclude}) \tag{10.8}$$

As before, one can solve for F, which is given as

$$F = \text{exclude}/(1-R) \tag{10.9}$$

Evaluation of Mandler-Jacoby Model

This model has been applied to data from a large number of experiments, and for the most part, the variation in parameters is sensible and consistent with the assumptions of the model. Specifically, the familiarity component is assumed to be due largely to automatic, perceptual processes, suggesting that experimental manipulations which would be presumed to have their effects on strategic or conceptual processing will leave the estimate of F unchanged. Without going into the specifics, that basic result has been obtained in several experiments (Jacoby, Yonelinas, & Jennings, 1997; Mandler, 1980).

Instead, I will return to the question: What do we mean by recall processes in recognition? Embedded in the estimation procedures are four important assumptions: (1) recall processes are separate and distinct from familiarity; (2) recall is relatively complete, (3) recall operates identically across the tasks which are used to provide estimates of F and R, and (4) recall and familiarity make independent contributions. Discussion of the first assumption is postponed until later. Assumptions 2 and 3 are discussed together below.

Commensurability, Completeness, and the Estimation of F and R

The third assumption (recall operates in the same way across estimation tasks) has been termed the commensurability assumption. Commensurability is assumed in Mandler's and Jacoby's procedures; however the estimation tasks are different. Mandler assumed that recall operates the same way in recognition as it does in cued recall. Jacoby explicitly did not make this assumption, but assumed that recall operates in the same way for inclusion and exclusion conditions. Given these differences, tests of commensurability are discussed separately.

Commensurability in Exclusion-Inclusion Comparisons. The commensurability assumption predicts that the probability of responding yes to the positive items in the exclusion condition will equal the probability of responding yes to those items in the inclusion condition. This prediction was confirmed by Jacoby (1991). Underlying the prediction is the assumption that recall is always complete and accurate, so that recalled items will not be misidentified. This assumption contradicts well-established phenomena: Recall is not always complete, as shown by tip-of-the-tongue results (Brown & McNeill, 1966; Koriat & Lieblich, 1974). One kind of information that can be missing is the information that identifies the source, that is, where or when a particular item or event occurred.

Recent experimental findings suggest that the completeness and commensurability assumptions do not always hold. Dodson and Johnson (1996) varied the similarity of orienting tasks between the sets of items which defined the exclusion condition. Following presentation of a list of anagram and read items, items in the second phase were heard for half of the participants and were word stem completions for the other half. Distinguishing between anagrams and word stem items in the exclusion condition was more difficult than distinguishing between anagrams and heard items, violating the equal-performance prediction. P(yes) for the positive items (anagrams) was .74 in the inclusion condition, but only .52 in the exclusion condition, when the negative set items were from word-fragment completion. A similar pattern of results has also been shown by Mulligan and Hirshman (1997). Similarity between exclusion sets makes exclusion difficult but has no effect on inclusion.

   Commensurability in Cued Recall-Recognition Comparisons. There has been no direct test of the commensurability assumption in Mandler's estimation procedures. There are reasons, however, to suspect that the assumption does not hold, and indirect evidence that it does not hold. With regard to the suspicions, most current models assume that cued recall itself relies on two processes, and it is likely that only one of them would operate in recognition. In the SAM model (Raaijmakers & Shiffrin, 1980), traces in memory must be accessed (sampling), and then once accessed, their contents must be output (recovery). In content-addressable retrieval models such as TODAM (Murdock, 1982, 1993), the Matrix association model (Humphreys, Bain, & Pike 1989; Pike, 1984), and MINERVA 2 (Hintzman, 1988), cued recall results in a retrieved vector which is noisy, and must be deblurred for output. Thus, when A is used to recall B, the information from the B trace must be processed further for output. It is reasonable to assume that such processes either do not occur in recognition, or if they do occur, they are facilitated by having the target items present. For example, for the test of AB, B may be recognized because A is used to recall it, but it seems likely that the output processing (recovery or deblurring) would be facilitated since the target is visibly present. Thus, cued recall performance may underestimate the contribution of recall in recognition memory.

   There is evidence for this in some of the fits of the two-process model to recall and recognition data. In fitting the model to data (Mandler, Rabinowitz, & Simon, 1981), the model predicted a .02 difference between item recognition for A or B alone and recognition of the AB pair. The data, however, showed a .09 difference between single item and pair recognition. This is precisely the result one would expect if cued recall probabilities underestimate the contribution of recall processes in recognition.

   A similar argument can be made for estimates of F from Rabinowitz, Mandler, & Barsalou (1977). The model assumes that for B items which do not allow recall of A, the probability of recognizing B alone, without the context item A, should be approximately equal to the estimate for F. In other words, without recall, recognition is based on familiarity only. Mandler reported that indeed, in Experiment 5 recognition of B items which did not lead to recall of A was .42 and the estimate for F was a respectably close .37. However, when Humphreys and Bain (1983) analyzed Experiments 4 and 6, and reanalyzed Experiment 5, a consistent pattern emerged; recognition of the relevant B items was consistently greater than the estimate of F. One explanation of the discrepancy is that recall was contributing to the recognition of the B items, even though B could not be used to recall A. If this is the case, then the cued recall probabilities will always underestimate recall in recognition.

There is indirect evidence against commensurability as well. According to Mandler and Humphreys dual process models, associative recognition is based at least in part on cued recall, but cued recall and associative recognition show different patterns of results for many experimental variables. Cued recall shows list composition effects for word frequency and item-strength, but associative recognition does not (Clark & Burchett, 1994; Clark & Hori, 1995a; Ratcliff, Clark, & Shiffrin, 1990; Hockley, 1992; Murnane & Shiffrin, 1991). Cued recall shows large retroactive interference effects, but associative recognition does not (Dyne, Humphreys, Bain, & Pike, 1989). Cued recall shows large forgetting effects, but associative recognition does not (Murdock & Hockley, 1989).

The Independence Assumption

Mandler assumed that the familiarity component is due to perceptual processing, and increases with repetition for a given item, but is invariant across other encoding manipulations. Consistent with this assumption, Jacoby described the familiarity component as perceptual fluency, and assumed that its operation was automatic. There have been many demonstrations consistent with this assumption (see Jacoby, Yonelinas, & Jennings, 1997; Mandler, 1980). Specifically, manipulation of several variables has been shown to effect the estimate of the recollective component, but have virtually no effect on the automatic component, which makes intuitive sense given most conceptualizations of automatic processing (Shiffrin & Schneider, 1977). Jacoby et al. (1997) showed that an alternative assumption of mutual exclusion between familiarity and recall did not fare well.

Curran and Hintzman (1995) put the independence assumption to a strong test by devising conditions in which automatic and conscious components of retrieval would likely show an inverse, trading-off relationship. The task was stem completion following presentation of a list of words. In the include condition subjects were instructed to use list words to complete the stems, whereas in the exclude condition participants were instructed to not use list words to complete the word stems. Manipulations of presentation time produced the predicted inverse relationship. In addition, Curran and Hintzman calculated correlations between A and R parameters for subjects and items. They found a positive correlation between A and R in the item analysis, indicating that in a general way some items were "better" than others, and a negative correlation in the subject analysis, showing the trade-off of automatic and conscious components. These results contradict the independence assumption; however, it must be noted that the task used by Curran and Hintzman was a stem completion task rather than a recognition memory task.

The independence assumption has been examined within Mandler's estimation procedure also. Bain and Humphreys (1988) constructed encoding conditions designed to increase cued recall, but decrease recognition of items in non-intact pairs. The only account of this within the two-process model is to assume that familiarity and recall trade-off, contrary to the independence assumptions of the model. Bain and Humphreys showed that estimates of F did vary inversely with cued recall, and concluded, "Mandler's assumption of the independence of familiarity and retrieval at the item level is incorrect, or the retrieval component is inadequately estimated by overt recall (*a violation of the commensurability assumption*), or the dependence of familiarity and retrieval at list level is the result of some list-wide trade off" (p. 116, italics added).

Finally, in an experiment described in detail later, Hintzman, Curran, and Oppy (1992) showed results suggesting that familiarity and recallability vary together. As the number of repetitions of a list item increased, frequency judgments for similar nonstudied items also increased unless subjects were able to use the non-studied item as a cue to recall the studied item (thus giving the nonlist item a frequency of zero).

Summary

The central assumptions of the Mandler-Jacoby model may indeed be wrong: commensurability may not hold, and recall and familiarity may not make independent contributions. But the big claim of these models may nonetheless be correct: that recognition operates on the basis of two components, familiarity and recall. Commensurability and independence violations may arise because recall and familiarity are not distinct within recognition memory tasks, and there may be subprocesses which are common to both recall and recognition components. It is important to distinguish between recall *processes* and recall *tasks*. To assume that recall processes operate in recognition is not the same as asserting that recall operates in recognition. Some subset of the subprocesses that operate in recall tasks may operate in recognition tasks as well. Just what those subprocesses are is not entirely clear. In the next section I describe how single-process models have evoloved to incorportate recall-like components.

The Evolution of Familiarity Models

Acceptance of the two-process approach requires a demonstration that the experimental results which support the two-process model cannot be explained by any familiarity-only model. In the early 1980s, several familiarity-only models were developed which could produce list-length and context effects, without appeal to recall processes. These models collectively have come to be called *global matching models*, and include TODAM (Murdock, 1982; 1993, the SAM model (Gillund & Shiffrin, 1984), Matrix association models (Humphreys, Bain, & Pike, 1989; Pike, 1984), and Hintzman's (1988) multiple trace MINERVA. For a detailed discussion of these models, interested readers may refer to original papers or two reviews (Clark & Gronlund, 1996; Humphreys, Bain, & Pike, 1989). Here I will briefly outline how global memory models account for list-length and context effects, and briefly describe their possible application to inclusion-exclusion differences.

Global matching models assume direct access to relevant information; however the relevant information is not restricted to the memory of the test item. Rather, the test item is matched to multiple memory representations in parallel. The familiarity of the test item T would be

$$F(T) = m(T,M_1) + m(T,M_2) + m(T,M_3) + ... + m(T,M_N) \qquad (10.10)$$

where each term represents the match of the test item to memory item M_i. This sum can be calculated in one of two ways depending upon the representational assumptions of the particular model. Separate traces may be stored in memory (SAM and MINERVA), and the familiarity may be computed by summing matches to individual traces as shown in Equation 10.10. Alternatively, multiple events may be represented in a single distributed memory, and the test item is matched to that single composite representation (TODAM and Matrix association models). These models make two recall-like assumptions, but incorporate them into the familiarity computation. Familiarity is based not only on stored item-specific information about the test item, but also on associative information and information about *other* items in memory. In earlier network models, associative information and other memory items were only relevant to search processes in recall. In the remainder of this section I discuss how global matching models have dealt with list length effects, context effects, and inclusion-exclusion differences. As a prelude, it is noted that global memory models appeared to have easy success in dealing with list-length and context effects, but in fact, these results proved difficult for global models, requiring additional modification.

List Length Effects

Global matching models can account for list-length effects because as the number of items stored in memory increases, the variance of the match distributions also increases. The difference between the expected familiarities for targets and distractors is unaffected, and thus the increased variance increases the overlap of target and distractor distributions. In addition to the variance increase, TODAM also assumes a decay function that decreases the strength of the composite memory trace as each additional item is presented. Although it may seem like list-length effects are dispensed with easily enough by global matching models, there is a devil in the details: The assumptions which produce list-length effects lead to other predictions which are not confirmed by data.

List-Strength Effect. All of the global matching models predict a list-strength effect, which is not shown in experimental results (Ratcliff, Clark, & Shiffrin, 1990). The list-strength prediction is that strength differences will be larger in a mixed list of strong and weak items than in a comparison between pure lists of all strong or all weak items. Strength has typically been operationalized as longer presentation times or increased repetitions. Strong items should be recognized better in the mixed list than in the pure list, and weak items should be recognized more poorly in the mixed list than in the pure list. The prediction comes from the assumption that the variance increases with the mean strength. The difference in the familiarity means, $F(T) - F(D)$, is the same for mixed and pure lists, but the variances are ordered $\sigma_{ps} > \sigma_m > \sigma_{pw}$ where ps, pw, and m denote the pure strong, pure weak, and mixed lists, respectively.

ROC Slopes. The list-length and strength predictions arise from the assumption that the variance of the familiarity distributions increases with the mean. A summary statistic, the ratio of the distractor and target variances, σ_D^2/σ_T^2, is the slope of the normalized ROC. For SAM and MINERVA this ratio is less than 1.0 because $\sigma_T^2 > \sigma_D^2$. As the strength of studied items increases σ_D^2/σ_T^2 should decrease because the target variance increases more than the distractor variance. As the length of the list increases σ_D^2/σ_T^2 should approach 1.0. TODAM predicts that the ratio should always be close to 1.0. Ratcliff, Sheu, and Gronlund (1992) showed that the ratio remained near .8 across strength manipulations. List-length results are not as clear cut: single-list experiments have shown the ratio increasing toward 1.0, but multiple-list experiments show a ratio constant near 1.0 (Gronlund & Elam, 1994; Yonelinas, 1994).

Context Effects

In global memory models, context effects arise because episodic associations are formed interactively, and it is assumed that when the verbal context is presented, people probe with the item cues and with the associative information in the joint cue. Thus, the familiarity of the joint probe AB is greater than the familiarity of AD. The interactive association assumption is instantiated differently in the various models: by mathematical convolution in TODAM, by outer product multiplication in Matrix association models, by multiplication of cue-to-trace retrieval strengths in SAM, and by a cubing function relating familiarity to similarity in MINERVA. Although the particular instantiation of the interactive cue assumption varies across models, the ability to account for context effects, *at least in principle*, does not. All of the models appear to have the proper machinery to handle context effects, and all of the models can discriminate intact from rearranged test pairs (Clark & Shiffrin, 1992). However, again problems lurk in the details.

Early applications of SAM to context-effect results may have appeared to show more success than was actually achieved. Clark and Shiffrin (1987) fit SAM to a wide range of test conditions which followed the study of word triples (ABC). Thirteen different test combinations of triples, pairs and single items were tested: ABC, ABC', AB'C", ABX, AB'X, AXY, XYZ, AB, AB', AX, XY, A and X, where primes denote items from rearranged study triples, and X, Y, and Z are nonstudied items. Three different decision rules were utilized, with instructions to respond "old" if: (a) all the items were studied together, (b) all the items were studied, or (c) any of the items were studied.

The version of SAM which fit the results incorporated encoding match assumptions, which boosted the familiarity of items tested with their original study context. In other words, the multiplicative combination of cue strengths was not sufficient to produce the magnitude of the context effects shown in the data. A fit of TODAM to the same data (Weber, 1988) was also unsuccessful. The version of TODAM used by Weber did not distinguish among the various distractor types. The versions of SAM and TODAM which were fit to these results were both fairly simple, and more complex models could be fit to the results (see Murdock, 1993).

Other context-effect related results also proved troublesome for global memory models. In a slight variation on standard context-effect methodology, Gillund and Shiffrin (1984) and Clark and Shiffrin (1987, 1992) compared recognition performance for single-item and cued recognition. Single-item recognition required discrimination between old (B) and new (X). The task for cued recognition was essentially the same except that the test items were accompanied at test by a clearly marked cue, denoted here by lower case (aB targets and aX distractors). High frequency words produced an advantage for cued over single-item recognition, consistent with standard context effects. However, low frequency words showed either no difference or a slight disadvantage for the cued condition. Clark and Shiffrin (1992) derived means and variances for the relevant familiarities for SAM, MINERVA, TODAM, and the Matrix model, and showed that the basic version of SAM could not produce a cuing advantage, and the other models could not produce a cuing disadvantage. Also, under some conditions Clark and Shiffrin showed high performance for intact-rearranged discrimination, but small or negative effects of context cues. Thus, contrary to some of the models, context effects and intact-rearranged discrimination were not closely linked, and none of the models captured the full pattern of results.

The success of global matching models in dealing with list length and context effects is not as straightforward as it might have initially appeared. Thus, we should be cautious in asserting that dual-process assumptions are unnecessary due to the success of these single-process models. Global matching models, however, can and have been modified to handle some of the problems described above, and the modifications change the models in ways that raise questions about the overlap between recall and recognition. Before discussing those modifications, we turn to how global matching models have been applied to include-exclude data.

Inclusion-Exclusion Differences

If the probability of responding old differs in the inclusion and exclusion conditions, the conclusion drawn from process-dissociation analyses is that there are recall processes operating in recognition. But should include-exclude differences *always* be interpreted as a recall effect? In the two-process model they must be, because there is no other mechanism within the model to account for such a difference.

Ratcliff, van Zandt, and McKoon (1995) fit a single process model to results of Yonelinas (1994) which were described quite handily by a two-process model. Participants in Yonelinas's (1994) Experiment 1 were presented with two lists of words, either both long or both short. In the include conditions, a test item is called old if it was presented in either list. In the exclude conditions, a test item would be called old only if it were from a designated list. Estimates of R decreased with list length, but estimates of F did not change. Although these results fit well within the two-process model, Ratcliff et al. successfully fit the SAM recognition model to the results of both experiments. How can a single-process model produce a dead-on fit to data which are taken as evidence of two processes? In SAM, for item recognition, memory is probed with two cues, the test item and context. The familiarity of a test item T is

$$F(T,C) = \Sigma_j \, S(T,M_j)^{w_T} \, S(C,M_j)^{w_C} \tag{10.11}$$

where T is the test item and C is the context cue. The two terms $S(T,M_j)$ and $S(C,M_j)$ give the retrieval strength between the test item and context cues and the memory trace of item j. The terms w_T and w_C are the weights given to the test item and context cue. These components are basic to the SAM model, and are not specific to the fit to Yonelinas's data. The context cue is necessary to focus retrieval on the relevant list so that the familiarity which is computed is the familiarity of the test item in the context of the study list, rather than the familiarity of the test word in general. The weights given to the cues are assumed to be under subject control to some extent.

In the simulation, Ratcliff et al. (1995) assumed a separate context cue for each list, and assumed that memory would be probed with a weighted combination of the test item and both list context cues. In the exclude conditions, the weight given to the context cue for the excluded list was lower than that for the included list. The conceptual assumption is that context could be used imperfectly to focus retrieval on the relevant list. Retrieval does not imply the retrieval of particular items, but rather refers to a global retrieval of the list. The result of this cue-directed focussing is to reduce the familiarity of test items from the excluded list.

In this case, SAM is able to give a fit to the results by assuming separate *cues* rather than by assuming separate *processes*. The moral of the story is that the include-exclude difference cannot always be taken as evidence for the operation of two processes; it may just as well be evidence for the operation of two cues which provide access to different information. Particularly when the exclusion is based on list membership, when multiple cues are clearly discernable, the multiple-cue account is a reasonable alternative to the multiple-process account.

Ratcliff et al. (1995) assumed that a familiarity-only version of SAM could not be fit to results of Jacoby (1991, Experiment 3). In that experiment, subjects were presented with a list of words which they read and anagrams which they unscrambled. A second list consisted of words presented auditorily. In the include condition, subjects were to say old to the read, anagram, and heard words (and new to new nonlist items), whereas in the exclude condition, they were to say old only to the heard words. Ratcliff et al. fit various versions of a two-process model to these results. One version of their two-process SAM model gave an adequate account of the data assuming that recall operated only in the exclude condition. The success of such a model seriously challenges the two-process approach to recognition in that it suggests that recall may not come into play at all unless subjects are required to reject familiar distractor items.

Other Evidence for Recalling to Recognize

Remembering vs. Knowing

Another approach to the measurement of recall and familiarity components in recognition requires subjects to indicate by self-report whether their recognition decisions are based on recollection or on other sources of information. Subjects respond "remember" if they recollect some detail or contextual information about the test item, and respond "know" for test items called old, but without such recollection. Tulving (1985) framed the distinction as one between conscious and unconscious memory. This may be reframed as a distinction between recollective and nonrecollective memory, or between recall and familiarity.

The interpretation of remember and know responses rests upon the assumption that subjects have a certain level of cognitive self-awareness and can use the terms in a consistent and meaningful way. Although this assumption seems unlikely to be completely true, the patterns of responding are consistent across experimental manipulations, and change in ways which are consistent with the assumptions of two-process models. The basic result is that experimental manipulations which increase recognition performance do so primarily by increasing the proportion of remember responses. Levels of processing effects, generation effects, list-length effects, and forgetting over time all show up in remember responses, with little or inconsistent variation in know responses (Gardiner, 1988; Gardiner & Java, 1991; Rajaram, 1993). This pattern of results is consistent with results from the process-dissociation procedure showing experimental manipulations typically affect the R component, leaving F unchanged.

The same question arises: What do we mean by recall processes operating in recognition? The definition of recall given in the experimental instructions is quite open: the conscious memory of "some aspect or aspects of what happened or was experienced at the time the word was presented (e.g., aspects of the physical appearance of the word or of something that happened in the room, or of what one was thinking or doing at that time)." (Gardiner, 1988, p. 311).

The alternative interpretation of the remember/know distinction is that it is a reflection of the subject's confidence, rather than an indicator of different processes. It is not surprising that people rate their remember judgments with higher confidence than their know judgments (Tulving, 1985). Furthermore, Donaldson (1996) has recently shown that the consistent result shown in almost all of the remember/know experiments, that accuracy differences are reflected in remember rather than know judgments, is *obligatory* within a simple unitary-process, familiarity-based model which maps remember and know judgments on to high and low confidence. To the extent that remember-know results can be interpreted as confidence differences, these results do not provide reliable evidence for the operatiion of recall processes in recognition. However, not all remember-know results follow this pattern, and the exceptions are sensible within the dual-process theory. Manipulations which would be expected to affect perceptual processing (Gregg & Gardiner, 1994), automatic components of recognition (Rajaram, 1993), or maintenance rather than elaborative rehearsal (Gardiner, Gawlick, and Richardson-Klavehn, 1994) produce an increase in know rather than in remember responses.

Word Frequency Effects

Common, high-frequency (HF) words are better recalled than low-frequency (LF) words, but LF words are better recognized. This reliable interaction is routinely presented as evidence that different retrieval processes underlie recall and recognition. Clark (1992) showed the same word frequency interaction comparing item and associative recognition, and suggested the same explanation: that item and associative recognition are based on different retrieval processes, and that associative recognition involves recall-like retrieval processes.

However, all the pieces of the recall account do not fit together nicely. Previous studies show that the HF word advantage for recall is eliminated or reversed if mixed-frequency lists are studied, but the LF word advantage in item recognition is invariant for mixed and pure frequency lists. If the HF advantage in associative recognition is due to recall then it should be reduced or eliminated in mixed frequency lists. Clark and Burchett (1994) showed, however, that like item recognition, and unlike cued recall, there was no interaction between word frequency and list composition for associative recognition.

The full pattern of results suggests that the word frequency results are not due to different retrieval mechanisms, but rather are due to differences in the storage of item and associative information. With the assumption that item and associative information are independent, any pattern of results for item and associative recognition can be obtained. The overlap between recall and associative recognition may be due to their common reliance on associative information, rather than similar retrieval processes.

Similarity Effects

Similarity effects have also been taken as evidence for recall processes in recognition. A distractor that is similar to one item or to many items on the studylist is more likely to elicit a false alarm, a result that is easily explained by a matching model. The variations and exceptions to this rule, however, may require recall-based explanations.

An exception to the rule has been shown by Brainerd, Reyna, and Kneer (1995). They showed that a semantically similar distractor was rejected more often than an unrelated distractor if the study-list item was tested just before the distractor test. They argued that the test of the target item made it easier to recall the study item using the similar distractor as a cue. The increased rejection rate for the similar distractor could also be due to a response bias, that subjects could not respond old to both the target and the similar distractor. However, the rejection rate of the similar distractor did not depend on what response was given to the target.

The similarity-based recall-to-reject account may explain some of the variation in similarity effects. False alarm rates are higher for distractors that are similar to many study items than to only one study item. For example, several experiments have shown high false alarm rates for category prototypes which were not presented among the training stimuli (Bransford & Franks, 1971; Posner & Keele, 1970; Reed, 1972). A similar result shown by Roediger and McDermott (1995) is that false alarm rates are very high for a distractor (sleep) when the study list contains several associates of the word (*bed, rest, awake, tired, dream, wake, night, eat, sound, slumber, snore, pillow*). False alarms are increased also for distractors which are similar to a single item in memory (Anisfeld & Knapp, 1968; Raser, 1972), but the effect is less reliable and smaller than that for distractors which are similar to many list items.

Two experiments (Hall & Kozloff, 1973; Shiffrin, Huber, & Marinelli, 1995) directly compare similarity to N items presented once each (NX1) and similarity to one item presented N times (1XN). In both experiments, false alarm rates were higher in the 1XN case than for the NX1 case. This difference may be due to recall. The NX1 items may be less likely to be recalled than 1XN items, reducing the possibility of a recall-based rejection. Or, it may be that items are recalled in the 1XN condition, but recall cannot be used as the basis of the decision to reject the distractor because recall of one similar list item does not necessarily mean that the similar test item is new. However, explanations without recall may work as well. For example, repetition of items may lead to differentiation, thus decreasing the similarity of targets and distractors (see Shiffrin, Huber, & Marinelli 1995; Shiffrin, Ratcliff, & Clark, 1990).

Repetition of Studied Items and Pairs. Hintzman, Curran, & Oppy (1992) presented participants with lists in which the items were presented between 1 and 25 times each. Global matching models predict proportionality in the frequency judgments for similar, but nonpresented distractors. That is, frequency judgments for a nonpresented item A' should increase proportionally with the number of presentations of item A, to which A' is similar. However, contrary to the proportionality prediction, participants showed a bimodal distribution with one mode at zero. In two of the experiments, the likelihood of JOF = 0 was U-shaped, first decreasing with repetition of A, then increasing.

Repetition and False Alarms in Associative Recognition. Clark and Hori (1995a) also examined repetition of pairs in an associative recognition experiment. Participants studied word pairs which were presented 1, 2, 6, or 12 times. Thus, target pairs could consist of items presented together 1 or several times; and rearranged pairs could consist of items presented in *other* pairs 1 or several times. Predictions of matching and recall-based models are illustrated in Fig. 10.1.

Repeated pairs have strong associations, and nonrepeated pairs have weak associations. A matching model sums over the associations, so stronger associations should produce higher false alarm rates for rearranged pairs from repeated study pairs. However, if recall is operating, correct pairings should be recalled more often for repeated pairs, producing lower false alarm rates. Consistent with this prediction, false alarm rates decreased steadily with study repetition

Similarity Effects in Forced-Choice Recognition. A complex pattern of similarity effects in forced-choice recognition also suggests the operation of recall processes. Tulving (1981) presented subjects with photographs, denoted A, B, C, and so on., followed by two-alternative forced-choice recognition tests. The two critical conditions are denoted A vs. A' where the distractor A' is similar to the target A, and A vs. B' where B' is similar not to A, but to studied photograph B.

The results showed higher accuracy but lower confidence for A vs. A' than for A vs. B'. Although global matching models can produce this pattern of results (see Clark, 1997; Hintzman, 1988), recall-based explanations are also reasonable. For example, the apparent similarity between A and A' may induce subjects to try to recall the correct item from the study list, using diagnostic features (those that are different in A and A') as cues. Because both single and dual process accounts appear workable, further research will be necessary to determine if recall is indeed the mechanism underlying the results.

For related procedures, matching models do not provide an account. Clark, Hori, and Callan (1993) modified Tulving's procedure for associative recognition. Participants studied word pairs, AB, CD, EF, GH, IJ, and so on. In the similar-distractor condition AB was tested against AD and AF, whereas in the dissimilar distractor condition AB was tested against CF and GJ. Note the item overlap in the similar distractor condition is not present in the dissimilar distractor condition. Global matching models make the same prediction for both item and associative recognition: an advantage for the similar distractor condition. However, associative recognition shows a dissimilar-distractor advantage. A tentative explanation offered by Clark et al. (1993) was that people had used a recall-based strategy, using words as recall cues. Such a strategy would favor the dissimilar-distractor condition because there are more cues, six versus only four for the similar-distractor condition.

Theoretical and empirical support have been found for the recall-based account. Nobel and Huber (1993) applied hybrid familiarity-plus-recall versions of several models, including TODAM, SAM, and MINERVA to the Clark et al. results. Of these, only the SAM model was able to produce the dissimilar-distractor advantage. This does not necessarily rule out hybrid versions of TODAM and MINERVA, as other hybrid models might do better. The important point is that the hybrid model did produce the dissimilar-distractor advantage for SAM, indicating that the recall explanation could work. Clark and Hori (1995b) also showed that the dissimilar-distractor advantage disappeared with very long study lists, consistent with the idea that the recall component in recognition would be disproportionately harmed by increases in list-length.

The dissimilar-distractor advantage may have non-recall explanations. TODAM stores item and associative information for each word pair. Recognition performance is optimized by weighting the associative information heavily at test, and giving relatively no weight to the item information. The similar-distractor disadvantage would be produced if subjects focussed on the item-level information more for similar-distractor tests than for dissimilar distractor tests. However, this would not account for why the result varies with list length.

A developmental study by Ackerman and Emmerich (1978) shows a result consistent with a recall model for associative recognition. Children studied picture paired associates, AB, CD, EF, and so on, each letter denoting a line drawing. At test, the children were given a stimulus term and four alternatives for the correct response, either B (correct), D, F, or X. Defined as a four-alternative forced-choice experiment (AB vs. AD vs. AF vs. AX), the match values for these pairs would make false alarms for the new item (AX) least likely, but in fact false acceptance of the new item was higher than for the rearranged responses. This result, contrary to the predictions of matching models, is explained by assuming that the rearranged responses are eliminated by recalling the correct stimulus terms for D and F.

Signal-to-Respond

In the signal-to-respond procedure, a test probe is presented to the subject, followed after some period of time, by a signal which indicates that the subject should respond as quickly as possible. Performance in the task generally increases as the interval between the presentation of the test item and the signal to respond increases. The increase in performance is well-described as an exponential growth to a limit, specifically,

$$d'(t) = A(1-\exp^{-R[T-I]})$$

where A is the asymptotic level of performance, R is the rate of increase, and I is the intercept, that is, the point at which performance first rises above chance. Taken together the intercept I and the rate R describe the retrieval dynamics in a given memory task, indicating the time at which the relevant information first becomes available (I) and the rate at which information accumulates (R).

Several experiments have shown a pattern of results which has come to be viewed as a signature for the operation of recall processes in recognition memory. The results show increases in the intercept and inverted-U shaped response functions. Such a case is illustrated in Fig. 10.1 which compares two tasks A and B. The bottom panel shows that the d' intercept for task B is later than that for Task A. The top panel shows the hit and false alarm rates. Note that for Task B the false alarm rate first increases, and then decreases, as the retrieval time is increased.

The explanation for the pattern of results for Task B is that incorrect information is available early in retrieval, leading to the increased false alarm rate, which is countered only by the delayed recall of correct information. A number of experiments have shown this pattern of results. The question is whether this pattern should be taken as definitive evidence for the operation of recall processes, or whether there are other alternative accounts.

Ratcliff and McKoon (1982, 1989) showed the pattern for semantic memory and sentence memory. In the semantic memory task, subjects answered questions such as "Is a robin a bird?" and "Is a bird a robin?" (yes to the first, no to the second). For negative questions, the probability of an incorrect response first increased, and then decreased, showing the inverted-U pattern. Likewise, following study of "John hit Bill", false alarm rates for "Bill hit John" showed a nonmonotonic pattern. The explanation is the same in both cases: The individual terms match, and this information is available before the order information.

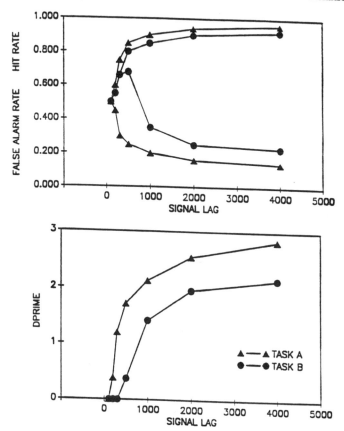

FIG. 10.1. Recall Signature in Response-Signal Results

A similar pattern has been shown for recognition for associations. Dosher's (1984) participants learned related and unrelated word pairs. Old and new test pairs were also related or unrelated. Related but new test pairs showed the inverted-U false alarm rate function. Similarly, for associative recognition Gronlund and Ratcliff (1989) showed inverted-U false alarm rate functions for rearranged distractors. Both results are tidily explained in terms of recall. In Dosher's experiments it is the recall of contextual information that overrides the semantic association strength. In Gronlund and Ratcliff's experiments, recall of the correct pairing (AB) presumably overrides the item level matches for A and D.

Although the delayed-recall explanation provides a tidy account for these results, they might also be explained in terms of information and cue differences. Rearranged distractors may only be rejected when the items are combined into a compound cue. The semantically-related but new pair may be rejected only when the pair is integrated with contextual cues. A "bird is a robin" may only be rejected when bird and robin are combined into a compound cue that specifies the relationship between the items. It is reasonable to assume that the construction of these compound cues requires time and conscious attention.

One might also explain these results in terms of item-level versus higher-level information. In all of the studies, except for Dosher's, the match of information at the item level might be obtained quickly, and would produce a false alarm. In Dosher's experiments, it is not the match of item-level information which produces the false alarm; it is the semantic associative information. The common thread might not be the level of the information, but the ease with which it is retrieved. Jacoby's distinction between automatic and conscious retrieval may be the key here. The inverted-U pattern may occur when incorrect information is likely to be automatically retrieved, and the correct information requires a compound cue, the formation of which requires conscious attention. This analysis is different than Jacoby's because it is not the retrieval process which requires conscious attention, but rather the formation of the appropriate cue.

An experiment by Hintzman and Curran (1994) is not easily explained without appeal to recall processes. Similar distractors differed from study items only in the addition or deletion of a letter s making the item plural or singular. False alarm rates for these similar distractors showed the inverted U-pattern, suggesting that the test item was used as a cue to recall the correct form of the word (and thus reject the incorrect form). It seems like a bit of a stretch to account for these results solely in terms of cue or information differences. Clearly, they cannot be explained by differences in item versus associative information, since all the relevant information is item-specific. However, one could explain the inverted-U pattern as due to the extra time required to combine the test item with the context cue, essentially the same explanation offered for Dosher's results. This version of the cue-combination account seems uncomfortably stretched in its reach to the Dosher and Hintzman-Curran results.

Further Evolution of Global Memory Models: Blurring the Familiarity-Recall Distinction

The distinction between familiarity and recall seemed clear-cut in 1968. Described within the framework of associative network models, recognition was based on information available from a node in the network, whereas recall required a search through the network. The recall-recognition distinction is blurred by the assumptions which define global memory models, that familiarity is based on information from all list items and their associations (rather than just the test item). However, although these assumptions were able to account for some of the early findings of recall-like recognition results, they appear to be insufficient to account for more recent results. This section describes recent modifications to global memory models which may blur the recall-recognition distinction even further.

List Length, Strength and Differentiation

Shiffrin, Ratcliff, and Clark (1990) showed that global memory models had difficulty in producing a list-length effect but no list-strength effect. The trick is to find a set of assumptions which eliminate the list-strength prediction while maintaining the list-length prediction. Several proposals have been offered, which change assumptions about the state of memory prior to list presentation (Murdock & Kahana, 1993), or the assumptions about encoding (see discussion regarding MINERVA, Shiffrin, Ratcliff, & Clark, 1990, p. 185), or the way in which test items are matched to multiple memory representations (Shiffrin & Steyvers, 1997).

Shiffrin et al. (1990) suggested a differentiation model to account for the missing LSE. The differentiation model assumed that as study time increased the associative strength to other items in memory decreased such that the two items would be less connected or less confusable. Shiffrin and Steyvers embodied this assumption in their model called REM. As more features of an item are stored, the item becomes less confusable with other items.

Such a differentiation mechanism may be able to account for the decrease in false alarm rates for associative recognition (Clark & Hori, 1995a), and may also account for the difference in false alarm rates for similar distractors from Nx1 and 1xN lists (Hall & Kozloff, 1973; Shiffrin, et al. 1995). A differentiation mechanism may also operate to some extent to exclude items in inclusion-exclusion experiments. In REM stronger items not only have a higher match to their own representation, but also a lower match to other items. This is the same pattern seen for anagrams in inclusion-exclusion comparisons (Jacoby, 1991); they are more likely to be included and more likely to be excluded. This is not to say that REM can account for inclusion-exclusion differences, but only that the differentiation mechanism may have the right properties.

Compound Cues, Associations, and Context

A number of experimental results may be accommodated by assuming that when multiple cues are available at test, they are in some cases (depending on task demands and time pressure) combined into a single joint cue. The formation of such a joint cue requires conscious, attentive processing, and the resulting joint cue contains information which is not available in either one of the individual cues.

The compound cue account may also be applied to the case in which one of the cues is list context. Such an account may be applied to Dosher's (1984) and Hintzman and Curran's (1994) response signal results. The cue-combination account of response-signal results seems quite different when applied to these results than when applied to the Gronlund-Ratcliff results. For Gronlund and Ratcliff, the cues are both words which are combined to create the associative cue necessary for intact-rearranged discrimination, but unnecessary for item recognition. However, the account changes when one of the cues is a context cue. The assumption here is that pre-experimental associations are accessed automatically, without a context cue, but retrieval of episodic associations requires combining word cues with context. Note also that a context-cue account was used to allow SAM to fit Yonelinas's (1994) inclusion-exclusion results.

One may question whether the context-cue account is anything more than a recall account in matching-model clothing. Presumably, the context cue focusses retrieval on the list, and without it, episodic factors such as list length, verbal context and episodic associations, and the specific word form would be missed. Thus, probing without context could indicate that a given item is familiar, but noting the item's singular-plural form or its verbal context would require probing with the context-item joint cue. Although the assumption is that both context and no-context cases involve global matching (only the cues change), the idea of focusing, taken to an extreme, that is, focusing on the contents of a particular representation (the episodic representation of the test item, if there is one), begins to sound like recall.

Explanations which rely on the use of context cues are always a bit tricky because it has been difficult to describe what is in a context cue. Smith, Glenberg, and Bjork (1978) referred to context as a "conceptual garbage can." Twenty years later our understanding of the information represented in a context cue, and how context cues are used, are still a bit lacking. One might argue also that the role of context is backwards in matching models, that context is not a cue used to probe memory, but rather is a kind of information retrieved from memory (as suggested in the instructions to remember/know experiments).

What is Recall? What is Familiarity?

All of this raises questions about what we mean by recall and familiarity. The term familiarity was used for the models of the 1970s and for global memory models of the 1980s and 1990s, but clearly familiarity does not refer to the same thing across all of these models. The scalar output from current models goes by various terms: familiarity, activation, match, strength, echo, and resonance - which may be less interchangeable than their interchangeable usage might suggest. Familiarity and matching may refer to different kinds of scalar output: Familiarity is often used to suggest item-specific information output from a lexical or semantic memory system, whereas matching may refer specifically to episodic memory, and may include associations between words and context-word associations.

We should be clearer, too, what we mean when we say "recall processes operating in recognition memory." This is often stated as if we mean that some particular item is recalled as a complete unit from memory. But if this is the only meaning for recall, we are sure to underestimate recall in recognition. Recall typically refers to the retrieval of item-specific content from memory (rather than a scalar), but how much content and how specific must it be to assert that a decision is recall-based? For example, for the test item HORSE, a person may be unable to recall and output the lexical unit *horse* from episodic memory, but may nevertheless vaguely recall that there were a few farm animals on the list, and one of them was a big animal, like a cow, or horse, or mule. If a person calls a test item old because he or she remembers only one feature of the test item, it seems reasonable to assert that the decision was recall-based, even though the person would be incapable of recalling the item. There may be many recall-like contributions to recognition that do not include the output of a complete unit from memory.

Conclusions

A great deal of evidence has been brought forward in support of the idea that recall-like retrieval processes operate in the course of making recognition memory decisions. This review presents only a sample of the evidence. What this review also shows is that much of this evidence is compelling only when very simple single-process models are considered. In the simplest familiarity models of recognition, local-matching models, other processes *must* be assumed, because the local-matching assumption is inadequate to account for much other than the simplest recognition results. However, when more complex matching models are considered, the picture becomes less clear. A conclusion one might draw is that recall-processes need not be assumed when more complex matching models are considered. However, it may simply be that recall-like mechanisms are being incorporated into matching models, but in different and more subtle ways.

Familiarity models of recognition have evolved considerably in the last 30 years, to the point where it may be important to distinguish familiarity from matching (lest the word familiarity should follow context into the conceptual garbage can). The summation of matches over multiple items and higher-order associations allows matching models to behave like recall-augmented models.

Assumptions about the formation of compound cues may also allow matching models to produce recall-like response-signal functions.

The familiarity-recall distinction may become even less clear if we consider the various ways in which recall may operate to retrieve vague or incomplete information (which may or may not be recoverable for output). It may be very difficult to distinguish between familiarity and recall-based models as the two approaches may be converging.

Summary

Atkinson and Shiffrin (1968) previewed what has in the last 30 years been a central question in the study of memory: Are recognition memory decisions driven solely by familiarity (matching), or is recognition based in part on recall-like retrieval processes. This chapter reviews theory and data, focusing in particular on evidence supporting recall processes in recognition memory. Arguments for recall processes often explicitly or implicitly assume the theoretical alternative to be a very simple local-matching familiarity model. When more complex familiarity models are considered, recall assumptions may be unnecessary. However, these more complex familiarity models take on many recall-like properties, blurring the distinction between familiarity and recall.

Acknowledgement

Preparation of this chapter was supported by National Science Foundation Grant DBS 9120911.

References

Ackerman, B. P., & Emmerich, H. J. (1978). When recognition memory fails: The use of an elimination strategy by young children. *Developmental Psychology, 14,* 286-293.

Anderson, J. R. (1972). FRAN: A simulation model of free recall. In G.H. Bower (Ed.), *The Psychology of Learning and Motivation* (Vol. 5, pp. 315-378). New York: Academic Press.

Anisfeld, M., & Knapp. M. (1968). Association, synonymity, and directionality in false recognition. *Journal of Experimental Psychology, 77,* 171-179.

Atkinson, R. C., & Juola, J. F. (1974). Search and decision processes in recognition memory. In D. H. Krantz, R. C. Atkinson, R. D. Luce & P. Suppes (Eds.), *Contemporary developments in mathematical psychology (Vol. 1): Learning, Memory and Thinking* (pp. 243-293). San Francisco,

CA: Freeman.

Atkinson, R. C., & Shiffrin, R. M. (1968). Human Memory: A proposed system and its control processes. In K. W. Spence & J. T. Spence (Eds.), *The psychology of learning and motivation: Advances in research and theory* (Vol. 2). New York: Academic Press.

Bain, J. D., & Humphreys, M. S. (1988). The relational context effect: Cues, meanings, or configurations? In G. Davies & D. M. Thomson (Eds.), *Memory in Context: Context in memory* (pp. 97-137). Chichester, England: Wiley.

Brainerd, C. J., Reyna, V. F., & Kneer, R. (1995). False-recognition reversal: When similarity is distinctive. *Journal of Memory and Language, 34,* 157-185.

Bransford, J. D., & Franks, J. J. (1971). The abstraction of linguistic ideas. *Cognitive Psychology, 2,* 331-350.

Brown, R., & McNeill, D. (1966). The "tip of the tongue" phenomenon. *Journal of Verbal Learning & Verbal Behavior, 5,* 325-337.

Clark, S. E. (1992). Word frequency effects in associative and item recognition. *Memory & Cognition, 20,* 231-243.

Clark, S. E. (1997). A familiarity-based account of confidence-accuracy inversions in recognition memory. *Journal of Experimental Psychology: Learning, Memory, & Cognition, 23,* 232-238

Clark, S. E., & Burchett, R. E. R. (1994). Word frequency and list composition effects in associative recognition and recall. *Memory & Cognition, 22,* 55-62.

Clark, S. E., & Gronlund, S. D. (1996). Global matching models of recognition memory: How the models match the data. *Psychonomic Bulletin and Review, 3,* 37-60.

Clark, S. E., & Hori, A. (1995a, July). *Recall processes in associative recognition, but no list-strength effect.* Paper presented at 7th Annual Meeting American Psychological Society, New York.

Clark, S. E., & Hori, A. (1995b). List length and overlap effects in forced-choice associative recognition. *Memory & Cognition, 23,* 456-461.

Clark, S. E., Hori, A., & Callan, D. E. (1993). Forced-choice associative recognition: Implications for global-memory models. *Journal of Experimental Psychology: Learning, Memory, & Cognition, 19,* 871-881.

Clark, S. E., & Shiffrin, R. M. (1987). Recognition of multiple-item probes. *Memory & Cognition,* 367-378.

Clark, S. E., & Shiffrin, R. M. (1992). Cuing effects and associative information in recognition memory. *Memory & Cognition, 20,* 580-598.

Curran, T., & Hintzman, D. L. (1995). Violations of the independence assumption in process dissociation. *Journal of Experimental Psychology: Learning, Memory, & Cognition, 21,* 531-547.

Dodson, C. S., & Johnson, M. K. (1996). Some problems with the process dissociation approach to memory. *Journal of Experimental Psychology: General, 125,* 181-194.

Donaldson, W. (1996). The role of decision processes in remembering and knowing. *Memory & Cognition, 24,* 523-533.

Dosher, B. A. (1984). Discriminating preexperimental (semantic) from learned (episodic) associations: A speed-accuracy study. *Cognitive Psychology, 16,* 519-555.

Dyne, A. M., Humphreys, M. S., Bain, J. D., & Pike, R. (1989). Associative interference effects in recognition and recall. *Journal of Experimental Psychology: Learning, Memory, & Cognition, 116,* 813-824.

Gardiner, J. M. (1988). Functional aspects of recollective experience. *Memory & Cognition, 18, 23-30.*

Gardiner, J. M., Gawlick, B., & Richardson-Klavehn, A. (1994). Maintenance rehearsal affects knowing, not remembering; elaborative rehearsal affects remembering, not knowing. *Psychonomic Bulletin & Review, 1,* 107-110.

Gardiner, J. M., & Java, R. I. (1991). Forgetting in recognition memory with and without recollective experience. *Memory & Cognition, 19,* 617-623.

Gillund, G., & Shiffrin, R. M. (1984). A retrieval model for both recognition and recall. *Psychological Review, 91,* 1-67.

Gregg, V. H., & Gardiner, J. M. (1994). Recognition memory and awareness: A large-cross modal effect on "know" but not "remember" responses following a highly perceptual orienting task. *European Journal of Cognitive Psychology, 6,* 131-147.

Gronlund S. D., & Elam, L. E. (1994). List-length effect: Recognition accuracy and the variance of underlying distributions. *Journal of Experimental Psychology: Learning, Memory, & Cognition, 20,* 1355-1369.

Gronlund, S. D., & Ratcliff, R. (1989). Time course of item and associative information: Implications for global memory models. *Journal of Experimental Psychology: Learning, Memory, & Cognition, 15,* 846-858.

Hall, J. W., & Kozloff, E. E. (1973). False recognition of associates of converging versus repeated words. *American Journal of Psychology, 86,* 133-139.

Hintzman, D. L. (1988). Judgments of frequency and recognition memory in a multiple trace memory model. *Psychological Review, 95,* 528-551.

Hintzman, D. L., & Curran, T. (1994). Retrieval dynamics of recognition and frequency judgments: Evidence for separate processes of familiarity and recall. *Journal of Memory and Language, 33,* 1-18.

Hintzman, D. L., Curran, T., & Oppy, B. (1992). Effects of similarity and repetition on memory: Registration without learning? *Journal of Experimental Psychology: Learning, Memory, and Cognition, 18,* 667-680.

Hockley, W. E. (1992). Tests of the mirror and list-strength effects for item and associative recognition. *33rd Annual Meeting of the Psychonomic Society*, St. Louis, MO.

Humphreys, M. S. (1976). Relational information and the context effect in recognition memory. *Memory & Cognition, 4*, 221-232.

Humphreys, M. S. (1978). Item and relational information: A case for context-independent retrieval. *Journal of Verbal Learning & Verbal Behavior, 17*, 175-187.

Humphreys, M. S., & Bain, J. D. (1983). Recognition memory: A cue and information analysis. *Memory & Cognition, 11*, 583-600.

Humphreys, M.S., Bain, J.D., & Pike, R. (1989). Different ways to cue a coherent memory system: A theory for episodic, semantic, and procedural tasks. *Psychological Review, 96*, 208-233.

Jacoby, L. (1991). A process dissociation framework: Separating automatic from intentional uses of memory. *Journal of Memory and Language, 30*, 513-541.

Jacoby, L. L., & Yonelinas, A. P., & Jennings, J. M. (1997). The relation between conscious and unconscious (automatic) influences: A declaration of independence. In J. D. Cohen & J. W. Schooler (Eds.), *Scientific Approaches to Consciousness. Carnegie Mellon Symposia on Cognition* (pp. 13-47). Mahwah, NJ: Lawrence Erlbaum Associates.

Koriat, A., & Lieblich, I. (1974). What does a person in a "TOT" state know that a person in a "don't know" state doesn't know? *Memory & Cognition, 2*, 647-655.

Mandler, G. (1980). Recognizing: The judgment of previous occurrence. *Psychological Review, 87*, 252-271.

Mandler, G., Rabinowitz, J. C., & Simon, R. A. (1981). Coordinate organization: The holistic representation of word pairs. *American Journal of Psychology, 94*, 209-222.

Mulligan, N., & Hirshman, E. (1997). Measuring the bases of recognition memory: An investigation of the process-dissociation framework. *Journal of Experimental Psychology: Learning, Memory, & Cognition, 23*, 280-304.

Murdock, B. B., Jr. (1982). A theory for the storage and retrieval of item and associative information. *Psychological Review, 89*, 609-626.

Murdock, B. B. (1993). Derivations for the chunking model. *Journal of Mathematical Psychology, 37*, 421-445.

Murdock, B. B., & Hockley, W. E. (1989). Short-term memory for associations. In G.H. Bower (Ed.) *The Psychology of Learning and Motivation* (Vol. 24, pp. 71-108). New York: Academic Press.

Murdock, B. B., & Kahana, M. J. (1993). List-strength and list-length effects: Reply to Shiffrin, Ratcliff, Murnane, & Nobel (1993). *Journal of Experimental Psychology: Learning, Memory, & Cognition, 19*,

1450-1453.

Murnane, K., & Shiffrin, R. M. (1991). Interference and the representation of events in memory. *Journal of Experimental Psychology: Learning, Memory, & Cognition, 17*, 855-874.

Nobel, P.A., & Huber, D.E. (1993). Modelling forced-choice associative recognition through a hybrid of global recognition and cued recall. In *Proceedings of the 15th Annual Cognitive Science Society* (pp. 783-788). Hillsdale, NJ: Lawrence Erlbaum Associates.

Pike, R. (1984). A comparison of convolution and matrix distributed memory systems. *Psychological Review, 91*, 281-294.

Posner, M. I., & Keele, S. W. (1970). Retention of abstract ideas. *Journal of Experimental Psychology, 83*, 304-308

Rabinowitz, J. C., Mandler, G., & Barsalou, L. W. (1977). Recognition failure: Another case of retrieval failure. *Journal of Verbal Learning and Verbal Behavior, 16*, 639-664.

Raaijmakers, J. G. W., & Shiffrin, R. M. (1980). SAM: A theory of probabilistic search of associative memory. In G. H. Bower (Ed.), *The Psychology of Learning and Motivation*, (Vol. 14, pp. 207-262). New York: Academic Press.

Rajaram, S. (1993). Remembering and knowing: Two means of access to the personal past. *Memory & Cognition, 21*, 89-102

Raser, G. A. (1972). False recognition as a function of encoding dimension and lag. *Journal of Experimental Psychology, 93*, 333-337.

Ratcliff, R., Clark, S. E., & Shiffrin, R. M. (1990). List strength effect: I. Data and discussion. *Journal of Experimental Psychology: Learning, Memory, & Cognition, 16*, 163-178.

Ratcliff, R., & McKoon, G. (1982). Speed and accuracy in the processing of false statements about semantic information. *Journal of Experimental Psychology: Learning, Memory, & Cognition, 8*, 16-36.

Ratcliff, R.,& McKoon, G. (1989). Similarity information versus relational information: Differences in the time course of retrieval. *Cognitive Psychology, 21*, 139-155.

Ratcliff, R., Sheu, C.-f., & Gronlund, S. D. (1992). Testing global memory models using ROC curves. *Psychologial Review, 99*, 518-535.

Ratcliff, R., van Zandt, T., & McKoon, G. (1995). Process dissociation, single-process theories, and recognition memory. *Journal of Experimental Psychology: General, 124*, 352-374.

Reed, S. K. (1972). Pattern recognition and classification. *Cognitive Psychology, 3*, 382-407.

Roediger, H. L., & McDermott, K. B. (1995). Creating false memories: Remembering words not presented in lists. *Journal of Experimental Psychology: Learning, Memory, & Cognition, 21*, 803-814.

Schwartz, B., & Reisberg, D. (1991). *Learning and Memory*. New York: Norton.

Shiffrin, R. M., Huber, D. E., & Marinelli, K. (1995). Effects of category length and strength on familiarity in recognition. *Journal of Experimental Psychology: Learning, Memory, & Cognition, 21*, 267-287.

Shiffrin, R.M., Ratcliff, R., & Clark, S. E. (1990). List-strength effect: II. Theoretical mechanisms. *Journal of Experimental Psychology: Learning, Memory, & Cognition, 16*, 179-195.

Shiffrin, R. M., & Schneider, W. (1977). Controlled and automatic human information processing: II. Perceptual learning, automatic attending and a general theory. *Psychological Review, 84*, 127-190.

Shiffrin, R. M., & Steyvers, M. (1997). A model for recognition memory: REM–retrieving effectively from memory. *Psychonomic Bulletin & Review, 4*, 145-166

Smith, S. M., Glenberg, A., & Bjork, R. A. (1978). Environmental context and human memory. *Memory & Cognition, 6*, 342-353.

Strong, E. K., Jr. (1912). The effect of length of series upon recognition memory. *Psychological Review, 19*, 447-462.

Tulving, E. (1981). Similarity relations in recognition. *Journal of Verbal Learning and Verbal Behavior, 5*, 479-496.

Tulving, E. (1985). Memory and consciousness. *Canadian Psychology, 26*, 1-12.

Tulving, E., & Thomson, D. M. (1971). Retrieval process in recognition memory: Effects of associative context. *Journal of Experimental Psychology, 87*, 175-184.

Underwood, B. J., & Humphreys, M. S. (1979). Context change and the role of meaning in word recognition. *American Journal of Psychology, 92*, 577-609.

Weber, E. U. (1988). Expectation and variance of item resemblance distributions in a convolution-correlation model of distributed memory. *Journal of Mathematical Psychology, 32*, 1-43.

Yonelinas, A. P. (1994). Receiver-operating characteristics in recognition memory: Evidence for a dual-process model. *Journal of Experimental Psychology: Learning, Memory, & Cognition, 20*, 1341-1354.

Chapter 11

Measuring the Time Course of Retention

Thomas D. Wickens
University of California, Los Angeles, U.S.A.

As everyone knows, the Atkinson-Shiffrin (1968) memory model contains both a short-term and a long-term component. The short-term component is a temporary holding buffer from which information is transferred into long-term store. This long-term information then is gradually lost or becomes unavailable as time passes.

In the quantitative versions of this model, information about the item accumulates in long-term store in an amount proportional to the duration of residency in short-term store. This information then declines exponentially with the time after transfer terminated. The information that can be recovered from an item rehearsed for r trials and tested after t trials, $t > r$, is

$$I = (r+1)\theta\tau^{t-r}, \tag{11.1}$$

where θ and τ are transfer and loss parameters, respectively. The long-term store information is translated into observable responses in one of two ways. In the original theory (Atkinson & Shiffrin, 1968; see also Atkinson, Brelsford, & Shiffrin, 1967; Brelsford, Shiffrin, & Atkinson, 1968), the retrieval probability is exponentially related to the information:

$$P(\text{LTS retrieval on trial } t) = 1 - (1-g)e^{-I}, \tag{11.2}$$

where g is a guessing rate. In other versions of the model (Freund, Loftus, & Atkinson, 1969; see also Atkinson & Wickens, 1971), the information is equated with the d' statistic from equal-variance Gaussian signal detection theory:

$$d' = I = (r+1)\theta\tau^{t-r}. \tag{11.3}$$

The actual recovery probability or d' at a particular delay is an average of the values given by Equations 11.2 or 11.3 over the distribution of short-term-store residencies.

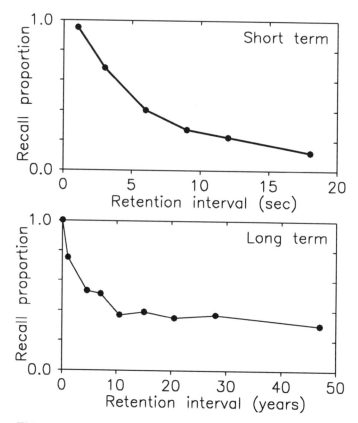

FIG. 11.1. Retention data derived by Rubin and Wen-zel (1996). Upper panel: Short-term retention (pooled data from Peterson & Peterson, 1959, and Murdock, 1961). Lower panel: Long-term retention (pooled from studies in Bahrick, 1983).

The form of the long-term retention function in Equations 11.2 and 11.3 was not central to the Atkinson-Shiffrin theory; the major contribution of the theory was to an understanding of the dynamics of the memory process and the relationship between the short- and long-term components. However, other researchers have been interested in the form of this function. My particular awareness of the recent work on this question was sparked by a paper by Rubin and Wenzel (1996) and a related paper by Wixted and Ebbesen (1991). The goal of these papers is to find empirically a form for the retention function. In particular, Rubin and Wenzel assemble many different retention data sets and fit them with a large collection of functional forms, looking for the function or functions that has the least error.

As illustrations, I take from Rubin and Wenzel's paper two forgetting functions with quite different characteristics. The top panel of Fig. 11.1 shows some results for short-term retention; it was created by combining results from several Brown-Peterson short-term memory studies using letter or word trigrams (Peterson & Peterson, 1959; Murdock, 1961). The bottom panel shows some results for long-term retention; it was created by combining six studies for the memory of campus locations (Bahrick, 1983). The time scales of these studies differ widely, as do the general characteristics of the retention levels. It is interesting to remark on these data with respect to the Atkinson-Shiffrin model. Within their model, these two functions must reflect different processes. The Brown-Peterson data would be interpreted as largely determined by the short-term buffer process, while the Bahrick data (except possibly for the point at $t=0$) has no short-term component and is determined by the dynamics of long-term retention, with the forms given above.

For a number of reasons, I am not optimistic about the likelihood of finding a form for the retention function on purely empirical grounds, although the attempt by Rubin and Wenzel to integrate many studies is an excellent way to start. First, there are simply too many functions that one might examine, with too little difference among them. Even restricting the set to those with "simple" forms gives too many alternatives. Second, the retention data from most experiments is too sparse to give very accurate parameter estimates or precise comparisons of functional forms. In most cases, retention is measured at too few time points. Even with data as extensive as those in Fig. 11.1, the number of points is only a few times the number of parameters. Third, there is enormous experimental variation over the corpus of empirical results; not least, there are many reasons to expect that such disparate procedures as recognition and recall will behave differently. Fourth, as the Atkinson-Shiffrin model illustrates, the retention process may be mediated by different mechanisms at different time scales, and there is no necessity for the time course of these mechanisms to have the same quantitative form.

In spite of these reservations, I agree with Rubin and Wenzel that it is important to take the form of the retention function seriously. For one thing, we need ways to capture the important and measurable characteristics of the forgetting process in a few interpretable parameters, so that they can be compared across experiments. For another, many theoretical interpretations of the forgetting process gives rise to specific forms of the retention function, and these forms can easily be incorporated in specific analyses. For a third, the general properties of this function can provide insight into the important characteristics of the memory system. In this chapter, I discuss some of these issues, expanding on remarks I made in Wickens (1998).

Measures of Retention

Retention can be measured in many different ways, and the choice of measure determines some of the properties of the retention function. The function that fits one measure will not be the same as the function that fits another measure. The most important distinction here is between measures of probability and measures of strength. In a probability representation, the probability that the item is recovered is described. For a recognition test, the probability is of a correct classification of an item; for recall it is of the recovery and generation of the item. Both quantities are directly estimated from an experiment.

Strength representations are much more varied. What is described is a latent variable that must be translated into a measurable outcome. This translation constitutes a model-dependent aspect of the representation. There are many ways to express strength. One possibility is as some more or less abstract measure of "information," such as that used in the Atkinson-Shiffrin model (Equation 11.1). Two other common representations use the d' statistic of signal detection theory and the strength parameter v of a Bradley-Terry-Luce choice model. The latter two representations are most appropriate when the retrieval is from a small set of alternatives.

Within each set of measures, certain transformations are mathematically determined. For example, a representation of the probability can also be written as such equivalent quantities as the odds ratio or the logit:

$$\text{odds} = \frac{p}{1-p} \qquad \text{and} \qquad \text{logit} = \log \frac{p}{1-p}.$$

These measures express the same information as do the raw probabilities, but their ranges are different, the odds ratio varying over a range from zero to infinity and the logit over the full real line. Different functional forms should apply to each measure. In a given situation, one of these quantities may be more simply related to other variables than the probabilities themselves, in the way that a linear model for the logit is usually simpler than a linear model for probabilities in statistical analysis (e.g., Wickens, 1989, Chap. 7). Similar variants exist for other measures; for example, the parameters of a choice model can be described in either multiplicative or additive form, and the signal-detection statistic can be either d' or the area under the operating characteristic.

Translation between strength measures and probability measures is not automatic. Equation 11.2 is more or less theory-free (although see below), but in general, the translation depends both on the task in which the retention was measured and on some model for the response process. For example, consider the signal-detection measure d' in a K alternative forced-choice situation. The foils are represented by a random variable X_n with density $\varphi(x)$ and cumulative distribution function $\Phi(x)$; the correct alternative by a random variable X_s with a density that has been displaced d' units to the right to $\varphi(x-d')$. The probability of a correct response equals the probability that X_s exceeds the $K-1$ realizations of X_n:

$$P(\text{correct}) = P[X_s > \max(X_{n1}, \ldots, X_{n,K-1})]$$

$$= \int_{-\infty}^{\infty} \varphi(x-d')[1 - \Phi(x)]^{K-1} dx. \tag{11.4}$$

Usually φ is taken to be Gaussian, in which case Equation 11.4 can be solved numerically (classically, as in Elliot, 1964). A similar calculation, using logistic distributions, relates the parameters of a choice model to probabilities. For small K, this calculation gives a reasonable result, but for large K it depends critically on the behavior of the noise distributions in the tail. Extreme-value theory may gives an asymptotic form for this distribution (for example, with Gaussian distributions, it has the Gumbel form discussed below), but in passing to the limit the specific link to d' is lost.

Response latency has also been considered as a response measure, with short-latency responses implying large item strength and long-latency responses implying weak item strength (Anderson & Milson, 1989). The linkage between latency measures and response probability is highly theory dependent, and I see no way to translate from one to another without a theory of the response process.

Characteristics of Memory Performance

Any observed retention function has a number of salient characteristics, including its largest value, its end point, its rate of drop, etc. These characteristics correspond roughly to properties of the fitting function. They are valuable in classifying performance and in descriptively grouping studies with similar properties. Any analysis of retention functions should find a way to cleanly represent these properties.

For standard retention functions, four quantities are most important.

- *The initial level of learning.* Associated with any retention process is the strength of the memory at the initial time point. Usually it is useful to extrapolate this value back to time $t = 0$, although in practice this point cannot be measured, as some delay inevitably occurs between study and the first test. In a probability model, this level can often be set to one; for strength models it is the original amount of learning.

- *The final asymptote.* Retention declines with the duration of the memory toward some asymptote. This asymptote may be at zero, but it is also possible for some strength to remain, even as $t \to \infty$. As with the initial level, the final level must be inferred, not directly measured.

- *The rate of forgetting.* Depending on the task and the amount of study, forgetting may take place rapidly or slowly. This characteristic certainly embodies the link between the units in which time is measured and the function—the numerical rate when retention time is measured in seconds will be slower than when time is measured in minutes. In probability models, particularly those that start from one when $t = 0$, this parameter also measures the resistance of learning to loss.

- *The balance between early and late forgetting.* The retention function, even holding the previous three characteristics constant, can vary in many ways. In complete generality, of course, a very large or infinite number of parameters are needed to completely specify the functional form. However, most of the variation over studies is captured by a single characteristic: the relative balance between early and late forgetting. How to represent this characteristic is discussed below.

In one sense these characteristics are separable. For many forms of retention function, it is possible to represent each characteristic by a distinct parameter in the functional form—examples are given below—so that they can be easily measured and compared across experiments. Whether they are independent in actual data is less clear. For example, it is quite possible for the degree of initial learning to affect the initial point, the rate of forgetting, and the final asymptote.[1]

Probabilistic Representations

One of the simpler ways to measure retention is by the probability of a correct response or, for recall, by the probability of a retrieval. This representation has several advantages: it refers to a clear dependent measure, it provides access to the ready-made analytical machinery of probability theory, and it opens the way to the theory of probabilistic failure processes. I explore here some possibilities for this representation.

Let the retention function $r(t)$ equal the probability that an item is retrieved from memory at time t. With a view to separating the four characteristics mentioned above, write this function as

$$r(t) = b + (a - b)[1 - F(ct)], \tag{11.5}$$

where $F(t)$ is the cumulative distribution function of some standard random variable. The parameters a and b are the initial and final levels:

$$r(0) = a \qquad \text{and} \qquad \lim_{t \to \infty} r(t) = b.$$

---

[1] An interesting approach to determining the usefulness of a functional form would be to examine the correlations among the estimates of its parameters over a series of conditions that varied such characteristics as the amount of original learning or the nature of the retention interval. From an empirical point of view, one would like to isolate the manipulation in as few parameters as possible.

For many sets of data, it is reasonable to set these parameters to one and zero, respectively, without formal estimation, so that $r(t)$ is simply the time-scaled *survival function* for the random variable:

$$r(t) = 1 - F(ct). \tag{11.6}$$

The parameter c here links the rate of forgetting to the units of measured time.

The distribution function $F(t)$ determines the fourth characteristic, the relative balance of early and late forgetting. This property is described by the rate at which items are forgotten relative to the number of items that can still be retained, a quantity known as the *hazard function*:

$$h(t) = \frac{-r'(t)}{r(t)}. \tag{11.7}$$

Thus, $h(t)$ expresses the chance that a still-remembered item is lost during the next short interval of time. When the hazard function is flat, then the forgetting rate for individual items is the same early and late in retention; when $h(t)$ rises, then early forgetting is less likely than late forgetting; and when $h(t)$ falls, then early forgetting is more likely than later forgetting. Hazard functions can quickly characterize the difference among forgetting processes. Fig. 11.2 shows a series of hazard functions for the long-term data that will be discussed below. As will be noted, they very much more dramatically than do the corresponding $r(t)$.

The particular characteristics of the forgetting process are determined by the distribution function $F(t)$. Several forms of function provide informative or plausible representations, and it is worth examining them to see their origins and interpretation. For the most part, the discussion below treats a as one and b as zero, so that the survival form of Equation 11.6 is appropriate, but each could be adapted as in Equation 11.5.

The exponential distribution. This distribution is created when items are lost as a homogeneous Poisson death process. In any short interval of time, a surviving item is forgotten with a probability that depends neither on how long the item has been retained nor on the number of other items that can be remembered. The exponential retention function and its hazard function are

$$r(t) = e^{-ct} \quad \text{and} \quad h(t) = c. \tag{11.8}$$

Note that the hazard function is a constant.

The assumption of constant hazard is unrealistic. Most real forgetting functions drop more rapidly at first. Simon (1966) has pointed out that a simple exponential function applied to all items is inconsistent with Jost's second law ("If two associations are now of equal strength but of different ages, the older one will lose strength more slowly with the further passage of time;" Woodworth,

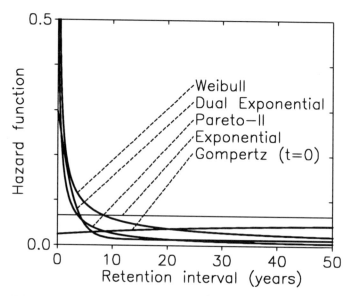

FIG. 11.2. Hazard functions for the theoretical functions described in the text, as fitted to the long-term data in the lower panel of Fig. 11.1.

1938).[2] Thus, the exponential function is most useful as a baseline to which data or other functions can be compared and as a component of more complex representations.

Fig. 11.3 shows exponential functions fitted to the two sets of data from Fig. 11.1. For the short-term data, the estimated decay rate is $\hat{c} = 0.135$, and the model fits well, accounting for 98.0% of the variability.[3] The fit is improved

---

[2] As discussed below, an exponential forgetting rate can be consistent with Jost's law if the items vary in their decay rates. Ensembles of items of different ages could have the same mean strength if the older items have smaller decay parameters. Another possibility is for the final asymptotes to vary (parameter b in Equation 11.5). Exponential retention functions are not the only ones that violate Jost's law. Any process that is Markovian in the retention level will violate the law, since two such processes with the same $r(t)$ are in the same state and have the same future course. For example, as the long-term store component of the Atkinson-Shiffrin model is formulated, the way that the information level changes (Equation 11.1) is the same regardless of how that value of $I(t)$ was obtained. An older trace that originally received much short-term rehearsal and transfer will have the same time course as a younger trace that received little rehearsal, thereby violating the law. However, in the complete model, the buffer process induces heterogeneity into $I(0)$, so that Jost's law again can hold.

[3] All fits reported in this chapter were obtained by numerically minimizing the sum of squared deviations between the observed proportions and the model probabilities, $\sum [y_i - r(t_i)]^2$. The functions were not transformed to linear form before fitting. Proportions of variability are measured by the ratio of this sum of squares to the sum of squared deviations of the y_i about their mean.

slightly by allowing an initial shift from zero, as if the effective $t = 0$ is displaced slightly from its nominal position:

$$r(t) = ae^{-ct} = e^{-c(t-d)}. \tag{11.9}$$

This model implies a displacement of $\widehat{d} = 0.51$ sec and improves the fit to 98.8%, not a large change is absolute terms, but one that eliminates a substantial proportion of the residual error.

For the long-term data, the one-parameter exponential function fails badly, accounting for less of the variability than the mean probability alone (the best parameter estimate, albeit hopeless, is $\widehat{c} = 0.066$). The two-parameter function of Equation 11.9 fits considerably better, but not sufficiently so to save the exponential function: with $\widehat{a} = 0.621$ and $\widehat{c} = 0.0230$, the variability accounted for rises to 67%. As the plots in Fig. 11.3 show, the observed retention rate drops more rapidly than ethe exponential functions at first and more slowly later. It is this characteristic of quick early drop and slow late drop that a better function must capture.

Dual Exponentials. A more satisfactory retention function suggested by Simon (1966) combines two exponential functions with different rate parameters. This function is probably best conceived as arising from a mixture of the effects of traces with two different forgetting rates. Let the rate parameter of the faster-decaying function be d times slower rate, $d > 1$, so that the function and hazard rate are

$$r(t) = \tfrac{1}{2}\left[e^{-ct} + e^{-cdt}\right] \quad \text{and} \quad h(t) = c\,\frac{1 + de^{c(1-d)t}}{1 + e^{c(1-d)t}}. \tag{11.10}$$

Both components influence the early portion of the process, so that the hazard function starts at $c(1+d)/2$, but the faster component drops out more rapidly than the slower, so that the slow component dominates for large t and the hazard asymptotes to c.

When $d \approx 1$ in Equation 11.10, there is little difference between the rates and the function is essentially exponential. The short-term data illustrate this situation: the parameter estimates are $\widehat{c} = 0.107$ and $\widehat{d} = 1.60$, and the quality of the fit is little effected by the second process (the variability explained climbs from 97.95% to 97.98%). A plot of this function looks so similar to the upper panel of Fig. 11.3 that a separate graph is not informative. In contrast, the second exponential term substantially improves the fit to the long-term data, with $\widehat{c} = 0.0128$, $\widehat{d} = 46.4$, and 93% of the variability explained. The top panel of Fig. 11.4 plots this function. The corresponding hazard function is shown in Fig. 11.2; its difference from the flat exponential hazard is very obvious.

A somewhat more general version of this exponential mixture representation is created by replacing the fraction $\tfrac{1}{2}$ in Equation 11.10 with arbitrary weights.

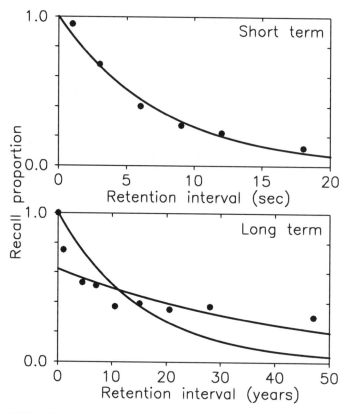

FIG. 11.3. Exponential functions fitted to the two sets of data in Fig. 11.1.

This version falls outside the convenient parameterization discussed above, so I do not pursue it here.

Pareto Distribution of the Second Type. A survival distribution that gives a good fit to retention data is the Pareto distribution of the second kind (Johnson, Kotz, & Balakrishnan, 1994, Chap. 20). It has a power-function form, but with the origin displaced so that $r(0) = 1$:[4]

$$r(t) = (1 + ct/d)^{-d}. \tag{11.11}$$

---

[4]The form $(1 + ct)^{-d}$ used by Wickens (1998) appears simpler, but its parameter values are harder to interpret.

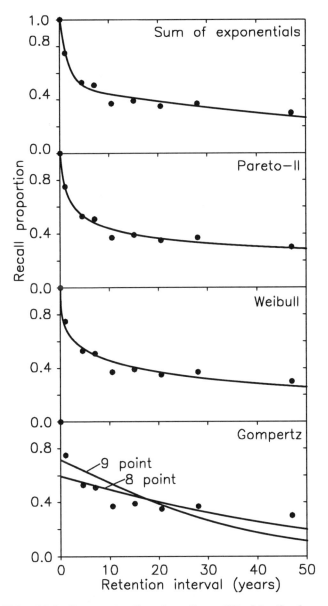

FIG. 11.4. Four retention functions fitted to the long-term data from the lower panel of Fig. 11.1.

Its hazard function starts at c and falls to zero at long times:

$$h(t) = \frac{c}{1 + ct/d}. \tag{11.12}$$

When d is large, the ratio c/d is small, and the dependence of the hazard function on t is minimized. As $d \to \infty$, the Pareto-II function approaches the exponential function e^{-ct}.

Fitting the Pareto-II function to the short-term data gives estimates of $\hat{c} = 0.139$ and $\hat{d} = 17.51$, which accounts for 98% of the variability. Consistent with the near-exponential form of the short-term data, $\hat{d}$ is large and $\hat{c}_{\text{Pareto}} \approx \hat{c}_{\text{Exponential}}$. Comparable values for the long-term data are $\hat{c} = 0.552$, $\hat{d} = 0.270$, and 96% of the variability. The estimate $\hat{d}$ is small and $\hat{c}_{\text{Pareto}}$ is very different from the specious $\hat{c}_{\text{Exponential}}$. As Fig. 11.4 shows, the Pareto-II representation fits these data well. The hazard function in Fig. 11.2 falls sharply, nearly asymptoting after 10 years, although, in contrast to the dual-exponential hazard function, it continues to decline to 0 as $t \to \infty$.

It is important to realize that a model of this simplicity cannot determine a single psychological process. Several distinct process models can give rise to retention functions with a Pareto-II form. Wickens (1998) shows that this form can be obtained from three distinct sets of assumptions about the dynamics of memory retention.

- *Heterogeneous items.* When the process is a mixture of exponential items with different rate parameters and these parameters have a Gamma distribution, then the composite retention function has the form of a Pareto-II distribution. This result has been used in a number of domains, and dates back at least to Maguire, Pearson, and Wynn (1952). In the context of memory models, the different exponential processes can arise because of items of varying strengths (thus, generalizing the dual-exponential model), because of averaging of observations across individuals (although that explanation appears not to be sufficient, see Wixted & Ebbesen, 1997), or because each item is represented by a variety of traces. Very likely all three sources of heterogeneity are involved. Because of their ubiquity, the various forms of heterogeneity are almost certainly a factor in any study.

- *Consolidation.* When items gain strength throughout the period that they are retrievable, their hazard function decreases with t. Such an increase in strength could be brought about by some form of long-term rehearsal process or by renewed storage created by either intentional or incidental retrieval. If the specific form by which this gain takes place is reciprocal in time, having the form $\alpha/(1+\beta t)$, then it matches the hazard function of a Pareto-II distribution. In effect, the representation is as a nonstationary Poisson process with a time-dependent rate parameter.

- *Competition.* Competition among the available items can also produce a process with a decreasing hazard function. At small t, most of the items are available, there is a great deal of competition, and the hazard rate is high; later, most items are unretrievable, and the hazard rate is low. If the effect of competition on an individual item is a power of the number of items, $h(r) = \alpha r^{\beta}$, then the Pareto-II form results. In particular, when the hazard is directly proportional to the number of available items, the retention function is a time-displaced reciprocal: $r(t) = 1/(1 + ct)$.

The fact that the Pareto-II distribution can be produced by these assumptions should not be taken as implying some special advocacy for that form. Different assumptions about the mixing distribution, the consolidation process, or interitem competition give different final distributions. Without further theory, the three representations are better viewed as explanations for a descending hazard function than as determinants of a particular functional form.

Weibull Distribution. A fourth functional form derives from the cumulative distribution of a Weibull distribution:[5]

$$r(t) = \exp\left[-\left(\frac{ct}{d}\right)^{d}\right] \qquad \text{and} \qquad h(t) = c\left(\frac{ct}{d}\right)^{d-1}. \qquad (11.13)$$

This form has a long history as a lifetime distribution (see references in Johnson et al., 1994, Chap. 21). In memory theory, it has been derived from one set of theoretical grounds (although as a strength measure) by Wickelgren (1972) and from a different set of theoretical grounds by Indow (1993, 1995b). As with the Pareto-II function, the parameter d controls the relative steepness of the hazard function. When $0 < d < 1$, the function has a falling hazard rate; when $d = 1$ the function is exponential, with a flat hazard function; and when $d > 1$ the function has a rising hazard rate. Presumably, for memory data, $0 < d \leq 1$.

The fit of the Weibull retention function to the example data gives $\hat{c} = 0.142$ and $\hat{d} = 1.05$ for the short-term function, accounting for 98% of the variability. The near unit value of d shows the exponential character. For the long-term data, $\hat{c} = 0.0167$ and $\hat{d} = 0.339$. Although the fit of the Weibull function is slightly worse that that of the Pareto-II function (91% of the variability vs. 96%), examination of Fig. 11.4 shows that the difference is at best of minor importance. The hazard function in Fig. 11.2 is quite similar to those of the dual-exponential and Pareto-II models, although with a shift to greater risks over the observed period.

Another version of the Weibull function is obtained by shifting the origin

---

[5] Rubin and Wenzel (1996) refer to the Weibull representation as an "exponential-power function." Wickens (1998) again uses an algebraically simpler, but less interpretable, form.

away from zero:

$$r(t) = a \exp\left[-b(1 + ct)^d\right].$$

This form is interesting because it allows a nonzero asymptote to arise intrinsically. After reparameterizing so that $r(0) = 1$ (an arbitrary value could also be used) the function is found to have five regions:

- When $d < 1$, the function is

$$r(t) = \exp\{b[1 - (1 + ct)^d]\}. \tag{11.14}$$

  The hazard function is increasing and the function asymptotes at $r_\infty = 0$.

- When $d = 1$, the function is exponential, with a flat hazard function and $r_\infty = 0$.

- When $0 < d < 1$, the function has the form of Equation 11.14, but with a declining hazard function.

- When $d = 0$, the function is the Pareto-II power function:

$$r(t) = (1 + ct)^{-b},$$

  which has a declining hazard function and zero asymptote.

- When $d < 0$, the function is

$$r(t) = \exp\{b[(1 + ct)^d - 1]\}. \tag{11.15}$$

  It has a declining hazard function and asymptotes to $r_\infty = e^{-b} > 0$.

This function fits the long-term data appreciably better than the unshifted Weibull, accounting for 96% of the variability. The exponent $\widehat{d} = -0.259$ puts it in the fifth category, which, with $\widehat{b} = 1.916$ and $\widehat{c} = 0.849$ in Equation 11.15, implies an asymptote of $r_\infty = 0.147$ (Fig. 11.5). This representation suggests an interesting way to identify the presence of permanent storage that is somewhat more intrinsic to the memory process than the separate asymptote of Equation 11.5.

Gompertz and Gumbel Distributions. The final function that I consider here is important because of its long tradition. The Gompertz distribution was originally proposed as a distribution for human lifetimes by Gompertz (1825). He noticed that the memoryless property of exponential lifetime distributions implied that a life annuity in such a population would have the same value regardless of the age of the holder, which is clearly an unrealistic property. His alternative has

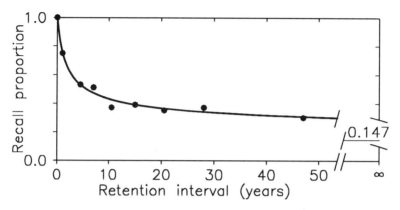

FIG. 11.5. A shifted Weibull function fitted to the long-term data of Fig. 11.1. Note the nonzero asymptote.

a survival function that is an exponential of exponentials and a hazard function that is a simple exponential:

$$r(t) = \exp\left[\frac{-b}{c}(e^{ct} - 1)\right] \qquad \text{and} \qquad h(t) = be^{ct}, \qquad (11.16)$$

for $c > 0$ (or, in Gompertz's form, $h(t) = b^t$, with $b > 1$). This function does not make a good memory model. The derivative of the hazard function is $h'(t) = bc^2e^{ct}$, which is always greater than zero, so that items have less resistance to forgetting as time passes. The best fit of a Gompertz function to the long-term data occurs in the limit as $c \to 0$, which (as the hazard function shows) implies an exponential model. In contrast to the human case, a life annuity on a memory item should increase in value as the item ages.

The importance of the Gompertz function here arises from the fact that it is the portion of the cumulative Gumbel (or "doubly exponential") distribution with positive arguments (Johnson, Kotz, & Balakrishnan, 1995, Section 22.8). This distribution has the form

$$r(t) = 1 - \exp\left[-e^{c(t-b)}\right] \qquad \text{and} \qquad h(t) = -b\,\frac{\exp\left[-e^{c(t-b)}\right]e^{c(t-b)}}{1 - \exp\left[-e^{c(t-b)}\right]}.$$
$$(11.17)$$

It arises as one of the extreme-value limit distributions discussed below, which gives it some plausibility as a memory model. The limit argument is not the only way to obtain this form. The long-term retention process of the Atkinson-Shiffrin model (Equations 11.1 and 11.2 with $g = 0$), after adjusting the parameters, has the form of Equation 11.17 with $c < 1$. The long-term process of that model is a Gumbel survival function displaced to allow an initial position less than unity. The final panel of Fig. 11.4 shows two versions of this function, one fitted to all the data, the other excluding the point at $t = 0$. Neither fit is satisfactory, again being constrained by its increasing hazard function (Fig. 11.2).

The inadequacy of the Gumbel form is qualified by the possibility that the distribution of initial strengths may be heterogeneous. An analysis like the one that led from the exponential distribution to the Pareto-II distribution applies here and can change the hazard function from ascending to descending form. The full Atkinson-Shiffrin model has a natural source of variable in the duration of transfer from short-term to long-term store.

Multiple Traces

The trace of an item can be treated a single coherent entity, or it can be treated as a collection of distinct elements. Many theoretical descriptions of memory are of the latter type. How these components are assembled and how they give rise to a particular response vary considerably. There are models based on distinct elements, models based on multiple pathways, and models based on collections of connections. In this section I examine some simple forms of this representation, using the principles developed above.

Consider a collection of N traces, each of which is lost independently with constant hazard rate. The survival function for the jth trace is exponential with rate parameter α_j, i.e., $r_j(t) = e^{-\alpha_j t}$. These elements can be combined to yield a response in many different ways, three of which are particularly simple.

Alternative Pathways. Suppose that each trace of an item constitutes an independent recovery route and that a given retrieval attempt uses one of these routes. If the chosen trace still survives, then retrieval is successful; if it does not, then retrieval fails. When the choice of route is random, the retention probability is the average of the individual retention functions:

$$r(t) = \frac{1}{N} \sum r_j(t) = \frac{1}{N} \sum e^{-\alpha_j t}. \tag{11.18}$$

When the traces are homogeneous (i.e., $\alpha_j = \alpha$, for all j), the pooled retention function is the same as that of the individual elements. However, although the average $r(t)$ is the same as the individual $r_j(t)$, the multiple paths give the alternative-pathways model an important property. Different retrieval attempts are likely to use different traces, so an item that is not retrieved on one attempt may be recovered on a later attempt.

More generally, the alternative-pathways model creates a mixture of processes with heterogeneous strengths. If $N = 2$, then the dual-exponential model results;

if N is large and the pathways have a distribution of strengths with density $f(\alpha)$, then Equation 11.18 becomes

$$r(t) = \int f(\alpha)e^{-\alpha t}d\alpha.$$

This integral is a heterogeneous mixture model of the type that gives a Pareto-II distribution when α has a Gamma distribution. Other mixing distributions produce different final distributions.

   Chained Links. Suppose that the traces are linked in a chain of associations, and that the item becomes unrecoverable as soon as one link of the chain is lost.[6] The retention function is that of the weakest link. The form of this function is found from the distribution of the minimum of a set of random variables. The item is recoverable only when all links still exist, so that

$$r(t) = \prod r_j(t). \tag{11.19}$$

With exponential random variables, recall is also exponential:

$$r(t) = \prod e^{-\alpha_j t} = \exp\left[-\left(\sum \alpha_j\right)t\right]. \tag{11.20}$$

The exponential nature of the composite function is also apparent from a consideration of the hazard function: because the individual link hazards are constant, the combined hazard also is constant until the first link fails.

   When the number of connections is large, it may be appropriate to approximate the form of this distribution by its limit as the number of links goes to infinity. With exponential components, the limit distribution is the Weibull function (as shown with the von Mises criteria given in Section 22.3 of Johnson et al., 1995). Within certain constraints, this result is independent of the actual form of the trace-retention function.

   The Weibull form here is somewhat surprising, in view of the fact that the distribution of the minimum is exponential for any finite N (Equation 11.20). Here, as in other ways, the extreme-value argument is more subtle than it seems at first. There are only three limiting distributions for maxima of random variables (the minima are the reverse of these distributions), and any parent distribution converges to one of these forms. Not surprisingly, which of these limit distributions applies depends on the shape of the component distribution function at the relevant end—the high end for the maximum and the low end for the minimum. Somewhat surprisingly, the form does not depend on the domain of the distribution function. For example, the limit distribution for the minimum or maximum of a set of uniform random variables has Weibull form and is not confined to the

---

[6]This argument has been developed for memory traces by Indow (1993, 1995b, 1995a).

range of the original variables. The key point is that as the number of terms becomes indefinitely large, the product in Equation 11.19 goes to zero for any t for which $r(t) < 1$. To obtain a valid limit distribution, the minimum or maximum must be scaled and shifted by a factor that depends on the number of variables involved.[7] See Colonius (1995) for a similar argument.

Parallel Pathways. The third approach treats the links as alternative routes to the response, all of which are explored. The traces act in parallel, and recovery fails only when all the connections are lost. The probability that the item cannot be recovered is the product of the probabilities that each of the individual traces is unrecoverable:

$$1 - r(t) = \prod [1 - r_j(t)]. \tag{11.21}$$

This representation requires the distribution of the longest-lived trace instead of the shortest. With exponential traces, the hazard is constant for any set of surviving traces, creating a probabilistic death process (Wickens, 1982, Section 10.2). The time course of the process is obtained by solving a set of simultaneous differential-difference equations that expresses the transitions among the network of states with different numbers of surviving traces. In a retention model, only the transition to the state where all traces are lost is observable, and the solution to these equations reduces to Equation 11.21.

With homogeneous exponential traces, Equation 11.21 leads to the retention function

$$r(t) = 1 - \left(1 - e^{-ct}\right)^N \quad \text{and} \quad h(t) = \frac{Nce^{-ct}\left(1 - e^{-ct}\right)^{N-1}}{1 - \left(1 - e^{-ct}\right)^N}. \tag{11.22}$$

On the face of it, it appears possible to use the fit of this function to estimate the number of traces involved (assuming the model to be correct). However, an analysis of the hazard function establishes that the model is unsatisfactory. Differentiation of the somewhat ungainly hazard function shows that for $N > 2$, $h'(t)$ is positive, implying an increasing hazard function. In essence, the older the process, the greater the chance that most of the traces have perished and the greater the hazard. Thus, this function cannot fit the long-term data. For a parallel-pathway model to be viable, either the traces cannot be exponential or they must have some interactive dynamic structure.[8]

---

[7]A comparable situation occurs with the central limit theorem for sums of positive random variables. As $N \to \infty$, the limit distribution of the partial sums $S_N = \sum_{i=1}^{N} X_i$ diverges to infinity. However, the distribution of the scaled sum $S'_N = [S_N - NE(X)]/N$ converges to a normal distribution, which, unlike the X_i, is on $-\infty$ to ∞.

[8]Professor Eric W. Holman has remarked to me that the distribution of survival time for a birth and death process (given by Kendall, 1948; see Bailey, 1964, Section 8.6) has a form that can be approximated by a Pareto-II distribution. This process has been used to model the survival of species

It is not possible to save this representation by passing to the limit of many links. The upper end of the exponential distribution is very different from its lower end, falling to zero instead of spiking to infinity. As a result, the limit distribution of the maximum is different from that of the minimum, now having Gumbel form. The survival function of this distribution has the same form as the long-term component of the Atkinson-Shiffrin function with which we started. As shown in Figures 11.2 and 11.4, it does not satisfactorily fit the long-term data, at least when its parameters are homogeneous.

Concluding Remarks

In the end, the goal of finding a single correct functional form form for the retention function may be unattainable. I am doubtful whether a single unique form can be expected to apply to all types of study and measure. However, we can certainly approach a solution more closely has been done yet. In this chapter I have described several considerations that should help characterize the form of the retention function. I have tried to show how a certain level of theoretical analysis can suggest both the constraints that the function must obey (others are in Wickens, 1998) and plausible forms for the function. The analysis is, of course, incomplete: any solution to the problem must ultimately draw on both empirical and theoretical treatments.

On the empirical front, there is a need to examine and compare various functions across different designs and data sets, a task begun by Rubin and Wenzel (1996). Pure goodness-of-fit measures alone are not sufficient to select a function, however. For a function to be useful, its parameters should map onto experimental manipulations in an orderly way. Purely empirically, one would like a good representation to isolate the effects of important procedural variables in a small or consistent set of parameters

Theoretical analyses have a somewhat different role to play. First, they can suggest useful functional forms to be examined. Some of these forms may derive from full-fledged memory theories, but they can also come from the types of less detailed treatment I use here. Second, these analyses should help to constrain the choice of model and to identify important characteristics that any satisfactory representation should have. For example, knowing that the hazard function declines immediately excludes a large set of potential functional forms, which then need not be examined empirically. This fact also suggests a number of process explanations, which could be investigated empirically. Third, and

---

of organisms. For memory processes, it could arise if each existing trace could both give rise to a new trace and be lost; the retention of a memory would then be tantamount to the survival of a species. If the loss rate exceeds the new-trace rate (perhaps for a little-used memory), then the retention probability falls to zero; if the new-trace rate exceeds the loss rate (perhaps for a much-retrieved memory), then retention has a nonzero asymptote.

most ambitiously, it is only through a theoretical or model-based treatment that the disparate measures of performance can be reconciled.

Summary

This chapter describes some probabilistic arguments that can help select a functional form to describe the time course of retention in human memory. Functions with flat or rising hazard functions (e.g., those based on exponential or Gumbel distributions) are unsatisfactory, particularly for long-term retention. Functions with declining hazard functions are more satisfactory (e.g., those based on Pareto or Weibull distribution, or on mixtures of exponentials). Models based on ensembles of separate traces are briefly considered.

Acknowledgments

This work was supported in part by a UCLA University Research Grant. I thank Eric W. Holman, Robert A. Bjork, and the Cogfog group for discussion related to this work.

References

Anderson, J. R., & Milson, R. (1989). Human memory: An adaptive perspective. *Psychological Review*, *96*, 703–719.

Atkinson, R. C., Brelsford, J. W., Jr., & Shiffrin, R. M. (1967). Multiprocess models for memory with applications to a continuous presentation task. *Journal of Mathematical Psychology*, *4*, 277–300.

Atkinson, R. C., & Shiffrin, R. M. (1968). Human memory: A proposed system. In G. H. Bower (Ed.), *The psychology of learning and motivation* (Vol. 2). New York: Academic Press.

Atkinson, R. C., & Wickens, T. D. (1971). Human memory and the concept of reinforcement. In R. Glaser (Ed.), *The nature of reinforcement* (pp. 66–120). New York: Academic Press.

Bahrick, H. P. (1983). The cognitive map of a city: Fifty years of learning and memory. In G. H. Bower (Ed.), *The psychology of learning and motivation* (Vol. 17, pp. 125–163). New York: Academic Press.

Bailey, N. T. J. (1964). *The elements of stochastic processes, with applications in the natural sciences.* New York: Wiley.

Brelsford, J. W., Jr., Shiffrin, R. M., & Atkinson, R. C. (1968). Multiple reinforcement effects in short-term memory. *British Journal of Mathematical and Statistical Psychology*, *21*, 1–19.

Colonius, H. (1995). The instance theory of automaticity: Why the Weibull? *Psychological Review*, *102*, 744–750.

Elliot, P. B. (1964). Tables of d'. In J. A. Swets (Ed.), *Signal detection and recognition by human observers: Contempory readings* (pp. 651–684). New York: Wiley.

Freund, R. D., Loftus, G. R., & Atkinson, R. C. (1969). Applicatins of multi-process models for memory to continuous recognitition tasks. *Journal of Mathematical Psychology*, *6*, 576–594.

Gompertz, B. (1825). On the nature of the function expressive of the law of human mortality, and on a new model of determining the value of Life Contingencies. *Philosophical Tranactions of the Royal Society of London*, *115*, 513–583.

Indow, T. (1993). Analysis of events counted on time-dimension: A soft model based on extreme statistics. *Behaviormetrika*, *20*, 109–124.

Indow, T. (1995a). *Retrieval sequences and retention curves: An analysis based on extreme statistics* (Technical report series No. 95-31). University of California, Irvine: Institute for Mathematical Behavioral Sciences.

Indow, T. (1995b). *Weibull form in memory, reaction time, and social behavior: Asymptotic distribution of minima from heterogeneous population* (Technical report series No. 95-04). University of California, Irvine: Institute for Mathematical Behavioral Sciences.

Johnson, N. L., Kotz, S., & Balakrishnan, N. (1994). *Continuous univariate distributions* (Vol. 1, 2nd ed.). New York: Wiley.

Johnson, N. L., Kotz, S., & Balakrishnan, N. (1995). *Continuous univariate distributions* (Vol. 2, 2nd ed.). New York: Wiley.

Kendall, D. G. (1948). On some modes of population growth leading to R. A. Fisher's logarithmic series distribution. *Biometrika*, *35*, 6–15.

Maguire, B. A., Pearson, E. S., & Wynn, A. H. A. (1952). The time intervals between industrial accidents. *Biometrika*, *39*, 168–180.

Murdock, B. B., Jr. (1961). The retention of individual items. *Journal of Experimental Psychology*, *62*, 618–625.

Peterson, L. R., & Peterson, M. J. (1959). Short term retention of individual verbal items. *Journal of Experimental Psychology*, *58*.

Rubin, D. C., & Wenzel, A. E. (1996). One hundred years of forgetting: A quantitative description of retention. *Psychological Review*, *103*, 734–760.

Simon, H. A. (1966). A note on Jost's law and exponential forgetting. *Psychometrika*, 505–506.

Wickelgren, W. A. (1972). Trace resistence and the decay of long-term memory. *Journal of Mathematical Psychology*, *9*, 418–455.

Wickens, T. D. (1982). *Models for behavior: Stochastic processes in psychology.* San Francisco: W. H. Freeman.

Wickens, T. D. (1989). *Multiway contingency tables analysis for the social sciences.* Hillsdale, NJ: Lawrence Erlbaum Associates.

Wickens, T. D. (1998). On the form of the retention function; Comment on Rubin and Wenzel: A quantitative description of retention. *Psychological Review, 105,* 379–396.

Wixted, J. T., & Ebbesen, E. B. (1991). On the form of forgetting. *Psychological Science, 2,* 409–415.

Wixted, J. T., & Ebbesen, E. B. (1997). Genuine power curves in forgetting: A quantitative analysis of individual subject forgetting functions. *Memory and Cognition, 25,* 731–739.

Woodworth, R. S. (1938). *Experimental psychology.* New York: Holt.

Author Index

A

Ackerman, B. P., 231
Acre, S., 165
Anderson, J. A., 35, 46, 54, 64, 73, 77, 80
Anderson, J. R., 63, 80, 216, 249, 264
Anderson, M. C., 106, 122
Anderson, N. S., 152, 162
Anderson, R. E., 83
Andrews, G., 143
Anisfeld, M., 230
Arbuckle, T. Y., 48, 57
Asch, S. E., 50, 54
Atkinson, R. C., ix, x, xiii, 1, 2, 3, 4, 5, 6, 9, 11, 13, 17, 21, 22 31, 35, 36, 37, 38, 51, 54, 56, 60, 61, 62, 76, 80, 84, 105, 110, 115, 119, 120, 122, 127, 133, 135, 145, 151, 162, 215, 216, 245, 248, 252, 259, 260, 263, 264
Azcowa, B. L., xiii

B

Baddeley, A. D., 60, 64, 77, 80, 121, 122, 127, 131, 145
Bahrick, H. P., 23, 246, 247, 264
Bailey, N. T. J., 252, 264
Bain, J. D., 36, 55, 64, 82, 105, 123, 132, 136, 220, 221, 222, 223
Balakrishnan, N., 254, 257, 259, 261, 265
Barsalou, L. W., 220
Basden, B. H., 88, 103
Basden, D. R., 88, 103
Battig, W. F., 109, 122
Bernbach, H., 59
Birtwistle, J., 133
Bittnor, L. A., 133
Bjork, E. L., 106, 122
Bjork, R. A., 62, 86, 106, 122, 181, 184, 202, 210, 213, 236, 264
Blake, M., 88, 103
Blesi, E., 210

Subject Index

A

Active
    memory, 19
    rehersal, 151, 153, 154, 158, 159, 160, 161
All-or-none vs. gradual learning, 3
Amnesics, 30
Anticipation vs. study-test method, 185
Architecture of models
    global memory models, 62
    item-processing models, 62
Array model, 68
    access to memory by serial, self-terminating search, 75
    generalization in, 75
    image vs. standard versions of, 70
    nature of features stored in memory, 71
    origin in context models of categorization, 68
    recall as special case of categorization, 69
    recognition as special case of categorization, 69
    responses based on measures of similarity, 69
Articulatory (phonological) loop, 146
Associations
    interitem, 87, 89, 93
    horizontal, 89, 97, 100,
    vertical, 89, 100
Associative
    information, 40, 47, 52, 56
    symmetry, 51, 54
Asymptote, 48, 49, 50, 51, 52
Atkinson-Shiffrin (buffer) model, ix, xiii, 1, 2, 5, 11, 13, 35, 36, 37, 47, 52, 151,
    153, 162, 165, 245, 248, 252, 259, 260, 263
    architecture of, 61
    control processes in, 63
    current status of, 63
    forgetting in, 63
    interference effects in, 61
    item distinctiveness, 63
    long-term buffer, 61
    memory stores in, 61
    recency effects in, 63

R

S

T

U